GOODBYE
HANGOVERS

Hello
Life

BOOKS BY JEAN KIRKPATRICK

Goodbye Hangovers, Hello Life
Turnabout: New Help for the Woman Alcoholic
A Fresh Start
On the Road to Self Recovery

GOODBYE
HANGOVERS

Hello Life

SELF-HELP
FOR WOMEN

JEAN KIRKPATRICK, PH.D.
Founder of Women for Sobriety, Inc.

BARRICADE
BOOKS

Fort Lee | New Jersey

Published by Barricade Books Inc.
185 Bridge Plaza North
Suite 308-A
Fort Lee, NJ 07024

www.barricadebooks.com

Library of Congress Cataloging-in-Publication Data

Kirkpatrick, Jean.
        1. Women—United States—Alcohol use. 2.
Alcoholism—Treatment—United States. I. Title. II. Title:
Goodbye hangovers, hello life.
HV5137.K54
613.8'1'024042

ISBN 1-56980-248-3

First Printing Barricade Edition
Printed in Canada

To the many

who seek help.

ACKNOWLEDGMENTS

So often we are prone to say, "I just finished writing my book," when we really mean to say, "I was able to write my book because so many others helped me."

I owe a deep debt of gratitude to the three women alcoholics who graciously consented to reveal themselves through the interviews that appear at the end of the book. For them, it was a painful trip back through dark corridors of lost time that they took because they knew their making this trip into their past would help so many others.

And last but not least, I wish to thank the thousands of women alcoholics with whom I have been in touch over these many years and for their candid revelations of painful experiences.

FOREWORD

When I was putting together my own book, *The Courage to Change*, I heard about Jean Kirkpatrick and Women For Sobriety. After reading some newspaper and magazine articles written about Jean and her views on women and alcoholism, I knew that I wanted to have her participate.

In advance of our interview in Quakertown, Pennsylvania—Jean's home base—she sent me a copy of her first book, *Turnabout*.

Jean's story of her own alcoholism made frightening reading. It was brutally honest and powerful. Jean really was able to capture on the printed page the pain, the despair, and the tragedy of herself—when she was trapped in alcoholism.

Her new book, *Goodbye Hangovers, Hello Life* is equally remarkable. This time Jean writes about the recovery process—life after alcohol. Drawing on her own personal experience and the wisdom of many women with whom she has worked, Jean deals with all of the negative emotions that immobilize the drinking alcoholic—worry, fear, guilt, depression, and loneliness. Once again, all of the power and the sensitivity of Jean's writing is here.

I think this book is important for three reasons.

First, it's about women and alcoholism and that makes the book essential reading. This area of study has been neglected for too long.

Second, Jean's twenty questions pinpointing "Am I an Alcoholic?" are clear, useful, and right on target.

Third, *Goodbye Hangovers, Hello Life* may introduce you to the support group, Women For Sobriety, that has helped many women with "drinking problems."

Jean is a pioneer in her writing about women and alcoholism and in her work as the founder and guiding spirit of Women For Sobriety.

I'm honored to be a part of this excellent book.

Dennis Wholey
The Courage to Change

CONTENTS

INTRODUCTION

Who is the woman alcoholic?

She is any race, any religion, any ethnic background, any age; single, married, divorced; homosexual, heterosexual, bisexual; with children, without children. She is a housewife, a workingwoman, or a combination of both. She is rich, poor, or middle-class. She has a college degree, or she may never have gone to school. She lives anywhere in the United States.

Why does she drink?

There is no one single reason why women drink. They may be lonely, bored, depressed, unhappy in marriages wrought with sexual conflicts, feel pressured handling full-time jobs and the responsibilities of families. Drinking makes them feel less nervous and unsure of themselves; that's why they drink.

The accepted number of women alcoholics in this country is 5 million. This figure represents the total population of Maine, Montana, Arizona and Alaska. Even more startling is to know that these women adversely affect approximately 23 million children—theirs.

Very few of these 5 million women are receiving treatment of any kind. A comparison survey released by the U.S. Department of Health and Human Services (1983) showed that only 22 percent of all persons in treatment are female.

That is the reason for this book.

There are essentially three kinds of treatment for alcoholism: (1) individual counseling; (2) attending a treatment facility (in-patient and outpatient); and (3) self-help, which is often used along with individual counseling in a treatment facility.

It is impossible to know how many women are in private counseling, but the number is surely low since women have little money for treatment, and counseling costs (as of 1984) are around $60 per hour. A reasonable guess is around 8,000 to 10,000 women. As for treatment facilities, Senator Paula Hawkins, chairperson of the Subcommittee on Alcoholism and Drug Abuse, noted in 1984 that there were 5,557 treatment centers for males and 375 for women, treating roughly 7,500 women. In the area of self-help Women For Sobriety (WFS) and Alcoholics Anonymous (AA) reach approximately 178,000 women, based upon available figures.

It is therefore easy to see that fewer than 200,000 American women alcoholics are being helped—less than 4 percent of the total.

One reason there are so few treatment facilities for women is that the prevailing view (still held by the majority) has been that an alcoholic is an alcoholic and that treatment programs need not distinguish between the sexes.

Then, too, there is the additional problem that women do not come forth for treatment. Sometimes the very people who should be encouraging the alcoholic woman to get treatment hold her back. It is not unusual for family members to urge her to "do something" about her drinking, yet when she wants to go outside the home for help, they do not want this to happen. What they had in mind, of course, was for the woman to stop drinking all by herself; they will encourage her, might even pour the alcohol down the drain to help. Because the public continues to view alcoholism as a moral, not a physical, issue and because women especially bear the brunt of this view, families do not want to risk the embarrassment and humiliation that might arise from having their alcoholics seek outside treatment.

Sometimes a woman alcoholic will turn to the family physician for help. Very often he is uncomfortable with her problem, seeing it as one that cannot be solved immediately, and so he treats it by prescribing tranquilizers. Out of a sampling of 603 women, almost one-fourth acquired an additional drug problem because of this kind of treatment from a family physician.

My own sobriety came about during the years 1970 and 1971. It did not happen as a result of treatment but, rather, from an examination of myself and my particular needs. Fifteen years earlier I had attended AA for a period of time but had then lapsed back into drinking. After again trying AA and finding it so male-dominated that it did not really speak to my particular needs as a woman, I devised a way to get sober through a trial-and-error method that later became the first self-help program for women alcoholics.

Since 1974 my work with women alcoholics has included many interviews and several surveys of attitudes and feelings. I have read about 35,000 letters from women alcoholics over these past ten years and during my own twenty-nine-year history of drinking and recovery. From this have come my conclusions about what women alcoholics think, feel, need, and want. More than ever before, I know that women *must* have certain elements in recovery programs if they are to be helped, not because their alcoholism is different from that of men but because they, as women, are different from men. This distinction is what has been missing. For too long programs for alcoholics have been designed by men, administered by men, dominated by men, and applied to women. For too many years we have merely treated "alcoholics."

The drinking behavior of women is different from that of men. Among women the greatest element is secrecy. In a recent survey of 603 alcoholic women only 2 percent did any significant drinking outside the home. Housewives enjoy an alcoholic's paradise. Alone and sequestered for the major part of every day, they have time *and* secrecy for uncontrolled drinking. In some cases this pattern is interrupted only by the serving of dinner and cleaning-up chores before bedtime, after which they are able to sneak downstairs and continue drinking in the quiet of night and a sleeping household. How easy it is to stumble to the bedroom and slip into bed unnoticed!

Nocturnal drinking is sometimes also the pattern for the woman who works outside the home and who has little "alone time." Her drinking often starts with cocktails at lunch and then continues seriously when the family is in bed and she is finally alone.

Very often the housewife believes she is "getting away" with her daily drinking, but the fact is that her family refuses to come to grips with the problem and simply ignores it. Many children who come home to a mommy who "has a headache" or a mommy "sick in bed" know exactly what is happening. Some of them search out liquor bottles and empty them with regularity, never mentioning it to anyone, and the alcoholic woman herself is not about to bring up the subject.

Although the special care a woman alcoholic requires is not always readily available, it is true that today women alcoholics are not getting as sick as some of us "old-timers" did. In my drinking days it was believed that nothing could be done to help until the woman hit bottom, but that is no longer true. Because media campaigns about alcoholism are having some impact, my kind of hitting-bottom alcoholic is not too visible these days. During my past ten years of working with women alcoholics I have seen relatively few who went the whole route. When I first attended AA in a city of one hundred thousand more than thirty years ago, there were about seventy-five men and five or six women at the meeting, most of whom *had* hit bottom. And we looked it. Our faces bore the physical deterioration for all to see: blotchy complexions and many small broken blood vessels around the nose. We looked hard. And old.

But this is no longer the norm. Perhaps it *is* the result of the media campaigns. Perhaps it is the new awareness of and emphasis on health and greater knowledge about diseases. Perhaps it is a greater concern about how we look. Perhaps it is the result of the "I'm responsible for my body" idea so prevalent now. Perhaps because more women are in the workplace...

Whatever it is, people don't drink as long as before without seeking help. Many women try to combat their problems alone, often not very successfully. But at least they make an effort. Women tend to go to libraries to look up "alcoholism" to find answers. Or they approach agencies via the telephone to get information.

At Women For Sobriety we often get calls from women who want us to send literature but won't give their names. The stigma of the woman alcoholic still remains, despite some very forward strides made recently by prominent women publicly announcing their alcoholism. Betty Ford, Joan Kennedy, Elizabeth Taylor, Liza Minnelli—all have brought some "class" to women alcoholics, but not quite enough. Small-town people still view "Mary Smith" as a "downtrodden woman" and don't equate her with Elizabeth Taylor or Joan Kennedy. Indeed, small towns tend to see Elizabeth Taylor or Joan Kennedy not as having a disease but as women with fast life-styles that finally caught up with them.

Public attitudes change very slowly, and the feelings toward women alcoholics have been negative for many, many years. Society's desire for woman to be "pure" continues strong and unabated, and another book could be written about the why of this obsession within American culture. For now, however, it is a fact that women alcoholics are subjected to a double standard. Male alcoholics who do something about their drinking problem are hailed as courageous. Comments about women alcoholics who try to do something about their drinking run something like: "It's about time she quit"; "Look what she did to Charlie's career"; "Those poor children!"

For the alcoholic woman with an already very weak ego this can tip the scales once again. If there is one thing an alcoholic needs for a successful recovery, it is encouragement. And so we come up against another of many reasons why lasting sobriety is extremely difficult for women.

For many women alcoholics the road to recovery is faced without the backup of families. Many have gone through divorces and, often, also have lost custody of their children. A study done in Canada a number of years ago, which has been quoted frequently as being applicable to the United States, indicates that for every ten women alcoholics, only one husband stays, while for every ten male alcoholics, only one wife leaves.

Women also often have financial problems that affect treatment. It is true that recovery can take place without money; both WFS and AA are "free" (they both take donations). But sometimes the alcoholism requires treatment in an institution at first, and it is this that women often cannot afford. And, as already mentioned, women prefer individual counseling because of the privacy it offers.

Self-help is the most effective answer in the long run, but it requires a strong desire to get well and a definite commitment to regular attendance (at WFS or AA); some women have difficulties with this.

Women alcoholics typically must deal with special problems, some of which helped cause the disease and others resulting from it. A high percentage of women have known sexual abuse and molestation, which they have hidden deep in their psyches, and there are often many guilt feelings, some arising from near promiscuity when deep in the throes of alcohol. As noted earlier, women are often dually addicted, with the second addiction coming through the family physician. But in my view, the most pressing problem is a woman alcoholic's lack of positive feelings for herself. She has had little or no self-respect before the onset of her alcoholism, and the drinking totally obliterates any positive feelings whatsoever. The building of a good self-image is paramount to recovery, and it is tied into a woman's feelings of dependency on others. Very often, emotional deprivation she has known as a child leads to emotional dependency in her adult years in marriage or other relationships. Then, too, from my experience I have found that a large number have had very poor relationships with their mothers, with adverse effects in later life. These feelings translate into an inability to make commitments in adult relationships; difficulty with decision making; sexual dysfunction; being nonparticipatory and passive in most things; marital instability and discord; feelings of helplessness, which lead to frequent bouts of depression.

This book is directed to women alcoholics so that they may better understand their special problems and the reasons they have had so much difficulty in achieving sobriety. And it provides a plan for recovery that may be used in conjunction with any other program or just by itself.

Hopefully, members of the professional alcoholism community will find some insights that they incorporate into current and future programs.

PART ONE

*D*RINKING

CHAPTER ONE

ONE WOMAN'S STORY

I don't know why I drank. But I did. And I drank lots. Lots and lots and lots, over two decades of drinking. Maybe it was because I was always alone, no brothers, no sisters, and parents too wrapped up in themselves even to know I was around. Maybe I drank because I always felt like a misfit, that I didn't belong anywhere or to anyone. I kept asking if I was adopted because I was sure I was. But they kept answering, "No, you're our little girl."

Maybe it was because of all the nights with baby-sitters over a period of at least ten years. Maybe that's it. Or maybe it's because I didn't think my parents loved me. Maybe...

Anyway, there must have been a reason. The more I try to find it, the more it becomes evident that there were many reasons. Probably the most relevant is that I felt unloved, uncared for, and at times unwanted.

Even though I was an only child, I certainly had aunts and uncles. I was also the only niece. That made for a lot of material spoiling and provided me with many, many toys. Anything new, I had it. But I still felt unloved.

Perhaps this is the only part of my life that wasn't average. Born in a small town in a rural setting in eastern Pennsylvania, I grew up on a quiet tree-lined street of modest single-family houses. My father was a salesman, a self-made man, filled with drive and aggression, who would have gone much farther in his career if my mother had not held him back. Every promotion he received she urged him not to take. Several fine offers came his

3

way but always had to be turned down if she was to be satisfied. Strange how such a strong and decisive man could be molded and changed by a small, selfish woman desirous of maintaining the status quo.

Never having received the nurturing from my parents I longed for, I crawled deeper and deeper into the dark part of myself, finding that pieces that should have been there were missing. And always I feared friendships and relationships and failed at them, going either too far or not nearly far enough.

Certainly the nurturing we all need was sadly missing in my life, and I was always looking for it. Throughout all my childhood I had fierce crushes on my baby-sitters, my teachers, my teammates; many people saw this as a predilection toward homosexuality. Now, in later years, I can clearly see that I was looking for a mother and for the tenderness and nurturing I yearned for. There was never anything sexual in my longings. I sought tenderness and understanding; I looked for a touch of a hand, a kind word, affection, attention. I was grateful to anyone who let me hang around.

There were the inevitable chants in the school corridors, but I didn't know what they meant, only that I was being taunted for something I didn't understand, naïve as that now sounds. I continued to follow my "best friends" home every night until I was told to stop. Humiliated, I did stop, never knowing why the bestowal of my complete attention on one person brought forth such enmity. Now I know, after all these long years. And the humiliation is just as strong as it was then.

My childhood loneliness was enhanced by my mother's adamant refusal to let me have a dog. Both my father and I wanted one, but her classic line was "A dog comes in this house, and I go out." Needless to say, my father didn't want a dog that badly.

My cousins, who lived fifteen miles away, also wanted a dog, and my father agreed to find one for them at one of the farms he visited. Find one he did, but it was in the middle of the week, so the dog stayed at our house until the weekend, when we could deliver it. For me it was love at first sight. When we delivered the dog, I remember making a terrible scene: crying; clawing; yelling in an hysterical way. This may have been the first time I experienced such hysteria as a result of something's being taken from me. It was to happen again in the years following.

This was surely one of my most traumatic childhood experiences. The extreme irony is that twenty-five years later, when I was remanded to a mental institution by a judge as fulfillment of a jail sentence, my German shepherd was taken in by my parents and my mother loved the dog as much as my father did. Isn't it strange how many times the things in life we feel will be terrible often turn out to be exactly the opposite?

I was ten years old at the time of the dog incident, and my loneliness was deeper than it had ever been. Years later this same black loneliness and emptiness came back full force in the isolation cell I inhabited for a week in the bowels of the psychiatric hospital. In the darkness I learned that we are forever and unalterably alone except for whatever spiritual conviction we may be able to muster.

As soon as I was able to drive a car, I spent many hours driving alone on rural roads, parking on a bridge, and listening to the gentle flow of the water on a summer evening somewhere in the woods, while deep within me I felt a nameless longing.

In high school there was never any question about my being "popular." I always was. I had a drive to be in everything and to work my way up: class president; on the basketball team; on the newspaper staff. Whatever activities there were in school, I was involved and usually somewhere at the top.

Like many others, I took it for granted that everyone had dates. I was "popular" and never had to be concerned come Saturday night. Because it was the thing to do, I dated, but I was never very comfortable. At home I was lectured heavily on what I could and could not do, what to be suspicious of and how to protect myself. It's not hard to understand why I was uncomfortable! I found it embarrassing and somewhat humiliating— and not too exciting—to be fighting off advances.

About this time I began to date a young man whose antics classified him as wild. Probably because he came from a very well-known, intellectual family, I was permitted to go out with him. What was delightfully different about him was that he was interested only in drinking and not in petting. It was almost as if he had to remind himself to kiss me good night, and then it was in an offhand manner.

At last I'd found someone to be comfortable with, and I began the first of my drinking on dates with him. Despite my naïveté, I did recognize that he seemed older and more worldly than the other young men. His grandfather was internationally famous, and J had had many more experiences than most of us in our high school class.

We finally were graduated, and I had managed to stay virginal. On graduation night I was with J, and except for a date a year later, after he had joined the RAF, I never again saw him. He took his own life after the war.

Being with J was the beginning of my drinking. We never drank large quantities—at least I didn't—but I remember being high. And drinking with him seemed more natural than anything else I had ever done. Although my mother never drank, alcohol was not foreign to me. It was always in our home, and almost all of my parents' friends drank. My mother would have liked it if no liquor had been present, but my father must have put his foot down on this issue because it was always around.

My father was never a heavy drinker. I can remember seeing him high several times but staggering only one time, and that was caused by a complication with his diabetes. But he drank or had a drink or two on almost every occasion. It was acceptable in our home, and there seemed nothing the least bit dangerous or forbidden about it.

On a Sunday night just before graduation I was in a very serious automobile accident. I was driving, and fortunately I hadn't been drinking. The accident occurred because I was inexperienced, having had my license for just twenty-nine days, and I was driving in an area unknown to me. My father had permitted me to take his brand-new Buick that Sunday night if I promised to stay on back roads. One of the back roads crossed a major highway, which was where the accident happened.

I sustained major injuries, not the least of which was a broken back. I was permitted to graduate with my class but had to make up some work later on. Perhaps the most serious consequence of the accident was that I was unable to go to college in Ohio as planned and had to remain close to home for treatment for my back and for a damaged kidney.

My father believed it would be a good idea in the interim for me to attend business college in Philadelphia, just thirty-five miles away, even though it was the very last thing I wanted to do. Moving to Philadelphia and living in an apartment dormitory began my long descent into hell that was to last, sporadically, for the next several decades.

Although I was unhappy at home, it was nothing compared to the loneliness, fear, and isolation I experienced in Philadelphia. Even now I can't believe the extreme feelings caused by this simple move. It was as if my life had ended. I was unable to sleep. I was frightened. It was like a nightmare come true. I felt abandoned.

I tried going to classes, but I hated them except for rapid calculation, at which I excelled. Business law and bookkeeping were simply out for me. Shorthand and typing were so far from any of my interests in life that I simply did not attend the classes. Instead, I began to drink in earnest. It was this period that set the pattern for my drinking: feeling rejected and abandoned, experiencing loneliness, feeling isolated and very frightened.

My days consisted of going to a few selected classes, having lunch, drinking with some of the fellows from the college across the street, then playing bridge through most of the night.

Now I am able to look at this period and see that the first signs of alcoholism were present. I was able to drink fairly sizable quantities of alcohol—a pint usually—in a short space of time without experiencing any hangover the next day. But there were times when I had blackouts—periods of which I had no memory.

My emotional upsets came from my not having grown up

like other people. As soon as I was away from home, I fell apart, and it was because I never had any growing up lessons. During all my years in school at home, I envied my friends whose parents took an interest in their work and helped them with their homework. Now I realize this is why I couldn't make it away from home. I had no established habits, no discipline, order, or self-responsibility. I did not know how to take care of myself. Maturity was missing. All this drifting, this homesickness, this sense of isolation and fear came from the emotional deprivation I felt. And it led to self-destruction, as it does in the case of anyone who is in such need of love and care and nurturing.

The only bright spot in my life during this time was receiving letters from Kirk, whom I had met just months earlier through my father's company.

Kirk was very different from any boys I had known. He was older—twenty-one to my eighteen—and he was very well traveled. Better yet, he was a very nice person, and I was instantly attracted to him. He was then in the army, and during the short period I was in college in Philadelphia he came to visit on his way to a new base in Shelby, Mississippi. During this visit he gave me his fraternity pin.

My absence from classes and my drinking prompted the dean to write several letters to my parents urging them to get professional help for me. These were never discussed with me, and it was only years later that I read them. They never followed the dean's advice.

The problems continued, and I was expelled from three colleges. I ran away and married Kirk; there seemed nowhere else to turn. I was not at all aware of the serious step I had taken, but for the moment it settled the question of college.

Kirk was sent to officers' candidate school in New Jersey, and we were able to be together on the weekends, my hometown being just a two-hour drive away. After Kirk's graduation we were off to his first assignment in Tucson, Arizona, and then, during the next two years, were stationed at a number of other bases. The base from which he was sent overseas was in El Paso, Texas, at the time, and as was our daily habit, we, the wives, were playing bridge when the separation came. Although we knew it was inevitable, it was a great shock, especially the way it happened. At 4:00 P.M. one day our husbands called us from Briggs Field to say they wouldn't be home that night. Neat and clean. No tears, no scenes. Numbly we women put away the cards, said goodbye to each other, and went back to our apartments to pack.

I had a fair supply of liquor with me, and I drove and drank my way home, taking four days to get to Pennsylvania. It was Christmas Eve when I arrived.

It was good being home, although I soon realized that my living habits were not those of my parents. It never occurred to me to live separately in my hometown, and my life with them had very tense moments. They were always after me about my drinking, which I now see as being much heavier than I was conscious of. But this was wartime, and life was anything but normal. The war years made everyone act differently. As I remember it now, it seems there was a party, a gathering of my parents' crowd, every night at someone's home. And of course, there was drinking, more than ever before, probably prompted by the anxiety of the times we were living in. Daily headlines bombarded us with our severe losses in the South Pacific, and the news, at first, was rarely good. Quakertown was a small community, and we all knew the boys that had left.

Although my drinking was heavy every night, it wasn't particularly noticed because of the crazy times we were living in. Everyone was displaying abnormal behavior. It was like being on a merry-go-round.

By the war's end I was eagerly looking forward to seeing Kirk, believing that we would settle down to live in Quakertown. However, that wasn't what happened or what he had in mind, and two years later, after much turmoil between us, it was obvious that we could not and would not live together. The differences that separated us were monumental. We both had changed greatly during the two years he had been gone, and it was clear to us how rashly we had acted in such an early marriage.

It was a very sad and upsetting time. During that period I had a nervous breakdown and was under psychiatric care for six months. There were so many conflicting forces. My mother wanted us to stay together no matter what. Kirk did, too, but I didn't, and I think his parents weren't keen for us to stay together. I only knew I had to be out.

After all the years that have passed, I now recognize but do not understand that I cannot handle change, nor can I seem to leave this particular geographical area where I live for any length of time. We had bought a ranch in Arizona, my favorite state, but I was unable to stay there. But that was only one of the problems, and it was comparatively minor.

My psychiatrist urged that I play tennis all summer, and take another shot at college, this time locally. My drinking was never talked about, although in retrospect I can see that I had certainly crossed the line from social to alcoholic drinking. All that summer I lived at home, played tennis all day and drank most of the night. My divorce was in the works, and I had applied to Moravian College to attend classes in the fall. However, because of my poor high school and college records, it was only after doing well in entrance exams that I was allowed to register for full-time attendance.

At twenty-seven years of age I was finally ready to study. College was right for me, and I couldn't get enough of it. Although I rushed to finish my degree, completing the four-year course in three years, I was also part of all the college activities, managing to make the *Who's Who of Colleges and Universities.*

But there was still my other life, the one apart from the campus: my drinking life. Next to my off-campus apartment was a neighborhood tavern that I frequented every night, becoming very good friends with the two waitresses and the bartender. It was like a family, I thought. These three took care of me on many occasions. I was always protected from men who tried to pick me up, and I was always seen home to my front door when negotiating by myself was impossible. And the next morning I was always back on campus, leading convocation in my position of convocation chairperson. When hangovers were too unbearable, I remedied them with a quick trip across the street from the campus to the Hotel Bethlehem.

None of this behavior seemed strange or unusual to me. Of course, I knew that not everyone was drinking in the same way, but my behavior did not disturb me, and I just can't understand why it didn't. Perhaps it was because there were always others who joined me; that they were always different persons evidently made no impression on me. It seems totally unbelievable to me now. But then? It seemed perfectly normal. Drinking to the alcoholic never seems abnormal.

My graduation from Moravian left me restless and again faced with the question of what did I want to do with my life. There didn't seem to be anything I wanted to do or be. Not that I lacked ambition and drive. I had both. But I yearned to know what it was I should pursue. I never did find an answer to that question until four years after I had quit drinking, when I knew I could help others. But that was a long way off. Between graduation from college and that time of helping others lay a life of tragedy and an unbelievable trail of hurting others. One of the serverest problems for an alcoholic in recovery is achieving self-forgiveness.

With a friend I spent a year traveling willy-nilly around the United States, having had my appetite whetted by the years of travel with Kirk, an appetite that has lasted all my life. When this phase ended, quite by accident I found a teaching position in Kansas and went there, running away from my restlessness and my problems, or so I thought.

The open desolation of Kansas was a revelation to me. Again I was emotionally torn apart because I'd left my home base. The school in which I taught had only thirty-three students in its graduating class. I taught English to grades nine through twelve and music to all grades. I started a high school newspaper and helped the upper classes put on class plays for the first time.

But my loneliness was unbearable. There were only two other faculty members, and both were married. There was one movie house in town that ran three movies a week. I went to every showing of all of them just to fill time and keep from drinking. Being alone in the middle of nowhere, I began to fall apart rapidly. I went to classes at times half-drunk and always hung-over. A young couple—he was the history teacher—tried to help me, but I was much too far gone. There were times I was stuck in snowdrifts because I couldn't handle my car, times I staggered into a liquor store for another bottle, fell up the steps of my apartment house, and stepped on my glasses, rendering them into a hundred pieces. There were days I missed school.

Finally, at midterm, I was asked to leave under the pretext of not having enough credits of the right kind to teach in Kansas. A very large good-bye party was given for me, and most of the students were in tears. It was a sad ending to a sad chapter in my life. I loved the children, but it wasn't the right kind of medicine I needed at the time. Love does not overcome alcoholism.

Driving home to Pennsylvania was a blur. I drove almost nonstop just before Christmas. It reminded me of that long solo journey at Christmastime, the drive from El Paso after Kirk had left for overseas. This was much the same—the same time of year and the end of a phase. But this time I was much, much sicker. I drank unceasingly all the way home.

Arriving around 4:30 A.M., I roused my parents from bed and expected a warm welcome, which I didn't get. It was obvious to them, but not to me, that I was drunk. My mother wanted to feed me, and I wanted to have a drink with my father. Instead, we had a family row, ending with my leaving, quite incensed.

I went to Allentown and woke up my friend Ann, who took me in. It was there that I stayed and drank for several weeks before getting in touch with AA.

Joining Alcoholics Anonymous was an act of desperation. I was no longer able to function as a human being. My life was totally out of control, and I, too, was physically out of control. My early months in AA were nothing more than attending meetings, meetings, meetings and talking, talking, talking. Giving my body a chance to catch up and rest was probably the best thing that had happened to me in my life. When I got to the Allentown group, there was a new approach to treating alcoholics with injections of ACTH. And of course, there were tranquilizers. I was not hospitalized but stayed with Ann, who lived just a half block from Phil, a doctor member of AA, who saw me every day for a few weeks. Withdrawal was painful psychologically and physically. For weeks the daily headaches were severe, but they finally began to lessen in length and severity. I didn't just *stop*. Well, I did, but then, after a week of AA, I went on a weekend bender. Again I stopped. This time it was for longer, and I believe it began to take. The reason was that I began to feel so much better. I was less frightened, my anxiety began to go away, and I felt less isolated and alone.

I went to AA in January after coming home from Kansas. By summer I was in graduate classes at Lehigh University, the academic challenge helping me maintain sobriety.

In the autumn I went to Philadelphia to attend the University of Pennsylvania and I lived in an off-campus apartment on Thirty-seventh Street. Although money was tight, I managed to get a small scholarship from the Carnegie Foundation. After the first year my scholarships and fellowships paid all my expenses up to the Ph.D.

These were extremely exciting years for me. I no longer attended AA, and hadn't from the time I went to Philadelphia. There were times I longed to drink, but I was too involved in learning. I had changed my objectives and now took an interest in American civilization, majoring in sociology. As always, I loved every minute of classes.

My first year was very difficult because I had to prepare to pass the advanced language examinations in German and French for my degree. In those years requirements for a Ph.D. were far more difficult than they are today. Every Friday night the university ran free classes in all languages for the doctoral hopefuls. Attendance was optional. Of course, I attended and can honestly say that despite my having had two years of German in high school and two years of college German, I understood nothing other than *the, and,* and a few other words. Our Ph.D. exam was in scholastic German so that we would be equipped to do research in the German language.

My life in Philadelphia was idyllic. I felt I had found myself. For the first time I loved living alone and savored every minute. I *knew* I was happy, a rarity in itself. My graduate classes were in American Civilization, which meant all American culture; American history, six semesters from colonial times up to the present; and six semesters of American literature. These were the basics. On top were courses in anthropology, sociology, psychology, philosophy, and the history of the American people.

We were permitted three attempts at each language exam. Having never had any French, I approached a friend of our family who once taught French and asked if she would help me; she agreed. I began with a French novel and a dictionary. The advantage was that we never had to speak these languages; we had to just *read* advanced French and German.

I worked hard at French during the summer months of my first year. By the time I returned to Philadelphia in the fall, I was able to pass my French examination. I took the German exam but failed it.

The only sour apple in my life at this time was the German exam. My whole academic future was threatened by it. I continued to attend class every Friday night, and I also engaged a tutor who worked with me three times a week. I would have to be successful and soon, that I knew.

Apart from the worry about German, my life was very, very happy. It was the first time I felt as if I were doing what I was supposed to be doing. Every day was a day to accomplish and learn. I smiled most of the time and felt exuberant. I was totally absorbed in my work and needed or wanted no one to disturb it. Ann wanted to see me, and a few times my parents dropped in to see me, but I could hardly wait to get back to my work. I was addicted to studying and learning. I simply couldn't get enough.

Because the city was very noisy, and I lived next door to a firehouse, which always made me feel very safe, I had a routine that minimized the noise and maximized the few hours of silence: I worked through the whole night and slept as the city awoke, from 6:00 A.M. to 10:00 A.M. From 10:00 A.M. to noon I read mail, planned my day, bathed and dressed, washed my hair, and got ready for class. After classes I went to the library until about 7:00 P.M., and after returning to my apartment, I ate and lay down for an hour to an hour and a half. My studying began at 9:00 P.M. and lasted until 6:00 A.M., when I really went to bed.

As rigorous as it sounds, it was perfect for me because I had never required much sleep at any time in my life. In my second year I experimented with sleep learning in order to store facts and statistics for my board examinations, which I was working toward—if I ever passed German.

After I got a tutor, much of my time was spent on German. I wanted it to be over and done with. After German classes on Friday night (I stayed for a double session), I went back to my apartment at ten and spent the entire night on German, doing vocabulary with a dictionary and then recording it. On Saturday, as I cleaned my apartment, I played the recordings over and over so that the vocabulary was embedded. By late afternoon, during the Metropolitan Opera broadcast, I was able to start the translation of the week's lesson in scholarly German from a German textbook.

It took another year of this intensive study for me to get up the nerve to take another shot at the exam. Finally, at the end of my second year, I passed the German examination and was notified that I was now a doctoral candidate.

I had been at the university for three and a half years and was coming close to the time of taking my board examinations, which every doctoral candidate dreads. This is the moment toward which all the years of work were directed. Unlike a medical student, who is tested each year along the way, a Ph.D candidate works for years before ever knowing if it was all in vain. The difference between a master's degree and a Ph.D. in those days was great, about four or more years of intense work.

As the board exam approached, I began to get very nervous,

worrying about failure and what I would do with the rest of my life. I still had no idea what I would do with my degree *if* I got it. Random thoughts included starting a women's college or trying to get into the United States Information Agency, which was a new agency in the 1950s. Thoughts of a government position were tempered by my history of alcoholism, knowing that it would probably hold me back.

As it turned out, all my worries were for nothing. Fate stepped in and settled my future. Well, perhaps it wasn't fate. Perhaps it was weakness.

During the summer months of my fourth year I was attending a party at the home of a writer in Quakertown, and I was superbly happy. Early in the evening my mother called to say that AA in Allentown—my friend and mentor Phil—called to ask if I would go with him to see a young male alcoholic in Quakertown who was in need of our help.

How I wish I had followed my selfish desire to stay at the party! But I didn't. I went, and it changed my whole life.

Since there was no AA group in Quakertown at that time, I remembered a man who sometimes went to Allentown with me, and he and I went to meet Jim, a young man in his early thirties. Jim's woman friend had called Allentown, and she was with him when we arrived. Jim was "totaled," and spending time with him at that point was futile. We made a few attempts at reassurance, left literature, and spent time with Jim's friend, promising we would be in touch early the next day.

The next day my male AA friend was at work, and I was left with Jim, whom I finally got to an AA meeting a day later. In the meantime, we spent hours and hours talking, sometimes with his friend and sometimes not. This was early August. By the time I went back to Philadelphia in late September my relationship with Jim was changing into a deeper relationship that I didn't want but seemed unable to control. As for his sobriety, as long as I was baby-sitting with him, he was all right.

It was great to get back to Philadelphia. I heaved a sigh of relief when I got to the apartment and back on campus for probably my last semester of classes. Jim called and begged to join me, but I steadfastly refused. After a week of this he used the oldest ploy in the world, and it worked. He got drunk and showed up unexpectedly, demanding attention and to be taken care of.

His moving in with me, and our relationship, did nothing for him and certainly nothing for me. In a strange way I seemed to be under his control. From the very beginning it was a sick, sick relationship. We played every game known to two people, and then we made up a few. We used each other, we destroyed each other, and—finally—we got drunk together.

My last semester is a blur to me. I was taking Dexedrine and Miltown to keep me going after the long nights with Jim.

One night, when I was studying for the board examination and he was demanding as usual that I spend time with him and I didn't, he went to the local bar and came home drunk. As if our ensuing argument weren't enough, with my playing the martyr, he went to the bedroom and took my pills. When I finished studying at dawn and went into the bedroom, I found him, cold and clammy. In panic I went next door to the firehouse and got help.

For a long time at the hospital we didn't know if Jim would make it. His friend who had originally called me about his coming to AA and I sat together hours on end, at times talking as if we couldn't say enough and then lapsing into long silences. Mary knew of our relationship but didn't seem very upset about it, something I should have heeded. But I was much too involved for that to be of consequence. Later I learned that Jim had had many affairs; he always returned to Mary after the woman he was seeing had been destroyed in one way or another. A few had committed suicide; others had attempted it.

I do not understand why I was so captivated. I shall never understand my total loss of self and total loss of control. In many ways I was ignorant of what was really happening to me, strange as that may seem.

At the hospital one of those very rare and almost unbelievable coincidences happened. The psychiatrist assigned to Jim's case happened to be the son of my mother's best friend! I hadn't seen him for years, but as children we had played together, and even in adulthood we had seen each other occasionally. It had been several years since I'd seen him.

After our mutual surprise George asked me to write about Jim as an aid to him, George. I did, and later George was to tell me it was evident from it that I needed as much help as Jim.

So the madness of my last semester was now filled with people: Jim recuperating and rebelling, appointments with George, and schoolwork. Occasionally Mary came for Jim when he was too drunk to drive or when I threw him out of my apartment. Also, a number of women with whom I was taking classes began to drop in often, something I would understand only later when I learned of Jim's brief affairs with them.

In the midst of all this I took my board exams and passed them by some miracle. Because I was high on Dexedrine, it was as if I were a robot answering the intensive questioning, and only part of me was really there. I drank water and chain-smoked through the entire four hours. The night before, Jim had gotten drunk and refused to leave the apartment.

A few days later I received word by telegram that I was the recipient of the Fels Fellowship, the first woman at the University of Pennsylvania to receive it. That I received it was a complete surprise, although I had gone through a number of candidate-eliminating lunches and meetings over a period of a year before the decision was made. However, my personal problems kept me from experiencing full joy. I wanted to stay in my apartment, close to the university library, to finish research for my dissertation. However, Jim now had a job as a flight instructor in Northeast Philadelphia and wanted me to live in that section of the city. It was a one-hour drive to the airfield every day, and he claimed this was the reason he was always drunk when he got home. He swore that his drinking would end and he'd go back to AA if we lived in the Northeast.

Reluctantly I gave up the apartment, and we went to the Northeast, where we leased a ranch-style house for one year.

Instead of Jim's doing the driving, now I did. That was okay with me so long as our lives settled down.

I took off a week from the university to move. Of course, I was riddled with misgivings, knowing almost certainly that I had made a terrible mistake. Yet I just went on with the moving. I decided I would make everything work and we could now live soberly. But the very first night in the new house Jim didn't come home until three. He was very drunk. And so it continued.

I was shattered, angry, weak, despairing, and beaten. Apart from everything else, I felt I simply couldn't do what was expected of me by the Fels Foundation. I very much needed help, needed a friend, but I did the easiest thing in the world—and the weakest: I started drinking. There seemed nothing left to save in my life. A few weeks after we moved, I learned that Jim was involved in an affair with Jody, a woman I knew rather well, and this time it was serious, or as serious as it could be with Jim. But every time I started packing to leave, Jim threatened suicide. And my drinking intensified until, one night, I turned the tables. I sealed the house, sealed the kitchen, and took an overdose of pills and booze before turning on the gas oven.

I awoke in the Lower Bucks County Hospital. A neighbors' dog had smelled the gas, and its barking brought them and then the police.

From the hospital I went to Quakertown to my parents' home, determined to end this nightmare I was living. A week of good food and the warmth of home made it easy for me to think I could do so. My plan was to go back, pack my things, move out and get back on my feet.

Then, one night when my parents were out for the evening, Jim arrived, sober, begging me to come back, all would be different. I held out for three hours. I went back with him.

Of course, it didn't last. Within a week Jim was again drinking and seeing Jody. One night, when he came home drunk and late, I confronted him, and he acknowledged his affair with Jody, saying he had no intention of ending it. She couldn't move in and live with Jim because she was married. I was the caretaker.

I lashed out physically at Jim, but I got the worst of it. After a number of head blows I was bleeding from the ears and mouth. Jim tied a string around my head before taking me for brain X rays. Again I was hospitalized for a few days, this time for serious injuries from the beating, and all of it was of my own making.

After this I no longer made any pretense of normal living, working, or studying. Every day was spent in a neighborhood barroom. Most of the time I was alone. Sometimes Jim would stop by and pick me up if he were able. Sometimes he picked me up as he was coming home from Jody's. Self-pity ruled me. Even the bartender begged me to quit drinking, told me not to come back, not to ruin my life. But his words meant nothing to me. I was hellbent on self-destruction. I became extremely ill, unable to drink my daily fifth of liquor, and finally I decided to see my old friend George, the psychiatrist.

Seeing him was a great relief. Of course he advised me to leave Jim immediately, and that same day I stopped at a house at Thirty-sixth and Walnut in the city and rented an apartment. Then I drove past the university and was overwhelmed with nostalgia and the nagging question of why I had let myself slip so far down.

Driving out to the Northeast, I felt alive, I felt hope, and when I got there, I started packing. When Jim got home, he wouldn't believe it, and the argument began. This time I held my ground, and this time he knew I meant it. So that night he stayed home, and we got drunk together, and the next day, and the day after that. I missed appointments with George, I lost the apartment, and I was right back in the rut again.

My drinking was now without end. I simply drank all day and all night long. Just straight. Always blended rye. I was always mildly stuporous. I loathed myself. I wanted only to die. There seemed to be no one loving me. My parents were condemning and judgmental, as they had every right to be. There was no one just to hold me and reassure me that everything would be all right. One weekend I drove to Allentown to see Ann, my closest friend, who was cordial and introduced me to the man she was about to marry. Feeling I was a third wheel, I quickly left. I drove to Quakertown on my way back to Philadelphia and found that my parents were not home. I went into the empty house and felt as if I were in a dream world, as if I had never lived there. My bedroom was still filled with my books, and I sat at my desk, and I felt as if I had never before done that. I felt strange and alienated and very, very lonely. I put my head on the desk and cried. Everything seemed totally unbearable, and I didn't know how to stop anything. I remembered that wonderfully apropos sentence *Stop the world, I want to get off.* I felt beaten. I was beaten.

After a long last glance at my room I left it and went to my dad's liquor cabinet in the dining room and took out a bottle of bourbon. After a long swig I took the bottle with me and left the house. There seemed to be no one in the world to whom I could turn.

Months trailed on, and nothing changed except that my downward slide went a little faster. Every cent I got from the fellowship was spent on drinking, and I had a very considerable amount of money. (Years later I offered to pay it back, but the Fels people were happy that eventually I finished my degree, some twelve years later.)

One night, while I was driving around looking for Jim and Jody, the persistent wail of a police siren cut through my mental numbness, and I tried, with great difficulty, to pull the car over to the curb. I was very drunk, and I knew it. Even worse, this was Philadelphia, and the city cops were unrelenting.

When I finally got the car stopped, I felt great relief, and my head slumped on the steering wheel just a moment before the policeman was at the door of my car.

"Okay, now let's see your license. Do you always drive drunk?"

Mumbling incoherently, I tried to tell him I wasn't drunk.

"Get out of the car and let me see your license."

Incensed, I got out of the car with great difficulty and then lunged at him, flailing fists and kicking him. From somewhere deep within I got the strength and anger of a caged animal. There was no way the policeman could take hold of me until he was joined by his partner. Together they slapped the handcuffs on me—tight—and drove me to the station house in the Northeast section of Philadelphia. After several hours there and a search of my person and their refusal to let me make a phone call, I was again handcuffed. This time I was put on the floor of a police wagon and driven twenty miles into the heart of the city, where I spent the night in jail in city hall.

During the night, that long, haunted night filled with the pitiful, heartrending moans and screams of women coming off hard drugs and alcohol, I managed to bribe a coffeeman with nine dollars I had hidden. I asked him to call George. He did.

The next day I was again handcuffed, put into the paddy wagon, and driven back to the Northest section. Now I was starting into withdrawal from pills and booze, and I hardly knew all that was going on. I knew I was in another jail cell, but I didn't care. I was sick, shaking apart, shivering, cold, nauseated. During the night I'd taken a few tranquilizers that I had managed to conceal, but now everything was gone. And now I had also lost my voice.

Not only was George in the courtroom, but so was my father. Shame enveloped me, and I couldn't bear to look at him. When I finally did, I saw how he felt. His face was ashen. If I were to rank the terrible moments in my life, this would be very close to the top of the list.

The judge gave me a severe lecture about all the advantages in my life and the opportunities I was throwing away, that I should not be there before him, wasting his time, and it was obvious he was angry. The sentence was six months and a $300 fine. I was charged with assault and battery of an officer, drunk driving, and resistance to arrest. After my psychiatrist had spoken, my sentence was commuted to a commitment in a mental institution under George's care.

With that my father came toward me and led me to his car. He was crying silently, but he put his arms around me, and I felt safe at last.

Even though George had medicated me before we left the courtroom, I was still unable to speak, so I just cried all the way to the psychiatric institution, which was quite a long distance. As soon as I was admitted, I was put to bed, and it was five days before I was able to speak. I was given Dexedrine in lesser and lesser doses until I was finally off it altogether.

My stay in the psychiatric hospital lasted for almost a year and was extremely traumatic. During that time Jim was not allowed to see me, although he made several attempts. (Later I learned that he had gone to Puerto Rico and had a flying job there.) There were twice-daily sessions with psychiatrists. And tests. Later there were shock treatments and experimental treatments using hypnosis and sodium Amytal for regressive hypnotherapy. And there were drugs, drugs, drugs. Alcoholism was never discussed. The psychiatrists who treated me believed that those of us who drank as I drank did so because we were emotionally upset. As soon as we were straightened out, they thought, we could drink like other people. Whenever I had weekend privileges, my drinking was never curtailed, and I was always brought back drunk, but I was never reprimanded.

When I was finally discharged, it was on the condition that I remain in Philadelphia, close to the hospital, so that I could be treated as an outpatient five days a week. This meant taking another apartment and living alone. It also meant more uncontrolled drinking.

It is a great sadness to me that when I finally got professional help, it was the wrong kind. To this day I cannot remember anything significant that was ever discussed during my three years of intense psychiatric sessions.

My new apartment was in West Philadelphia, and one week after I had moved in, Jim returned from Puerto Rico, and we took off from there. This time we haunted Philadelphia nightspots, all on the seedy side, especially after 2:00 A.M., when we went to private clubs to drink until 5:00 or 6:00 A.M. Most of the time I missed my psychiatric appointments, and when I did make them, I was usually drunk and was dismissed.

Then I had to move home. My father's money had simply run out after all the years of psychiatrists, hospitals, apartments, drinking money, and car expenses. He had exhausted almost $175,000 on my care.

When I moved home, Jim followed. He no longer attempted to work, having inherited a large sum of money from a distant cousin who had conveniently died.

Although my parents did everything possible to keep me from seeing Jim, I would simply leave home and not come back for days. Jim's and my relationship was mainly that of drinking buddies now, with occasional sex. We valued the drinking buddy part much, much more than the sex. We both were free to kill ourselves slowly. And we did just that.

The sordidness of this period of my life is just not describable. Nor can I write about it. I was absolutely hooked on alcohol and drugs. Much of the time I didn't know who I was or where I was. There were times I found myself slumped over in a car seat, parked on a street in a place I couldn't identify.

If there was ever a person who lived a charmed life, I did. I was lucky to have survived.

I totally ruined life for my parents, but I was unable to see it. I embarrassed them all the time and made their lives pure hell. At last, at my urging, my dad helped me to buy a home—an old farmhouse on the edge of Quakertown. He made the down payment and the mortgage payments, even though I had every intention of getting a job. However, I was much too sick to do so. Sylvia, one of the psychiatric nurses from the hospital, came to live with me at the urging of my parents, but this didn't do very much to change my life. I continued to do just as I wanted to.

Jim came to my house very often, but his drinking hit a bad turn. On a dark night in Philadelphia, on the expressway, his motorcycle hit a car, and his leg had to be amputated. During the next months he visited me daily, sometimes staying over. Sometimes Sylvia had to put both of us to bed. One day he was late coming. Two hours later Mary called to say that Jim had used a shotgun to blow off his head. There was a note for me and a ring.

After that the days were gray and long. Even though I had always been aware of the destructive element in our relationship, part of me grieved. But part of me felt released.

At last I was emotionally free to begin the long road to recovery.

CHAPTER TWO

THE BIG DECISION

So you really want to quit. Is this the first time? The second time? Perhaps the fiftieth time? Or is it the thousandth time?

If you are anything like me, you will answer, "Yes, this is at least the thousandth time I've made the decision to quit drinking."

It is natural to wonder why it is so extremely difficult to quit drinking when all it brings is physical hardship and emotional bankruptcy. Even knowing that alcoholism is a disease and that we've lost all control of our drinking doesn't seem to stop us, does it? We know this truth, yet we go ahead and drink, day after day, week after week, year after year, always trying to prove that the diagnosis of alcoholism is wrong. Somehow we are still able to fool ourselves into believing that one of these days we are going to be able to control the amount we drink and put an end to this nightmare of erratic behavior that others find offensive. We know that with time and concentration we will control our drinking and subsequently our lives. Right?

How do I know this? I know because I was once where you are now, and all I can say is "Thank God I'm no longer there." This doesn't mean that I don't have compassion for you because I do. I know how you are suffering emotionally, physically, and spiritually. I have a great desire to help you, and I think I can.

I can't offer you a magic formula, although that is what you are hoping for. I also know that at this point you are not really looking for a way to quit drinking; you are looking for a way to drink without losing control.

In simple words, you are looking for a way to escape being an alcoholic.

That's the part that we must get straight right now. The fact that you are reading this means you are concerned about your drinking. But now let's find out if you are an alcoholic. Okay? Here we go:

1. Do you end up having an argument with your spouse every time you drink?
2. Do you try very hard not to drink before a certain hour every day?
3. Do you ever drink because you are nervous about going to see a doctor? Going to the dentist? Starting a new job? Going to a funeral?
4. Do you ever drink because you are afraid of doing something and think a few drinks will make it easier and will relax you?
5. When you drink, do you make an effort to drink slowly so that people won't notice you?
6. Do you sometimes miss going to work on Monday morning?
7. Do you sometimes keep a bottle in your car just so it's handy if you want it?
8. Have you ever had trouble finding your car when you've been drinking?
9. Do you ever feel uncomfortable about getting rid of empty bottles?
10. Do you ever try to find different places to get rid of your liquor bottles?
11. Do you ever have trouble stopping drinking once you get started?
12. Have you ever had trouble remembering things that happened while you were drinking?
13. Have you discovered that you get less flak

from family members if you sneak a few
drinks and don't do all your drinking in front
of them?

14. Do you ever want to take a drink the next
    morning after drinking the night before ... to
    recover faster?

15. Do you believe that you have a serious
    drinking problem but are afraid to mention it
    to anyone?

16. Have you ever told yourself that you really
    ought to give up drinking?

17. Do you find that drinking makes you feel
    less insecure and less vulnerable?

18. Have you found that it helps to have a drink
    or two before going to a party and that it
    makes you feel less nervous?

19. Have you ever bought your liquor at several
    different stores because you didn't want to go
    back to the same one?

20. Have you ever noticed any changes in your
    drinking habits?

In answering the twenty questions, did you learn something
about yourself and your drinking? Do you now *believe* you have
a drinking problem? Or do you still deny being an alcoholic? A
social drinker, a person without an alcohol problem, would have
answered no to all twenty questions. Did you?

Most of us go through three stages before winning our fight
with alcohol: admission; surrender; acceptance. Now is the time
for you to *admit* that you have a problem with alcohol so that you
can begin to work toward recovery.

ADMISSION

Do you want to quit? Usually we quit drinking the day we
can no longer stand ourselves. This day is often hastened when

those persons whom we love have had enough of our behavior and leave us.

The day for that last drink comes closer when the person you love most says, "Okay, I've had it. You've punished me just far enough. I'm not going to put up with your behavior any longer. I refuse to let you yell at me the way you do. I cannot take your insults anymore. And I know that you will never keep your promises. I've had it, and I'm leaving."

Of the hundreds, perhaps thousands, of alcoholics I've talked to or whose letters I have read over the past several years, the clearest message I have received is this: When the whole world falls in on us and we are left alone, we are finally able to find the strength to quit drinking. Perhaps we quit on that day because we are so scared that we cannot sleep or eat or make sense of anything. Fear dominates us, and we are more frightened than we have ever been before. We want to crawl under the bedcovers and whimper about the unfairness of life.

Out of this fear, however, comes the strength to give in. Many times we have wanted to but couldn't. It takes an event of great consequence to make us act. Some people are fired, some lose an entire family, some lose both before quitting drinking.

I was never fired, but I was left alone. And even though I wasn't fired, there were strong implications that I *was* being dismissed. Politely, I was let go because of a "technicality."

Neither have I experienced a husband's leaving me because of drinking. Although I am divorced, it was not because of alcohol, so I have never shared that experience with those who are going through it now. However, I did experience a time in my life when the staunchest of my friends, everyone who meant anything to me, finally gave up and left me, and I felt more alone and isolated than I have ever felt before or since. Not only was I torn apart inside and scared, but I experienced a total sense of disconnection with all other human beings.

That was the day I seriously began to quit drinking. Several years ago a newspaperwoman who interviewed me wrote that I had quit cold turkey. This is not exactly true, and indeed, I hadn't told her that. Naturally the last drink that any one of us has is certainly the day in which we have ended our drinking cold turkey. But what I mean to say is that I did not drink up to a certain day and then quit forever. The way I stopped drinking was in fits and starts, even though I wanted to stop suddenly and never drink again. My pattern was to quit and to be certain in my mind that I'd quit, but then, after several days or weeks of feeling wonderful, I would be certain I had made a mistake and would begin to drink again. Then, filled with guilt and remorse, to say nothing of the hangover and shaking hands, I would quit *again*, certain that *this* time was forever.

But the pattern of stop and start, with longer intervening periods, happened over and over, so I do not have any real knowledge of the last time I had my last drink.

For those of you who are waiting for the magic word on how to quit, this may not be the way for you to do it. I have known thousands of alcoholics who have simply quit and never had another drink after they called on self-help groups or therapists or who did it alone. Perhaps it depends on how sick you are or the kind of personality you have. It may be that you wake up some morning with the worst hangover you have ever had and say, "This is it." Or you may be fired from your job and you say, "This is it." Or perhaps you're in an automobile accident and, with the help of a court and a judge, you are kept away from alcohol for thirty to sixty days, and that is the way for you. It may be, too, that you reach a point of such self-disgust, life being filled only with guilt, remorse, depression, loneliness, desperation, anger, and quarreling, that you are able to call for help.

There is no one way to quit. For most of us it does involve self-disgust, when we reach a point we cannot and do not want to go beyond, a point beyond which we can no longer struggle. At this point some people want to end it all by committing suicide. Some do, and many hundreds of others try, even if subconsciously the will to die is not present. I well remember a holiday period when I had been drinking and suffering mightily from hangovers plus much emotional stress. One day, when I woke up, I knew it was the day I would commit suicide. I did not think about it, but my despair with my life was so great that something beyond my thinking mind knew I would end it. Obviously my life did not end that way, but I know that I was not fooling that time, for it took several doctors several hours to ensure my survival.

Self-disgust is the factor that finally leads to surrender—to the decision to quit at last.

There is no way out of alcoholism. Many of you may be saying, "Well, I'm not an alcoholic yet. I just have problems with drinking. Every time I drink I feel terrible, but I'm nothing like all those people described. I don't drink often. I drink only once a month and only on special occasions, so I'm really not an alcoholic."

Well, let me lay this on you. You *are* an alcoholic and need to admit it and surrender just as all of us must do. How little you drink makes not one whit of difference; it's *how* you drink. Getting into trouble requires surrender. The keynote is what happens when you drink.

SURRENDER

When we surrender, we must learn that alcoholism is a terminal illness. There is no way out and no turning back. We have it and must surrender to its dictate: abstention.

Only two things will happen if you continue to drink: You will probably die from it or some complication it causes, or you will be a person cut off from others and unable to function socially in any acceptable manner.

More people die from the complications caused by excessive use of alcohol than die from being drunk. The introduction of so much alcohol into one's system damages brain cells, damages the muscles of the heart, and creates a condition known as esophageal varices, which is the breaking down of the small blood vessels in the throat. Alcohol eats through the lining of the stomach. It can create pancreatitis. It has everything to do with cirrhosis, fatty globules in the liver that either interrupt or halt its function, ending in death.

You can see there are many reasons why you must surrender and accept the fact that you are an alcoholic, that you have a terminal illness, that it will not go away and will probably get worse, despite the many experiments you may have heard about on learning to drink moderately. Surrendering now may add years to your life and allow you to move along the road marked "Happiness," impossible as that may seem.

Many years ago I heard a man say that he didn't miss drinking anymore. "I never think about it. It never enters my mind." At the time I thought I had never heard anything so preposterous, yet now, after twelve years of sobriety, I am able to say that very thing. Others may be able to make that statement even before twelve years have gone by. It is different for everyone. However ridiculous it may now appear to you, there will be a day when drinking doesn't figure in your life or your thoughts. That was one of the biggest surprises to me, and I know other recovered alcoholics feel the same way. It's amazing to realize how much of our lives was involved with and consumed by thinking about drinking. While we are involved with that kind of life, we simply don't know how warped our thoughts are: *Where will I get the next drink? When is the next party? Will the liquor stores still be open when I finish work? Where can I get rid of these empty bottles? I can't visit the Joneses because they never serve liquor. How can I avoid a hangover before that important appointment?* And on and on and on.

It takes only a few weeks of not drinking to begin to realize how one's life was totally dominated by such thoughts. As we get more into the nondrinking life, we begin to understand many things. This new knowledge comes with our acceptance.

ACCEPTANCE

After the early stages of Admission and Surrender, you move into Acceptance. You have finally begun to see that there is no way out of this box. You may try to get out of acceptance. I know I did. I really squirmed, and the more I squirmed and tried to go back to drinking, the more it became obvious to me that I was trapped, stuck with the knowledge that my drinking days were at an end.

Acceptance can and should be a comfortable place. It is where you are when you have given in to the inevitable; it is the final acknowledgment that you are an alcoholic. It is much harder for women to accept the word *alcoholic* than it is for men, and rather than have recovery be hung up by semantics, it is better for some women to avoid the use of the terrible word. In that case, word it differently: Accept the fact that you have "a problem with alcohol" and "are unable to drink" and that every time you do, you "get into trouble" or "can't stop" or "something bad happens." This suggestion has frequently drawn criticism from those who believe that it keeps women from accepting the truth. My counterargument is that if a woman starts to get the help she needs through simply admitting that alcohol is her "problem," then much is accomplished. The true nature of her disease will soon become abundantly clear to her.

The problem with the word *alcoholic* comes from public perception or, rather, lack of perception of the person so described. Generally the public sees an alcoholic as a person who spends most of his or her life moving between lying in the gutter and sleeping in a flophouse. It comes as a shock to nonalcoholics to learn that fewer than 4 percent of the 15 million alcoholics in this country fit that picture.

Because social drinkers' behavior is so different, they cannot understand the life of an alcoholic. Social drinkers drink when they choose to drink and only the quantity chosen. Thus to them the word *alcoholic* conjures up the derelict. This is why so many alcoholics really have a problem accepting the truth about their disease. Many true alcoholics share the picture seen by the social drinker at first because they were reared in the same culture. Just the other day I had a phone call asking for help from a woman who was barely able to speak at 11:00 A.M. She said, "I know I'm not an alcoholic *yet,* but I have been doing a lot of drinking during the day, and I have been missing work."

This woman's alcoholic drinking was probably discernible years before, but most all of us are ignorant about alcoholism and don't want to learn. I, too, had great difficulty in believing I was an alcoholic, thinking *they* were much worse than I was. As I look back now, almost no one could have been worse than I was.

All this affects acceptance. We keep thinking we are not yet at that point, that we have all the time in the world, so our problem is not serious. An easy way to accept your problem, and its seriousness, is to dwell on the truth that every time you drink, you have arguments and display behavior that isn't the real you and that your drinking creates other difficulties in your life. Too often we are convinced that our drinking helps us face the problems of our lives. For some very strange reason, most of us are able to convince ourselves of this for too long a time.

As mentioned earlier, acceptance of the true nature of your drinking may have to come from the loss of someone close to you, the loss of friends, or the loss of a job. Or it may have to come from your loss of self-respect. It usually takes this kind of personal tragedy. This is the sad part of our disease. We get pretty far down the hill before we start back up. But we do not have to go the whole route.

In the long run acceptance may be the easiest part of recovery. We give up drinking, and then we come to know ourselves. Often this is a great awakening. We begin to learn *why* we turned to alcohol in order to cope with life's problems. We begin to see, even though crudely at first, what makes us tick, and sometimes this is not pleasant.

Almost all of us began drinking in an effort to ease the pressures on our lives. Some of us crossed the line into alcoholism but still tried to use alcohol to solve problems. Of course, when we recognize and accept our alcoholism, the time has come for us to begin working on our problems in other ways. We drank to cope, so when we quit drinking, we must learn new and better ways of coping. In many ways our new sobriety will really depend upon how quickly we can learn the new ways of coping, ways that are not self-destructive.

To maintain sobriety, which has thus far been elusive to us, we are going to have to learn new ways of living. These new ways will reshape our whole lives. This is the processs of recovery. We are going to remake our lives in ways that will provide us with the things for which we have deep-seated emotional needs.

The name of the new game is self-sufficiency. Of course, when we quit drinking, we are attempting to achieve lasting sobriety. It is necessary for us to understand how this can happen. We must learn that sobriety is built upon our conceptions of self. It is true that almost all of us with drinking problems do not really know who we are; we do not have true assessments of our capabilities. And it is necessary for us to know these things to maintain and enjoy sobriety. How many people have you known who are sober but that's about all you can say for them? Many are simply "dry" but are not happy. That is the tragedy of an uneasy sobriety.

Recognize now that sobriety does not mean an end to "living." Indeed, it is just the opposite. By following the suggestions in this book, you will find the greatest happiness of your life and a truly remarkable sobriety, one without sweat and pain, one without uneasiness.

Your main desire should be to learn how to change your life. This will come about with practice and some guidance. It will happen with a change of thinking patterns. I learned that my thinking was entirely wrong. I believed all the terrible things that had happened to me were simply due to my bad luck, to ill fortune. How wrong I was! It was *I* who had created these negative happenings. They didn't just happen to me out of the blue. It was my negative thinking and my negative actions that had created them. It was then that I realized that I had to change my way of thinking in order to change my life.

It is difficult to get into positive thinking as soon as alcohol is removed because we are not feeling very good. When the alcohol is first taken away, we feel very, very negative. The person that initially emerges is not really the true person. It is someone very frightened, very nervous, very uptight, and generally not very pleasant. We usually have frequent headaches during this early period, and we have many thoughts about wanting to drink. There are many times when we are struck by the thought *Is it really worth this?* Many times feelings of paranoia take over. We begin to believe that everyone is talking about us, watching us. But these feelings are part of the final withdrawal; they are not the real us. And you may be lucky and never experience these feelings; certainly not everyone does.

If you are one who experiences these feelings, know that they go away. The real you begins to emerge when you start to be in charge of yourself, and this happens gradually because you have been dependent for so long. Dependency on alcohol kills desire for self-fulfillment. It totally destroys any feeling of self-sufficiency.

Negativity has been the pattern of our thinking, and indeed, it along with the alcohol has almost destroyed us. The two, alcohol and negative feelings, are long-time bedfellows. In sobriety we change these feelings. We turn them around. We begin to make our emotions productive for us rather than destructive to us and others.

We begin the process by seeing ourselves as capable people, not as the beaten-down, incapable failures we have been imagining ourselves to be. Too often those who try to achieve and maintain sobriety fail because their thoughts stay in the same rut of guilt, remorse, upset, anger, depression, and more remorse. Many continue to see themselves as emotional cripples and thus impede sobriety.

You are at the crossroads. You have made the decision to quit; you have moved through the three early feelings of (1) admission, (2) surrender, and (3) acceptance; and you are now ready to look at yourself in an objective way occasionally. Later you will be able to view yourself objectively most of the time, but in these early weeks it is very difficult to begin to sort out emotions. Just knowing that most of what you have been feeling and experiencing has been almost totally negative will help you a great deal. In fact, at this time it is beneficial to begin to write down your feelings in a small record book. Take time to record all your feelings, feelings that seem to have been controlling you in these last years, the drinking years. I would guess that they will surprise you.

When you are able to believe once again in your own capability, you will no longer be an emotional cripple. You will not engage in emotional conflicts that continually upset you or that make you feel guilty. In fact, once you are able to see yourself in the true light of your capability, you will no longer have to use or even think about the use of alcohol as a means of coping.

Yes, it would be great if we did not have this illness, this disease, this thing that is terminal. But the truth is we do have it. We are alcoholics and can no longer handle alcohol. This is what forces us into being different persons. It is the motivation to change. And that is really a marvelous opportunity, for when we change our self-perceptions, we will be much stronger persons.

If someone were to say, "We'll erase your alcoholism and you can drink again," I guarantee you that having learned your new way of life, you would never consider taking up that proposition. There would be no need to. You would not need a drink to help you with your life or with the situations in life. You would not want to drink to dull your senses or to escape life because you would find an exhilaration with life that you had never before known. The exhilaration that I am telling you about comes to you from the inside when you learn all that you can do, all that you are capable of, without the debilitation of alcohol.

Aim high. Sit down somewhere and write on a sheet of paper what you want to do in your life, what you want to accomplish, what you want to have, where you want to go. Too often we fail to see life stretching before us in the image of a road. We get bogged down in small details. Most of us spend more time planning a picnic or a weekend camping trip than we ever spend planning our lives.

I don't know why this is, why we are so unimaginative with our lives. I was more than forty when I learned about goals and life planning. Now I have a one-year plan, a five-year plan, and a ten-year plan. You should begin doing this, too. It will help with your recovery. It will put hope and zest into your life. You will not feel that all is useless and hopeless.

Begin now to make a list of what you want to do: return to college; start a business; become a realtor, or a lawyer, or a rock cutter. You may simply want to take up a hobby in a serious way. I have found that part of this process is being imaginative in one's thinking. Many times there are things we wish we could do but think is impossible. Why? Because it seems ridiculous? Because we think others will make fun of us? Or do we lack the belief or the drive or the intensity to do it? Are we too lazy? Or does it always come back to our feeling that others will laugh, will make fun of us? So what? Let the world laugh. Who cares?

In your new sobriety you are going to learn how to develop *you*. You are not going to care too much what others think of you. When I say that, I don't mean that you will defy society as we all once did in the days of our drinking. Now, in sobriety, you will begin to assert yourself in independent ways. You will broaden your horizons. You will begin to make plans for your life. You will begin to feel enthusiasm for things you never did before.

Now is the time to live. Now is the time to become all those things you always wanted to be when you were trapped in a narrow tunnel of addiction and self-destruction. Now you are free to be everything you want to be. It takes planning, and it takes a belief in self, and it takes enthusiasm and desire. Invest your life with these, and you will never again want to drink.

When you begin to assess, like, respect, and love yourself, you are then able to love others. You are then able to be useful to others.

Quitting? Yes, now you know how. Simply put down the

bottle. Put away the glass and quit. It is your choice. It is always your choice. Nobody is telling you to quit. But make the decision today. If you have a drinking problem, end it. Take charge of your life. Take charge of yourself, and launch yourself into the adventure of the new you, beginning with the belief and knowledge that you are a competent, capable person.

PART TWO

SOBRIETY

CHAPTER THREE

UNDERSTANDING YOUR DEPRESSION

The slumped form in the corner of the couch was me. How long I had been in that position, unconscious of the people and sounds around me, always depended upon how long the nurses let me stay that way. Although I was dressed, it was only because someone was paid to dress me. No other reason. I was beyond caring about myself or how I looked. I was beyond caring about anything.

This period of severe depression lasted several months. It occurred during a time when I was hospitalized for a "nervous breakdown," that quaint and meaningless term used to describe any condition other than "normal," whatever "normal" may be. I was there because of my alcoholism, but this was almost totally ignored.

In my state of depression I was oblivious of everyone and of everything going on around me. I had pulled into myself all the outer radar one normally uses to communicate with the world. Neither my mind nor my body functioned, nor did I want them to. Worst of all, somewhere in the recesses of my mind I knew how impossible I was being, but I couldn't change any of it. Whatever reaction I caused in others by my uncommunicative behavior made no difference to me. I no longer cared what anyone thought about me or my behavior. There were times tears rolled down my face, but I didn't know what I was crying about. There were times I was unaware that I was crying. Most of the time I simply seemed to stare into space, unfocused.

And then it left. I began to want to recover, and I still do

43

not know exactly how the change came about. It became apparent to me that I had been somewhere, way down in a frightening place to which I never wanted to return. I also knew that when I was in this deep black hole, I was always trying to get out but couldn't do it. It was like being deep in a dark vat and clawing helplessly and hopelessly at the shiny sides in an effort to raise myself and crawl out, with each attempt being frustrated by some force that continued to push me back down into the darkness.

I had been somewhere that I couldn't describe to others, nor did my psychiatrist understand the terror I had felt at not knowing how to come back. I had lost touch. And I had also lost the link to the human chain of existence.

Experiencing such depression is devastating and almost indescribable. It is a feeling of loss, a feeling of emptiness. It was, for me, the feeling of a terrible weight pushing me down toward the bottom of what was a bottomless black hole.

Disillusion with ourselves and life leads to depression. It was no accident that I suffered my worst period of depression at the lowest point in my life. I had lost—thrown away—everything I worked so hard to get, my Ph.D. It had been there in my grasp, and I'd thrown it away.

Studying the classical explanations of depression has given me new insight into that period of my life. Experts see as the basis of depression the woman's loss of self-esteem or feeling of value. The woman suffering from depression thinks about herself, *I am no one, I am no good, I am nothing. No one loves me. It's not worth it. Who could love me? I can't cope any longer, I hate my life, everyone will be better off without me. My life is over. I am nobody, I am nobody, I am nobody.*

These devastating feelings of worthlessness, coupled with feelings of helplessness, are expressed by almost all women alcoholics at some time or another, usually when they are first into sobriety. The feelings can last for years if the real reason is not recognized and dealt with. Experiencing depression during drinking days is common because alcohol is a depressant. However, in sobriety our depressions no longer come from alcohol. They arise from the almost total lack of good feelings about ourselves. Taught to be passive, giving, nurturing, caring for the needs of others, we are stripped of any real feelings about ourselves. As women we feel undefined in anything but subservience.

Drinking helped many of us to have quite different feelings about ourselves, fleeting though they may have been. Drinking helped us feel strong, resilient, powerful, confident, able to take on the whole world. Alcohol gave us a voice to say no and even to say "I won't." Remove the alcohol, and we are right back to the real us.

This kind of thinking is what overpowerd me when I was hospitalized. Feeling like nothing and feeling totally worthless, I wanted only to sink to the very bottom of the black pit into which I seemed to be falling. At the time I didn't think about suicide. That happened later, when I was out of the hospital. I had tried suicide when I was with Jim, but in the hospital I was simply not thinking or feeling at all.

Thoughts of suicide and attempts at suicide are very real among depressed persons, especially women alcoholics. The old saying "If someone threatens suicide, we know she probably won't do it" is completely untrue. They *do* do it, and many attempt it, as did I, on several occasions. Jim talked of it many times, yet I was so taken up with my own depressions that I wasn't really listening hard enough. Often this is the case. The depressed person hangs around with another depressed person so that helping each other is simply out of the question. *Both* are in dire need of help.

Threatening suicide may be a bid for attention, but it is a real threat and should never be taken lightly. Although the number of attempts that fail is ten times higher than those that succeed, it is from the group that fails that the later "successful" suicides will emanate. Refusal to take people's threats seriously may lead them on, as if they were being dared to do it.

An alcoholic woman I knew over a period of five years very often talked about suicide. Indeed, she made many attempts, and because they were never successful, although a few came very close, I made the grave error of thinking she would probably never die in that way. I was wrong. She did die that way after at least a dozen false attempts that I can remember, and I was told there were many, many more. Were the others practice? Or a warning? Or a declaration?

The very worst thing we can do when someone threatens suicide is to treat it lightly. For the general population, suicide ranks tenth as a cause of death, but it ranks much higher among college students, and recently we are seeing a very high rate of suicide among teen-agers. Among alcoholics suicide rates are also very high.

The feeling of loss of control permeates everything young people do. Loss of control is surely to be observed in the rock videos so currently popular, symbolizing the loss of control the young feel within themselves.

Need we look much further for the answers to suicide among the young?

Certainly all suicides are committed by depressed persons, yet it is also true that not all depressed persons commit suicide. Instead, they are emotional cripples trying to grapple with life and its myriad complexities.

Of course, the very nature of some of the symptoms of depression often masks it to others. These symptoms can be:

> Sleeping difficulties
> Feelings of failure
> Weight loss or gain
> Inattention or lassitude
> Easily crying
> Inability to concentrate
> Restlessness
> Tiredness
> Low sexual drive
> Poor appearance
> Trouble with decision making
> Difficulty with remembering

Agitation
Inability to see humor in anything
Trouble with relationships

From these symptoms we can easily see that people may be depressed without even knowing it. Many low periods in my own life have included a number of these symptoms, yet I would have described myself not as depressed but only as "down." One of these periods occurred when I stopped drinking. That period of depression lasted, on and off, for almost a year.

During that time I was unable to get a job and I had much difficulty with relationships. Of course, one of the most traumatic experiences of an alcoholic is making the transition from drinking friends to nondrinking friends. Often we don't have any nondrinking friends since we long ago alienated them.

The depression of the alcoholic in this period is due to the great feeling of loss that comes from losing the security of dependence upon alcohol. It also comes from being adrift without relationships and from a deep feeling of wondering, *Who am I?* The loss of self is perhaps most acute at this stage of recovery.

We know that the person suffering from depression seems to be dead inside. We see only the shell of what once was an alive personality. It is as if the internal fire of life were snuffed out and only the body were left in a state of shell shock. Nothing we suggest the person do seems to change this condition of death in life.

For therapists the most difficult problem is reaching the person. Too often I have been in touch with severely depressed persons who simply can't be reached for certain periods, yet to give up is to lose the person. The depressed person must go from being inner-centered to outer-directed. Several years ago I made a cassette tape about the depression experienced by alcoholics, and as a way of getting the alcoholic outer-directed, I suggested the listeners become involved with large ideas that would put their thinking on a different plane. Sometime later a woman wrote to me and said about the tape, "You asked me to get involved with large ideas at a time when I wanted to know how to get out of bed."

It is true that many severely depressed persons cannot even get out of bed, cannot comb their hair or manage the simplest function, but very often this kind of depression requires medical attention. This was the case of the woman who wrote to me.

Of course, even for depressed persons who do not require medical attention, it is difficult to become outer-directed. During the period when I spent days on a couch in a slumped-over position, the last thing in the world I could have done was get myself involved in large, challenging ideas.

There is a very wide gap between those experiencing depression and those who are not. When we are well, we believe that the depressed person just needs to be shaken, scolded, spanked, or pushed into some action—any action. Yet this is not the course to take. It is true that we must somehow reach the depressed person, and this may severely try our patience. On the other hand, when we ourselves are deep in depression, we want only to be left alone and to be understood.

Depression often is a warning to us that we are not dealing with our feelings, that we have suppressed or withdrawn from emotions that are too upsetting to face. We experience that terrible feeling of helplessness and loss of control, loss of the persons we once knew ourselves to be. Oftentimes we used alcohol to mask and suppress bad and disturbing feelings, but now, with the alcohol taken away, we are again in the trap of having to face the upsetting emotions or withdraw. More often than not we withdraw.

It is very important for you to know that almost without exception, a recovering alcoholic knows a period of depression. For some, especially women, this lasts a long time, and it is probably the most difficult period experienced in getting well and back on the right track.

It is a period during which we are ready to give up because getting sober doesn't seem worth all these negative feelings. We also tend to have feelings of self-pity. We look for "justice," believing that because we gave up alcohol, we should automatically feel marvelous, as if we had never been drinking. And then our depressions deepen.

In essence, depression is a form of dying, a kind of emotional and psychological death. We give up on ourselves. In a state of depression we no longer seem to have the will to live. The depressed person denies the present and tries to live in the past. The recovering alcoholic tries to run away from the discomfort of the recovering process, of reality, of being without the once-reliable coping substance—alcohol.

The need to avoid reality at all costs derives from the inability to stand one's self. Hostile and angry feelings try to surface but are quickly smothered. Then the depression sets in. To the alcoholic, it is easier to deal with than are anger and hostility. These emotions come too close to revealing the underlying true feelings of insecurity, immaturity, feelings of being nobodies in a complex world of somebodies.

As much as we may want to turn away, these are the revelations about ourselves that must be faced and dealt with.

My period of depression and anxiety was very long-lasting. As a woman I had a severe struggle discovering anything of myself, as most women do. Men seem somehow better able or better equipped from childhood to find an inner core of self than women do, perhaps because few of us women had any help with self-esteem as children. We were taught to be caretakers, followers, peacemakers.

Suffering from a loss is a great part of depression, and the loss is usually that of the self. This is why the person feels dead inside. One loses the sense of one's self because one loses self-awareness. With its loss, only the shell of the person remains.

The psychiatrist Dr. Alexander Lowen believes that the person is the body and the body is the person. He contends that when the body is meaningless, or "dead," the person ceases to exist as an individual with a definite personality. He sees this as the condition known as depression. He also believes that the loss of aliveness is expressed by the depressed person in his or her constant discussion of lack of feeling, of desire, of interest. According to Dr. Lowen, early oral needs, as well as needs to be held and supported, to experience bodily contact, to suck, to be warmed, and to receive attention and approval, have gone unfulfilled. In maturity this is revealed through an inability to be alone; a boasting, attention-grabbing personality; a hyper-sensitivity to cold, and a dependent attitude.

We must certainly see that the inner emptiness displayed by all these feelings cannot ever be filled by another person because fulfillment must come from inside, must come from self.

The moot question is how this can happen when a depressed person lacks faith in his or her self, looks to outside sources for help and fulfillment, and cannot turn to an inner strength. Obviously the difficulty of successful help for us when we are depressed is that no one can reach us. Despite our knowing that others are trying to help, we simply are unable to respond. The hopelessness and despair, the collapsed sense of self make it impossible for us to be treated successfully in a short time. Because the suppression of feeling is at the bottom of depression, it is useful to find out what is being suppressed. Very often, for the alcoholic, it is anger and feelings of guilt, to say nothing of the feelings "I am nobody, and no one cares."

For the past twelve years I have not had any alcohol, but I can't say that the day I stopped drinking was the end of trouble. It was the end of my creating trouble, but it was the beginning of a long road upward. As mentioned earlier, between not drinking and the start of the upward climb there are a few stages in which we seem to be in a downward spiral. From the time of the last drink we move into the discovery of our feelings and, at first, seem to find only negative ones. We discover a number of feelings we have long suppressed.

LOSS OF SELF

The feeling of being a nobody was easily remedied over the past several years by our use of alcohol, which provided us with a whole new set of feelings about ourselves. I well remember the first few times I drank during my teen-age years. Before drinking I felt unloved, unpopular, undesirable, and a hundred other *un*'s that one can think of. I wanted to be popular. I wanted to be noticed. I wanted to be the "life of the party." And when I first had a few drinks, it seemed as if I had found the nectar of the gods. Just a few drinks, and I began to believe I was all those things I wanted to be. I felt as if I were oozing charisma. My personality changed, and I had the dynamic feelings I had longed for. And all this happened with so little effort. Just a few drinks! I had unearthed the new personality and the new person that were to serve me for the next several years.

We drink for so many years and we become so adjusted to this created person that we no longer know who we are, who we *really* are. Our bottle personality is so ingrained that we keep on with the drinking in order to keep it alive and functioning. And in this way we truly become enslaved. After several years we can no longer function without this use of alcohol. We are now both physically and emotionally addicted.

It is not difficult to understand, therefore, that when we give up the alcohol, we are truly without a sense of knowing who we are. We are adrift in emotions that require a skipper and none is present. We hear others saying to us, "Just give it time. You will soon feel better." And that is true. Physically we soon feel better, and we ask, "Why don't I feel emotionally wonderful? Why do I feel so lost, so nowhere?" This is when we experience depression.

Often this period of depression is also a period of anger. "Why me? Why? Why? Why?" We flail about and want to shout, "Damn them all anyway. They can all go to hell!" The anger comes from our feelings of being trapped and unable to escape the inevitability of the truths which we have been avoiding for such a long period of time. Sometimes our anger becomes anxiety, and our uneasiness makes us feel as if we would jump out of our skin unless something happened to relieve it. We are experiencing feelings over which we seem to have no control. And it's true. We have feelings that we don't understand and that we have long suppressed. Sometimes we suppress them again, and then we are back in depression.

Because anxiety is such an uneasy condition, our minds force us back into depression. Depression makes everything in our lives come to a complete stop, while anxiety annoys us into attempted actions. Anxiety and anger are harder for us to deal with than depression, which is an extremely passive emotion. We do nothing, despite the discomfort, which we learn to handle rather well. As we experience more and more of the anger and anxiety, our loss of self fades.

As we begin to find ourselves, our loss of the use of alcohol starts to become secondary. Our feelings of anger and anxiety are helping us get in touch with ourselves, and these new feelings make us restless, make us want to do something, even though we don't yet know what. We are still in the basement in feelings about ourselves; we feel very pessimistic, helpless, and often extremely apprehensive. We still feel totally worthless and useless, totally without friends. We feel adrift.

This period of depression may last for several weeks or as long as two years. For women alcoholics it is almost always longer than it is for male alcoholics, and for very many reasons. Frequently women do not have jobs to go back to, their lives are more often in shambles, and they are more often alone than males are. The family of a male alcoholic is more likely than not to be intact and functioning, so that he is cushioned during this period. Furthermore, women often have another problem to handle at this time, and that is another addiction, usually to prescription drugs, such as Valium. And as we've seen, most women, as it was with me, have almost no feelings that can be translated into self-value and respect. In recovery, as women we have much longer roads to travel than men do.

Recovery for all alcoholics seems to have a great deal to do with the finding of self, and for men their loss of self through alcohol seems to be linked to their understanding of their true roles in life and society. With women it is all that plus not even having a starting point. Both sexes, however, must first find and identify their inner cores before recovery in the truest sense can ever begin to happen.

Loss of self means explicitly that there was a self to be lost. Some alcoholics do not have this. Role confusion was, in fact, what led them to alcohol. The "I don't know who I am" and "I am nobody" feelings must first be changed to "I am somebody" before a lifetime of sobriety is possible. There is a large body of written thought that establishes the truth and ways in which the change can be accomplished. Solomon even stated it, saying, "For as he thinketh in his heart, so is he" (Proverbs 23:7).

Indeed, we have been proving this all along. We thought of ourselves as nobodies, and that is exactly what we became. We became even more: We were *drunken* nobodies. Our plan now, for our first step forward, is to begin thinking of ourselves in positive ways. And very often we must begin to create these persons for ourselves.

In our depression this is difficult, for we have reneged on life. We have withdrawn and pulled back and away. But now we must learn to work for ourselves and to know that the hopelessness and the pessimism we feel can be transitory if we understand *why* we are depressed and *how* we can correct it.

The whole of recovery depends on our wanting to change.

Negative thoughts have caused our sufferings; positive thoughts can bring us our emotional cures. People who go through life thinking, *I am nothing, I deserve nothing*, get exactly that from life: nothing. It is the original cop-out.

For alcoholics it is extremely difficult, almost impossible, to believe that we create our own reality. This can be understood by looking at hypochondriacs. They complain about particular ailments for a long enough time, and then they have them. Their minds have created them, and their physical bodies go along with their minds.

Thus the dilemma. The depressed person must want to emerge from the deep hole of depression and must want to change. But not wanting to do anything, not wanting to uncover emotions, not wanting to be a part of life are at the base of depression. And alcoholics are well experienced in escaping from reality. I know.

How can we come out of this blackness that has enveloped us? We can begin by having mental images of ourselves as active, alive persons. We can help this process by being aware of our dark, negative thoughts and changing them into positive thoughts. We can put on paper some of our thoughts, both negative and positive, and then cross out the negative ones.

We can also think about putting the pieces of our life back together, about how this can be done and how we are now capable of doing it without the physical debility caused by alcohol.

We must remember at all times that we are looking for a lasting prescription for life. We must see this period of depression as a stage we have to pass through on our way to complete recovery. It is a transitory period if we force ourselves to do what we must do to get out of it and to move forward. See this period of depression as the period in which we are getting in touch with ourselves. It is the time when we are beginning to uncover ourselves, layer by layer. This is the first revelation. Moreover, it is a revelation in which we are free of the masking effects of alcohol. This is why the feeling of despair is sometimes overwhelming. When we first see our sober selves, we are certainly not enchanted with what we see. We want to hide, to cover up, to escape.

As we move along this road of self-discovery, we will begin to gather certain truths about life that have always evaded us. Or perhaps we have evaded them. Perhaps the most important is learning that negative emotions destroy only us, no one else. And we will also learn that life can be a triumphant experience only when we are triumphant people. Nothing positive ever happens to negative people. They have created their own worlds of reality into which nothing positive can penetrate.

That's what depression is: a world of shielding negative thought, an escape into the depth of self, a mask behind which we have hidden those thoughts that hurt us. It is a place we have crawled into so far that we have lost ourselves. We no longer know who we are. It is a tomb of our own making.

CHAPTER FOUR

BATTLING
(AND OVERCOMING) GUILT

Who among us has never experienced it?

Feelings of guilt and remorse overpower many of us, and women alcoholics, as a group, have been the victims of guilt feelings to an excessive degree. Society continues to excoriate us long into our sobriety. On the other hand, men seem to experience more remorse than guilt, and society more quickly forgives them. They are not held quite as accountable as women. As a whole, society is just not crazy about alcoholics and is downright uncomfortable with and unforgiving of women alcoholics—perhaps because the disease comes too close to too many people in an embarrassingly annoying way.

Guilt is not just an ordinary, everyday emotion like anger or worry. It is a long-lasting, debilitating agent that invades, overpowers, and consumes the individual. It is like a wild and hungry animal that feeds on ego and character.

Guilt is a destructive emotion that cuts us into shreds. We are unable to function adequately so long as we experience guilt. We act differently, apologetically. We are in emotional chains. One dictionary says of guilt: "A state of having done wrong." How terribly inadequate this definition is. Of course, we believe we've done wrong! More than that, guilt is a feeling of having done something unforgivable to another or others. It is our inability to forgive ourselves that makes up the feeling we call guilt. When we speak of feeling remorse, we are speaking of how sorry we feel that something has happened; remorse does not contain within it the self-flagellation that guilt does.

Strangely enough, many women can be made to experience guilt by the attitudes of others, of society, family members, friends, all of which are transmitted to us by their actions toward us. Guilt is transmitted by attitudes as well as by actions.

The feeling of guilt nurtures a sense of failure and unworthiness. It is a garden of fertile soil for the negative feelings we feel about ourselves. Now, in our attempt to recover from alcoholism, we are ripe candidates for overwhelming feelings of guilt that can destroy our very fragile sobriety.

As women we feel unreasonable guilt feelings:

— For being away from our children while holding jobs
— For *not* feeling guilty when we think we should
— For being bored with housework
— For drinking at home
— For buying something for ourselves
— For being assertive about something for ourselves
— For things we've done that produced pleasure
— For spending grocery money to buy liquor
— For not being receptive to sex with our spouses
— For not being perfect women
— For wanting something more out of life than we have
— For wanting anything for ourselves
— For expressing dissatisfaction
— For feeling relieved when our children leave home
— For feeling independent
— For our spouses' extramarital affairs

Although many of these feelings of guilt are unreasonable, they do not seem so to us. As we gradually pull ourselves out of depression, we are faced with these new overwhelming feelings and even begin to feel guilty because feeling guilty feels right!

Many turn to self-help groups at this point. All we see there are happy and relaxed faces, and again we wonder if we are in the right place. Certainly these women can't understand what we are feeling because they have surely never been through it, been through what we are going through. We nurse our feelings and suffer.

During these early months of sobriety it is really best for women to attend women-only meetings, for the addition of subtle male-female play is just not conducive to women's talking at this juncture. Too often we turn to males to avoid talking about ourselves.

Guilt produces a feeling of being weighed down by an unshakable heaviness. These feelings can be physical and are often expressed by headaches, anxiety and uneasiness, a sense of being trapped in a cage with a wildcat. I know. It was once a constant for me.

The power of guilt has been a very strong force in the hands of many clergy, helping them to keep the flock on the straight and narrow. Christianity in particular has seen woman as the perpetrator of evil and sin, luring Adam into unforgivable behavior. Although the tale of Adam and Eve is not now as popular in clerical exposition as it once was, the allegory is as strong as ever, though not vocalized.

Through the ages women have been perceived as not clean, as persons to be forgiven but given a wide berth. In the name of religion many groups have regarded the menstrual cycle as a time of impurity, a period during which women were to be banned. Even reproduction carried an element of not being clean, being impure. This does not even take into account the "husband's tuck" or the making of woman more to his liking.

Needless to say, males created these attitudes, and through the ages women have been viewed as inferior to men, second-class citizens. All these years later women are still trying to free themselves from the stigma of the expulsion from the Garden of Eden.

Equality is still not at hand, nor have the attitudes of society changed all that much. As mentioned earlier, alcoholic men usually experience remorse rather than the feelings of guilt women experience. They do not know quite the same self-condemnation as female alcoholics. Between male and female is a world of difference; one need only look at recovery rates to see it. Feelings of guilt and shame restrict women's rise from the depths of depression, making it much longer-lasting. For some it is never-ending. Guilt has been heaped on women, most often by all the males with whom we are associated: fathers, husbands, brothers, employers, and sometimes doctors and clergy.

Society has certain expectations of both sexes. For women several roles are allowable, but the "perfect housewife" is by far the most acceptable to everyone, except perhaps to herself. Surely this role is the one still most preferred by society. It maintains the pecking order; woman is in her rightful place. This woman is neatly dressed, is clean and sparkling, speaks softly, and has no definite opinions on world affairs. If she does, they are better not voiced—that is, if the social balance is to be kept.

Her perfect grooming keeps people from believing that she's done a day's work, but her house is in perfect order. Her husband's dry cleaning and laundry are perfectly managed, and their home runs smoothly. She is an excellent cook and shops for food to get the best buys, keeping in mind the saving of pennies, always saving money wherever possible.

She is the devoted wife. She entertains the right people for her husband's career, not for her own liking. She keeps their children well dressed and clean, and they reflect her high standards of good, well-ordered living.

Sexually she is responsive, whether or not this feeling is genuine. This is how it is supposed to be, and she fulfills her wifely duty. She makes no demands, nor does she ever discuss her feelings, or lack of them, with her husband. This is simply not in her role, as it is defined.

The perfect housewife sees to it that she has the perfect figure. Her husband occupies her total interest, and pleasing him is her career. When they are in public, she is his showcase. She mirrors his success, wearing the clothes and the jewelry his position can support. Her role is to enhance his social status, and when asked who she is, she replies, "I am John's wife." Her status is his; her social position reflects his business success or failure.

And there the fairy tale ends.

Gradually, very gradually, this image of women is being changed. It took the latter third of the twentieth century and men like Alan Alda and Phil Donahue to add their voices to those of women to change society's view of women. Women are now beginning to be seen as people with desires, wants, faults, and definite personalities of our own. More than that, it has taken all these years for the truth to come to the surface, a truth women have known all along: that women carry an unfair share in marriages. More often than not both husband and wife are in the workplace most of the day, yet at day's end the woman is still expected to make dinner, do the dishes, bathe the little kids and put them to bed, take the older kids to Little League or school play practice, manage the laundry and cleaning, plus do the grocery shopping, while the man has a drink, reads the newspaper, watches the news on television, and waits to be served dinner.

When recognition of our equality was sought by women, men complained and women felt guilty!

It takes several generations for social attitudes to change, and we are still in the very early stages of this totally new view of women. Despite the gains we are making, slowly but surely, most have not yet been able to change their psychological conditioning. Although the relationship of man and wife has had to undergo a change because so many women work outside the home, women still react with feelings of guilt. Indeed, this particular conflict is the gem of guilt producers.

Men, too, have had difficulty in psychological adjustment to the new order of the world. Many a man's ego has had trouble accepting the need for his wife's income to keep the family secure, and he has sometimes treated her working as a hobby she enjoys indulging in. His inability to accept both her working and its absolute necessity often urges him to actions and words that make her feel more subservient than ever before. "Why isn't dinner ready? It always was before." Or, "When are you ever going to do the laundry? I have no clean shirts."

The demands of husbands and the attitudes of society conspire to make workingwomen feel guilty. Being overpowered by feelings of failure, women are kept from any feelings of pride in what they are doing. They are denied the pride from being a co-provider for the family that should rightfully be theirs. Instead, they are made to feel they are letting the home fall apart. The thought that both husband and wife are equally responsible for running the home is still foreign to most men, only natural after growing up being waited on and cared for by women. Why shouldn't the pattern be repeated in their own homes when they marry?

Very few women are able to handle this kind of pressure, no matter how unfair it is. Our conditioning as women has been so thorough that we usually feel guilty of failing as wives rather than speak up and say, "We both work and should both share the work at home equally." This is beginning to happen more frequently, but let us not forget that every day there is an increasing number of divorces.

There is a persistent belief that the work men do is important, while the work women do is not. Unfortunately this has been true for years. Females who wanted to enter the field of medicine were always taught to be nurses; young women wanting to enter business were always told to be secretaries. What else could they possibly be?

At last this is changing.

Perhaps the most common guilt among women is the feeling that they have abandoned their children during their hours at work. Not having children myself, I can speak only of what I have seen among the thousands of women coming to our self-help groups. Perhaps part of that guilt comes from a woman's feeling that society disapproves of her being away from the home, and should anything happen, she is responsible.

Of course, there is some truth in this. Children coming home to empty houses have been tagged latchkey children, and they are vulnerable. It places women in a dilemma every day and produces the guilt package labeled "Failing as a mother."

These feelings of guilt are experienced by almost every workingwoman I have ever spoken to. In women alcoholics these feelings are amplified. Women alcoholics already have built in superstructures of self-beating; add some large doses of guilt, and recovery from alcoholism is delayed by years.

What of the women who do not work? At least the workingwoman has something to feel good about, that her efforts are helping provide for her family, and sometimes she knows that all the stress and the criticism are worth it. But the woman at home is not so fortunate. In some cases her desire to work is thwarted because of her husband's feelings of inadequacy: "What would people think?"

For many of these women the entrapment by social attitudes has contributed to new descriptive phrases in our language: *the housewife's syndrome* or *the housewife's dilemma*. What is behind all this is the boredom women feel being at home all day. Many women, instead of screaming out loud, "I'm bored to death," turn their feelings inward, feel very, very guilty—and drink.

Many women, now in their forties and fifties, were led to believe that keeping a perfect house is a full-time job and that any feeling of frustration or boredom is just not acceptable, not justified. These women experience feelings of guilt when their children are grown and leave home. Why? Because they suddenly feel freed from being mothers on a daily basis within the structure of home. Yet they are unable to express this feeling, for society does not recognize it as acceptable. Gradually this, too, is changing. It's about time.

Women who cannot express their feelings of boredom at being at home or who cannot express their feelings of joy and freedom when the children leave home internalize their feelings of guilt. It takes the form of self-punishment and self-destruction by way of pills, alcohol, or deep-seated depression, expressed in crying, anxiety, insomnia, and an unreachable, indescribable sadness, and sometimes in anger.

A bored, angry, depressed woman often turns to alcohol to alleviate these unbearable feelings of guilt and pain. And such a woman may become the dual user of alcohol and prescribed drugs. Not knowing how to handle these feelings of guilt, many women turn to family doctors for help, and they, more often than not, prescribe tranquilizers.

Thus, in recovery, women alcoholics, far oftener than males, have two addictions to deal with. For them handling their feelings of guilt in rational, acceptable ways in recovery is a serious problem of an entirely different kind and sometimes requires the help of a professional therapist.

These particular feelings of guilt experienced by women are not usually known to men because of their different cultural conditioning. All of us, however, experience guilt when we feel, or are made to feel, that we have failed to do what is expected of us. Sometimes we experience guilt when someone dies. Many studies show that men in war feel extremely guilty when their buddies, standing next to them, are killed. They feel relief that it was someone else, not themselves, and this thought produces extreme feelings of guilt. They experience both sorrow and relief, and this can cause lifelong guilt feelings.

Very often many of us feel extreme guilt when family members die. We go through the litany of "Why didn't I do more?"; "Why didn't I call once a week?"; or "Why wasn't I more concerned?" We review our entire relationship with those parents (or brothers or sisters), and we concentrate our thoughts on the shortcomings of our behavior—our assumed insensitivity to their needs, the arguments we had, and the words we rashly flung at them in moments long ago.

These feelings of guilt come from the realization that we no longer have the opportunity to say, "I'm sorry," and from the inevitability of death, which we irrationally believe we might have postponed if only we had done something differently.

There are times when I believe we use guilt as a way to forgive ourselves for behavior we feel is unacceptable. If we experience guilt, we can tell ourselves we are really paying for something that happened. Eventually we may be able to relax.

Just as a family member's death is a great producer of guilt, so is divorce. Feelings of guilt stay with us a very long time after divorce. We feel guilt because our marriages failed, and even though our partners may have been the ones to walk out, we feel that we, alone, failed. The entire disruption is our fault.

Divorced people usually spend a very long time deciding to marry again, for they carry within themselves fear of another failure. Women are particularly likely to be guilt-ridden by marriage failures. When the marriage fails because of a woman's drinking, she will carry the guilt for many years. Then the game of "If only . . ." can sometimes be the single cause of failure in recovery. But this occurs when self-indulgence continues and the alcoholic stays inner-directed, inner-oriented.

It is an unfortunate fact that most alcoholics are led to behave in ways, when we are drunk, that are extremely difficult for us to forgive. We feel extreme guilt for what we have done to others, advertently or inadvertently. Sometimes we are guilty of passing guilt on to others in subtle ways. When something is wrong in our lives, how often do we say to another person, "Well, if you hadn't . . . " implying, of course, that it was the fault of the other person and we are blame-free? There is also the phenomenon that we are so overcome with guilt we have acquired from other persons we look for opportunities to pass it on.

Oh, how we all long to be blame-free! Yet how few succeed!

Of course, there is also guilt by association. We sometimes feel accountable for anything our parents did that may be socially unacceptable or morally taboo. And all of us who drink know what families can do to us. There are occasions when a person has had long periods of sobriety, in some cases many years, yet the spouse will say, "I'd love to go to the party with you, but I'm afraid you'll drink again and humiliate us the way you used to."

When this kind of guilt is passed to us from others, we must learn to see it for what it is: a form of one-upmanship. We are being intimidated; it is the holier-than-thou attitude. We are made to feel weak and erring, while our spouses are strong, good, moral, and unimpeachable. And then we react to this, many times, by going ahead and doing exactly what it was suggested we might do: We drink and create scenes. Then we *really* feel guilty. We've blown it again. We tell ourselves that what we did was unforgivable, but we ask for, sometimes beg for forgiveness. And then we usually acquire a larger dose of guilt from our spouses, who can now say, "I told you so."

The person who experiences feelings of guilt is always the victim. There are instances in which real issues are clouded by interactions. I know of one instance in which an innocent person became victimized by a feeling of guilt that was imposed on her. She left a chronically sick husband who happened to get worse after she left him. Of course, his family began the condemnation of her: "How could you do that? You are his wife!" They added, "We can never forgive you."

She began to react. She couldn't sleep; her work suffered, and she was fired; she had constant headaches and became listless. Her life changed radically, and all she could think was, *I did it, I did it, I did it. It's all my fault.*

Totally forgotten were the reasons why she had left him. He was always ill, and there had never seemed to be a right time to leave, even though she had wanted to over the many years he beat her and sexually abused her.

Although her cause was "just," it was she who was destroyed by the guilt created by others. All reason was gone, and only devastating emotion remained to destroy her.

In our drinking days we are often the victim of the guilt others create in us. True, we do enough to create our own guilt, but it is also true that we acquire a large amount from those surrounding us whom we have hurt. Forgiveness for our thoughtless actions is sometimes long in coming.

Moreover, we may have been victimized as children by our parents, who may have been victimized by their parents. There seems to be an inevitable chain of guilt linking us to parents who often rear us with threats that are surely guilt-producing. Some of the more usual ones from our mothers are:

— "If you don't do as I say, you'll be sorry."
— "I've sacrificed so much for you and see how you pay me back!"
— "Why do you love others and not me, your mother?"
— "Do as your mother says or you'll be sorry."
— "Just think how you'll feel when I am gone."

All these are guaranteed to carry a lifelong warranty. They are almost never-failing if we do not do something to remove the devastation they create.

Then, in our years of marriage, we collect another group just as devastating: (from husband to wife):

— "If you weren't gone all day, the children wouldn't have such terrible grades in school."
— "Ever since you started working, the house looks like a pigpen."
— "You never give the children enough of your time. No wonder they get into trouble."
— "If you wouldn't drink so much, we wouldn't have these problems."

Women alcoholics are self-condemning because of our fragile and, more frequently, nonexistent feelings of self-value. For us, self-condemnation is as easy as falling off a log. Perhaps this is what provides us with our excuses to drink; these negative emotions set the atmosphere for nice bouts of self-loathing.

The real question is, How do we exorcise these feelings of guilt so that we can get on with our recovery? How do we get rid of the feelings of "It's all my fault. Everything that is wrong was my doing?"

There is a school of thought that believes that continued discussion of the things we did while drinking will keep us sober, that if we keep our unforgivable past behavior close to us, we will have insurance for not drinking again.

However, it has always seemed to me that reliving that period when we displayed our worst behavior is just not the road to happy and continuing sobriety for women alcoholics.

But how to get rid of guilt feelings? After a lifetime of trying, I can say first that one very important way to relieve guilt stands out: It is to know, and to grasp the knowledge, that the past is gone forever and that we can never change what happened but that we *can* change how we feel about the past.

Secondly, and just as important, is to know that our perceptions of the past are very probably inaccurate. Usually nothing is as bad as our minds have made it or as bad as others have made it in reminding us of it. Because we are prone to self-condemnation, we must always remember that we have probably greatly enlarged what has actually happened. We must add to that the real knowledge that we are alcoholics who have suffered a real sickness, which led us to actions for which we were not totally responsible because of the condition we were in.

Thirdly, we must see the value of being centered in today and the future, not in the past. We must remind ourselves of this every day. It is of the utmost importance.

Fourthly, we must know that our deep guilt comes from our fragile feelings about ourselves. In recovery we must spend endless time providing ourselves with strong self-images so that we can begin to have some honest feelings of self-value. Our poor feelings about ourselves permit us to be real patsies for the accusations of others: "You're no good. You never were, and you never will be," and on and on and on.

Unfortunately we have come to believe these accusations, hurled at us over many, many years of our drinking. What is true is that most of us have done unforgivable things to ourselves and to those we love. *We must acknowledge them. But we must do it without a continuance of self-condemnation forever and ever, till death do us part.*

As alcoholics we have a great range of personalities among us, but in the largest sense, most of us are as decent as anyone else. We are sometimes more sensitive than others because of immaturity in some areas of our emotional life. We are just not all that different from the general population, but our years of drinking have left us vulnerable and hypersensitive, and this hypersensitivity is the part of us that quickly seizes upon "I'm no good, and I never will be."

This is just pure and simple rot. Now is the time to get feisty and ready to do battle with those overpowering old emotions, those old feelings. Too long have we felt powerless to do anything for ourselves. Now is the time to assert ourselves and take charge of self-defeating, negative emotions.

Recovery is a process of upward mobility. It is the process of unloading old baggage and acquiring new thoughts to deal with life's problems. We cannot deal with life until we deal with ourselves.

Our triumph over guilt feelings begins with our belief that we are not powerless to rid ourselves of them. Recovery is the time to see that our earlier willingness to take the blame for everything came from our poor feelings of self, came from our "doormat" feelings.

Forget the past. Plan for tomorrow. Live today.

CHAPTER FIVE

FEAR AND WORRY:
THOSE NASTY NEGATIVES

To achieve a successful and happy recovery, we must first of all identify and then remove the negatives from our lives. I have already pointed out that the first negative stages we go through when we stop drinking are periods of depression and then feelings of overwhelming guilt.

Perhaps the next most identifiable period is that which is dominated by fears and worries. As we emerge from the darkness of depression, we become much more attuned to our troubling feelings. We have sleepless nights, and we experience anxiety that makes us feel as if we were jumping out of our skins. We are constantly on edge. Most of this comes from the fears that are beginning to surface.

Fear is probably best described as anticipation of danger, while worry is daily encounter with it. Sometimes the difference is hard to distinguish. One woman told me she believes fear is quick and immediate while worry hangs around, taunting us, lingering for endless time, nagging us to sleeplessness.

Before writing this chapter, I began thinking about the early days of my sobriety, about how those days and weeks were plagued with feelings of worry and with many fears. Sometimes I had difficulty in identifying whether it was a fear or a worry I was feeling, and then I asked, "Can we know one without the other's being close behind it?"

I have noticed that I can fear a number of things but that I don't necessarily worry about them. The reverse is also true. One person may worry about not having the bills paid, while another may worry about the bills' not being paid and fear the possibility of a resultant bankruptcy.

Fear seems to be a degree more serious than worry; it seems to be a step beyond. Worry seems a lighter, more surface emotion, one that can really be worked on. Fear is a stripe of a deeper cut.

Later, as we mature, we may come to accept death without feelings of fear, but we may worry about *how* we will die. We begin to worry about not having enough insurance, about our children's not being able to go to college, about a host of things that might happen far in the future.

We may worry about a recurrent sore throat and fear that it is cancer because of the years of drinking; we have heard that alcoholics have a higher incidence of throat cancer than the general population.

Worry seems to be the everyday glue of our life, while fear is that awful sharp feeling we experience when we are thrown into areas of the unknown. Worry nags at us; fear haunts us.

Perhaps our most common fears are these:

    Death
    Failure
    Rejection
    Financial ruin
    Old age
    Incurable illness
    Drinking again

With the exception of the last, fear of drinking again, almost all people experience the same general fears, although some of us are better equipped emotionally to handle them than others. These fears constitute the unknown, which is usually what we worry about.

Our fears change as we get older. When we are children, we fear death. When we are in high school, we fear rejection by the opposite sex. When we are in college or working at a job, we fear failure. When we are first married, we fear financial failure.

When we are middle-aged, we fear that our marriage might fail or that our children will be killed or get into serious trouble. When our spouses die, we fear being alone. When we get older, we fear ill health. And at the very end, we may again fear death as we see it inevitably approaching. Our fears seem to be related to our ages; their weight shifts into a different gear of intensity as we move into different periods of our lives.

Change breeds fear. Change is very difficult to handle for many of us. In my own life I found that change always threw me into an intense drinking bout, and still, after twelve years of sobriety, I have trouble handling change in my life, even if it is for the better. I have observed that other alcoholics are just as apprehensive of change, and it seems to me that it comes from our deep-seated insecurities. We want to hang on to that which we know, even if it's not the best of all worlds.

When change occurs in my life now, even after all these years of sobriety, I still am out of sync for several weeks. No longer do I think about having a drink, but I am definitely affected in other ways. This happens with just a small change, too, like sleeping in an unfamiliar house for several nights.

Dramatic changes in our lives, the big ones—loss of a spouse, loss of parents, loss of children—affect everyone to some degree or another. These changes strike a note of fear in us. We wonder what is to happen. Our security is shaken at its very base.

The unknown factor is that which causes us to experience fear. During the worst years of my drinking I would awaken in the middle of the night, profusely perspiring and aware of being so frightened I wasn't able to call out. It was all I could do to get out of bed and cross the room to turn on the light. Then I began to feel comforted to a small degree. But why? It wasn't the dark I was afraid of, but it certainly intensified my feelings of fear of the unknown. As soon as the light was on, I felt comfortable, seeing that I was in my own room and among my own things. My fears had sprung from the depth of my insecurities, made all the worse by the bountiful lacing of alcohol.

Fear—the experiencing of it—humiliates us.

Too many of us with drinking problems have tiptoed through life, afraid of this, afraid of that, afraid of being rejected, unloved, unwanted, undesirable—afraid of just about everything that makes up life. A few stiff drinks have taken care of these feelings in the past. But now what do we do, where do we stand, how do we proceed?

I began to realize that most of my new sobriety time was spent being upset, worrying about this, worrying about that. I seemed always to be in one of two states of emotion: worried or very frightened. Then a magic day arrived. I came upon a sentence that really changed my life. And it can change yours, too. It was a simple sentence, a simple admonition. It merely stated: *We can be bothered only to the degree we permit ourselves to be.*

That's it, that's all there is to it, but what a piece of valuable information. Just think, it tells us that *we* are in total control of our feelings if we permit ourselves to be. We are bothered to the degree we permit ourselves to be bothered.

Stumbling upon this thought transformed my life. Before, I had always believed that I was the victim of feelings of fear, of worry. I believed that was the way I was and nothing could change that condition. But when I discovered that *I* could change the whole situation, my world changed. That this was possible had never occurred to me before.

We have seen that whenever we fear something, anything, we usually worry about it. We spend valuable hours worrying about being in debt, growing old, getting incurable illnesses, forgetting that we already have one, alcoholism, which is never cured but only arrested. Sometimes this excessive worry causes us other illnesses in our sobriety. I have seen many alcoholics become very ill during the early months of the sobriety, even though most of the illnesses are psychosomatic. They come from our inability to cope with, or even to recognize, what is happening to us. Others simply worry, worry, worry. Sometimes we worry ourselves right into a relapse of drinking.

Early sobriety is a very difficult period in which to hold ourselves together. We are coming from a condition of willful anesthetizing to a state of having to face life's realities of bills, family problems, job concerns, and our own shaky sobriety. It is a renaissance, but it also carries the same lack of coping mechanisms that led us to drink in the first place.

There is the terrible realization that life is filled with problems, big and small. In my early sobriety I had great difficulty handling my problems. I wanted them all to be solved so that my life would be serene and even. I was extremely proud that I recognized my problems and was making an attempt to solve them, but no sooner had I almost solved the problems I had identified than a new set confronted me. And that is where my frustration almost got out of hand. To this day I have trouble accepting that I will always have unsolved problems in my life, that this is a condition of living, that there will probably never be a time when everything will be in apple-pie order. I suppose the more complicated one's life is, the more problems there will be. This realization must be uppermost in our minds in our new lives of sobriety. I think, too, that it is very important we realize that some of the urgency to drink came from our desire to escape the reality of these problems in our lives. But now the moment of truth is at hand. Probably what is the most startling truth is that we are better able to handle situations than we believe we are.

Let's try an imaginary situation. Suppose you've slept through your morning alarm and you awake a half hour late. In a cold sweat you hurry to your car, hoping that you will be able to make up the lost time by really moving through traffic. When you get to the door of your apartment house, you see it is raining very hard and you need an umbrella, so you go back to get it. More time has elapsed, and you are quietly saying things under your breath. Finally you get to your car only to find that of all mornings, this is the one you have a flat tire. You just can't believe it, but it's true.

You first feel anger, followed by disgust and frustration, and then fear sets in: You could lose your job. Automatically you begin worrying about this very real possibility. You can't put it out of your mind. Your entire trip to the office is spent worrying about the possibility of your being unemployed.

This is a very clear example of how we worry about what *might* happen. We create harrowing images of being fired, of having to go on unemployment, of being without any security. We are dominated by the mental images our fear and worry have caused. Sometimes imaginary possibilities so dominate us that we act irrationally and fail to take care of solving our problems in the most expeditious way—in this case, calling our employer and then taking a taxi or bus to the office, leaving the fixing of the tire until later.

During one period of my life I had great difficulty in getting a job, having been in a mental institution for almost a year and being unable to teach when I was released. So I looked for other employment and found a wonderful job with a large department store, where I started as a clerk and then moved up to the position of buyer. It was a job from which I derived great self-satisfaction. It had many elements, all of which I loved. There were days when I went into the store three or fours hours before it opened because I so loved my work.

Right after I was made a sportswear buyer, it became part of my job every week to go to New York City to the different manufacturing houses to order merchandise. In the early days I had to go with the merchandise manager, whom I disliked very much. He was very demanding, and in the beginning, when I made many mistakes, he pointed them out and soundly criticized me for them. Our trips to New York were awful for me. He talked little, walked very fast, was unpredictable, and was difficult to be with. And I learned very little from him because I was always afraid of making a mistake and incurring his disfavor.

Then, one morning, when I was to meet him at the bus in Allentown at six-thirty to leave for New York, I overslept. Normally I require very little sleep, and do not sleep through an alarm. On that morning I did. My frustration and anger with this man led me right into a period of worry and fear. I really feared losing my job, and I worried about it the entire trip to New York, having taken a later bus to meet him at our first manufacturer. When we met, nothing was said. I was treated all day to a cold shoulder and only clipped sentences. Later I discovered that firing me was very much out of the question because of my work record, but—more interestingly—*his* job was in question, for he was an alcoholic, a drinking alcoholic, whom I totally failed to recognize.

How many hours had I wasted on what might have happened? Perhaps this kind of apprehension is with us much of our lives. As I write, I can think of at least a dozen other occasions in which I experienced great apprehension, which did not change the outcome one iota. I just suffered unnecessary wear and tear.

During our drinking days we submerge all our apprehensions in several stiff drinks. In sobriety we find we are extremely vulnerable, assailed by nameless fears and terrors. Indeed, our basic tendencies are to maximize rather than to minimize every problem. We are sometimes paranoid about what is happening around us, believing it all is purposefully planned to compromise us, to jeopardize us. This is a delusion of early sobriety: that the world and those around us are out to get us one way or another. There will be times when we still awaken in the middle of the night, shaking and afraid of demons that possess us. Although these fears are nameless, they are very real in the terror they produce. As time moves on and we learn more about ourselves we get stronger and stronger emotionally. The early period, however, is the most difficult.

When I was going through this period, I tried to ease my feelings by writing them down. I developed the habit of forcing myself to identify as much of the upset as I could. There were times when nameless fears awakened me in the middle of the night, but I began to know what they were all about. I sensed that my fears came from deep feelings of guilt and shame from remembrance of actions committed while drinking which I had earlier permitted myself conveniently to forget. As time went on, I forced myself to haul these memories into the open and made myself accept that they had happened. My fears were coming from my inability to deal with these negative and humiliating memories. I recall I sometimes broke out into a cold perspiration that came from my feelings of disgrace. I was very tempted to drink again, to get away from these realizations, which were often horrible—the raw, inexcusable conduct I always had thought was for others. I'd thought my own standards were so much higher, but I found in my new sobriety that I had been as capable of bad behavior as anyone else.

In new sobriety we come face-to-face with much of ourselves that is startling and offensive. We learn we have dark sides that we have used alcohol to avoid. Alcohol has served to anesthetize us from actions that were unacceptable to our sober, moral, social selves, and unless we now begin to see this as a part of ourselves, we will probably fail in our sobriety. The best way to accept it is to know that we were deluded by the use of alcohol, and this is a very sound reason for our forsaking its use forever.

The experiencing of fear seems to be related to the degree to which we feel secure. Of course, I'm not talking about being attacked by a bear, when a feeling of fear provokes a person to immediate and defensive action. I refer to the kind of everyday fear we alcoholics seem to enlarge, the fears that lessen with the daylight hours, fears that are not really concerned with reality. Fear of failure is in this category. Certainly it is normal to think about the possibility of failure, but to alcoholics this particular fear becomes blown out of proportion. It dominates our lives, and it makes succeeding almost totally impossible.

In sobriety we must start to recognize the fears that are without substance and those that come to us out of real and deep-seated emotions we are trying to hide. The first group, fears without real substance, may usually be dealt with if we simply write them down on a piece of paper to identify them and to see that they are not real. This should be done frequently in the beginning. The oftener we write them down, stare at them, and think about them, the faster we will no longer fear them. What happens is that what we have identified as "fears" are really not unmanageable.

The second group of fears is of a different caliber and is far more difficult to deal with. It is not uncommon for some alcoholics to require therapy when they experience these fears and if one is able to afford it, it should be seriously considered. Those unable to afford therapy—very likely the majority—must devise ways to expurgate and identify these frightening feelings that usurp serenity and sleep.

Fear can be a devastating emotion, and we are surely on a quick route to relapse if we don't spend time trying to understand why we feel as we do, learning the origin of our fear and then learning how to get over it.

Too often we look at others and, seeing their happy faces, are led to believe that they know little or no upsets in their lives. Then we feel even sorrier for ourselves. Of course, our perception is almost always incorrect. There is no life without problems or sorrows. Those people who appear carefree have probably learned the secret we must learn: Problems bother us only to the degree we permit them to.

Fear can be dealt with as soon as we learn what it is we fear. When I made my jaunt into self-discovery, I found that authority frightened me unreasonably. It took me some time to identify my fear, but it always came back to authority. For example, some years ago I was involved in several small traffic accidents and was confronted by policemen. In each instance my heart was racing and my hands were sweaty. I had the very same reaction when I received a notice from the Internal Revenue Service. My reaction of fear started before I even opened the letter. This also happened every time I received a letter from a law firm.

During my growing-up years I realize now that I was in the shadow of a strong authoritarian figure, my father. My irresponsible behavior very often was corrected, and when I did something of which I knew he disapproved, I experienced a racing pulse and sweaty hands. I knew I was in for it. During my adult drinking years I ran up against authority far too many times, most all of which were extremely unhappy occasions.

Identification of fear does not necessarily remove it—even

now I still feel uncomfortable and frightened in some circumstances—but my fear is not as irrational as it once was. Now I
know *why* I feel it.

Spend time with yourself discovering what you fear and why
you fear it. This will lessen the nighttime horrors. It will also
begin to get you in touch with yourself and your feelings. I have
found that we who drank are usually strangers to ourselves. And
sobriety—recovery—requires getting to know ourselves.

Right now you may be thinking, *It's easy enough for her to
write about it, but she doesn't know the number of problems I have,
or she wouldn't be so glib with her advice.*

Of course, that's true. Each of us has different problems,
different worries, different fears. However, the specifics of your
problems, and how they differ from mine, are really not important. That we each have problems is important, that we each
know fear is important.

Most of what we fear is the unknown. Identification is half
the battle. Perhaps someone close to you might quickly and easily
tell you what it is you are frightened of long before you yourself
could identify it. It is certainly worth trying; it's happened to me.

Fear is one of the worst emotions we can experience. It
causes us to act irrationally because we react out of panic. There
is usually a time in our life when we come up against stark reality
and have a glimpse of all the pitfalls. We have an inkling of what
may happen to us. And we are afraid. My stark brush with reality
came with my mother's death. Although she had been totally
helpless for several years, my mind still permitted me to live in
a dream world within which I was depending on my mother. I
was unable to accept the truth, nor could I acknowledge that the
responsibility for her care was, and had been, totally mine. I feared
the reality too much to see it. I wore blinders because I was afraid
that were I to see my full responsibility, I might have failed.

The wearing of imaginary blinders is not always bad. Fear
escalates when we focus on how much we dread something's happening. Sometimes we need this masquerade, this protection. But

not in recovery. That is the time we *must* take off the blinders and find the truth of our feelings, of our fears.

We should see our steps to recovery as an upward climb, and the first three phases are the most important: working out of that first stage of depression; uncovering our guilt feelings; and identifying our fears and our worries.

In each of these stages of recovery we can put certain actions into motion, and as soon as we do, we hasten the process of getting on top of our alcoholism. Depression, guilt, and fear are all stages in which we will undergo the greatest temptation to begin drinking again. These stages are extremely uncomfortable. They make us squirm and feel uneasy because they feature the feelings that we tried to submerge but that continued to accumulate.

Now are the days and weeks of reckoning. These days and weeks will be the most uncomfortable of our entire recovery, and it is important to recognize this, for it will help, knowing that once we are through this rough time, the rest is almost a piece of cake.

CHAPTER SIX

LONELINESS

Can we ever forget the loneliness of alcoholism?

The noisier and more complex our society becomes, the more acute our loneliness. Each of us is so involved in so many aspects of life that our loneliness creeps in at odd moments unexpectedly, often shocking us by its intensity. If there are times we are forced to slow our busy lives, we become aware of this loneliness and the roof falls in. Startled, we say, "But I'm with people all the time. How can I be lonely?"

When we are forced to quit drinking, we become acutely aware of how lonely we are, and we wonder why because so many people surround us. But the more we are around people, the lonelier we become.

Eventually we realize that loneliness cannot be driven away by being with people. We recognize that our loneliness is an ache somewhere deep inside which one cannot reach, cannot explain, cannot touch, and has no idea how to ease. Looking into the past, we begin to see that we often drank because we were lonely. And the more we drank, the lonelier we became. Is there any loneliness that can compare with that which we knew when drinking?

I have always wondered if we in this century are lonelier than people in other centuries who lived in quieter times without radios, televisions, video rock, supersonic jets. Were Emerson and Thoreau lonely in the same way we are? Or were they less vulnerable to feelings of loneliness because of their self-reliance? Their books describe solitude, not loneliness. They describe being close to nature and being renewed in spirit.

Too often we of this century dismiss this as outmoded ro-

80

manticism and impractical nonsense. We mistakenly believe it is better to be constantly involved in activity and to put things of a spiritual, meditative nature into abeyance. We believe that to be busy is not to be lonely.

Many times the strength of the loneliness that grips us alcoholics also blinds us to a reality of another kind. We are unable to see the love others have for us because we feel terribly alienated. This feeling of alienation is at its height when we drink. When we are lonely, we are empty and that makes us unfeeling. There seems to be a void in the very center of our being. We are inattentive to our families. Often they suggest we get out more, be around people more, join groups, get into crowds. But crowds aren't the answer. Loneliness comes from inside us, and it has developed from feeling unfulfilled.

This feeling of being unfulfilled leads lonely people to overeat, to overindulge in alcohol, to overdo in almost every area of life in a vain effort to fill the spaces within. Too often, when we quit drinking, we continue the pattern with chain-smoking, drinking endless cups of coffee, eating excessive amounts of candy, all in a futile effort to fill the void.

Could our loneliness come from our feeling that there is no place to go, that our lives are without meaning? Or does it come from a sense of alienation?

Because my life is extremely busy and full of people, appointments, travel, writing, many of those whom I serve just assume that I am never lonely. But a full life does not always mean that. It certainly helps, and it is far better than an idle life, but it alone does not mean one is no longer lonely.

Feelings of alienation and loneliness can strike at any time. I remember one Saturday evening when I was sitting in the Pittsburgh airport. Never have I felt such loneliness and a total sense of isolation from all the people who were milling about me. For one of the very few times in my life I wondered if my decision not to have children, made so many years before, had been wrong. The people I was seeing were families, and they all seemed happy and carefree.

I am now sure that my feelings of loneliness and isolation came from the time of night, the day of the week, and the fact that I was weary, having just ended a long and grueling speaking tour. I wanted to be home, not in the Pittsburgh airport with several more hours of travel before me. Yet at times when we are in such a bleak situation and when we are especially tired and wonder why we do in life what we normally enjoy doing, we feel particularly disgruntled, unfulfilled, and unhappy. We feel alone—terribly alone and very much unloved. We are like children at summer camp, wanting to be home, no matter how many chores we must do when we get there.

It is frequently said that we are our loneliest at parties, in roomfuls of people we don't seem to identify with. Often the merriment and gaiety enhance our sense of alienation, and we want to run away because we feel we don't belong. Our identity with the group is in question. We feel lost and out of place. It's as if there were no way to bridge this gap. We only want to run—or drink our way out of the uneasy feelings.

Almost all alcoholics feel this way much of the time. We feel outside life, and we meet this with inappropriate actions. Our low tolerance for uneasy feelings, for personal discomfort prompts us to escape in the only way we know. Others experience this feeling of being apart from life, but they do not use the escape we do. How many times have we heard a president say how lonely it is at the top? Almost every president in my lifetime has spoken of the lonely feeling, of being apart from everyone, the total isolation of the position.

Of course, it is difficult to feel great sympathy because each of these men tried to move heaven and earth to reach his elevated position. That he feels alone and out on a limb is of his making. This leads us to question whether or not our loneliness is of our own making.

Our feelings of loneliness and the accompanying feelings of isolation sometimes possess us when we begin to realize that we are—each of us—totally alone in life. Every once in a while this truth strikes us, and as we get older, we become more frequently aware of our absolute aloneness in this temporary state of life. Aloneness and loneliness are two different emotions, but we often feel loneliness when we become aware of our aloneness.

Sometimes, when I've experienced a crisis in my life, I've had a feeling that someone was in the situation with me, only to find that this was a subconscious deception on my part. I was alone all the time. This kind of experience can lead to a new feeling about God, a Superior Being, Buddha, or an Oversoul. The realization that we are alone leads us to crave a union with someone who will always be with us, who doesn't ever become discouraged with us and leave, someone who thinks we are wonderful. These are similar to the reasons why we feel close to our pet cats and dogs.

Suddenly we embrace not religion, but a Spiritual Mentor. We are now certain that we have found the answer. We have found a way to combat our nagging inner loneliness. As with all things, we immerse ourselves wholly and believe that our problems are now over, that we have "recovered" and need nothing else.

Returning to the world of reality that we have so long evaded, we face the fact that some of our contemporaries are no longer with us, death having claimed them, a fact we were able to ignore during our drinking years. We begin to acknowledge the deaths in our own family, aunts or uncles, perhaps a cousin or our grandparents. A second wave removes our parents from our lives, and sometimes a classmate or two. Then a few more friends our own age are suddenly and swiftly removed from life, and again we feel threatened and alone. Our perceptions of life are revised, and we make many decisions with our own mortality in mind. Now our loneliness becomes more pronounced unless we are soothed by our Spiritual Mentor.

Just at a time when we need them, we find that our close friends are not there. Even worse for us, the alcoholic, we are without friends as we come into our new sobriety. We are left only with drinking buddies, who do not now fit into our new life. We are adrift.

One of the most harrowing periods of our recovery is this

one in which we are are so alone. Despite our families' trying to understand what we are feeling, few ever really know, and our feelings of alienation grow more intense. We wish to turn to others, but there are no others. Our drinking buddies don't understand why we are trying to stay sober. They thought there was nothing at all wrong with the way we were drinking or the things that happened to us at those times. "What's the matter with you? You can't be an alcoholic! Why, they're all in the gutter. Look at you; you're in good shape. Sure, you take a drink too many now and again, but hell, we all need to escape sometimes, eh?"

And these are our friends?

This period of being in limbo stretches into a long time. New friends are not made overnight. It takes an inordinate amount of time to change not only the persons we spend leisure time with but also our entire social structures.

At this time we can help ourselves immeasurably by becoming members of self-help groups, for there we find others who have been through what we are now experiencing. There we find soulmates. Sometimes, in time, we find friends.

In the meantime, however, it is a shattering experience to find that all the things we have seen happen to others—their periods of loneliness and despair, which we drank our way through—have suddenly come to us. All the years before, we have been saying to others, "Cheer up. It will change. Just have another drink, and everything will get better."

No words help. In fact, when we are overcome with this awful inner loneliness, nothing that others do for us seems to help. We have to work it out in our own way.

When I stopped drinking and found myself between social groups—my drinking pals and the new friends I hoped to have—my worst enemy seemed to be elongated time. Never had an hour been so long, or a day had so many hours, or a week seemed so endless. Never before had I realized how drinking had sped up time. Now, in my new sobriety, time stretched into nowhere in a straight line that had no visible end. Loneliness was like a fever that nothing could reduce or remove. It seemed as if the whole world were running on a schedule into which I didn't fit. Everyone seemed to know where he or she was going, but I stumbled around directionless.

To ease my loneliness during this period, when I had no real feelings about myself, I often sat in the parking lots of the many shopping malls in our area just watching people, like a deprived voyeur trying to get a focus on happiness. Frequently I'd prowl the stores, listening to conversations that were not mine to listen to, watching people interact, imagining their lives, filling in the spaces with ideas about them. I made myself believe they all were happy while I was terribly lonely and miserable. I began to resent their being together, as if the whole world seemed to be paired while I was alone. Many times I wanted to drink. I began to think, *I'll show them*, a real signal of the trouble I was in.

I was far enough along the road to recovery by then to recognize that were I to drink, I would again have to go through the same difficult stages I'd already been through to get to where I now was. So I shelved the idea of drinking. There were times when I began to lapse back into the old "nobody loves me" routine, and feeling sorry for myself was added to my feelings of loneliness.

But I began to know that my loneliness came from inside me, and being in crowds of people would do absolutely nothing except make me feel lonelier.

As my feelings of loneliness persisted and intensified over the weeks, it seemed to me that I was doomed to be alone and lonely, and I felt very threatened by this feeling. Even worse, these feelings were beginning to devour me. Like all other negative feelings, the longer we permit them to be a part of our emotional selves, the more they are compounded.

During this period I was withdrawn, moody, and unable (unwilling?) to get interested in anything. I overate, mostly junk foods, and I indulged myself in the belief that nothing would ever change, certainly not for the better.

In retrospect, I believe the reason for the intense loneliness during this part of recovery is that we are unequipped to handle this no man's land. We have begun to work ourselves through and out of depression and guilt feelings, but now the nothingness sets in, and we seem to have nowhere to go. We are extremely vulnerable during this period because it should be the starting point for wanting to "get with it." We might feel the urge to "get on with life" once or twice only to sink back into loneliness and isolation again. It is easy at this point to fall back into being afraid. Fear and self-pity can become very destructive.

Instead of doing anything about my feelings, I endured them. Because the period was so prolonged, I became a victim of the side effects of loneliness left untreated. It made my new sobriety seem like a curse rather than an exciting adventure in living.

Perhaps I avoided finding a solution because I wanted to indulge myself in a prolonged period of self-pity. The only positive part of this period in my life was that I didn't revert to drinking, although I don't know how I avoided it, feeling as negative as I did.

Where is the solution? Since we can't find the answer in walking endless miles in shopping malls and eavesdropping on conversations not meant for our ears, we must try to fill the emotional void with solid, unrelated actions. My error was in hoping for, and expecting, a miracle in emotional fulfillment. Since the chances of this happening are about 1 in 10 million, the answer must be found in mental activity, doing something new, learning something new, something that involves our entire concentration, that takes us out of ourselves.

I took courses in real estate and finally got my license as a salesperson. Although I have never used it, studying for it and taking courses over a period of a year almost completely occupied me. At least the activity took the edge off my loneliness, and I didn't feel isolated from the world of living beings while I was in classes. Although I did not make any real friends, I did make new acquaintances, people with totally different life-styles from mine, and it was interesting to find that even if their problems were not exactly like mine, they were worried about family problems, they were concerned about money, and they felt doubts about what the future would hold. I began to notice that the difference between them and me was that they didn't express the self-doubts or the fears or the self-pity I permitted myself to swim in. I perceived them as being much stronger emotionally than I was, thereby giving myself an excuse for my emotional self-indulgences of weakness and negativity.

Learning about real estate required all my concentration because everything about the subject was new to me. The vocabulary was strange and foreign-sounding, and I discovered that I was the only one in the class who had never had anything at all to do with real estate. It meant that I had a great deal to catch up on. But this was the solution I needed to get me through this terrible period.

Each solution is different. Make certain, however, that you choose something you know very little about.

Sometimes there will be a family conflict you will need to overcome. Family members sometimes feel they must be with the recovering alcoholic every minute of the new sobriety, and this can become very smothering and a great incentive to escape with a drink. At this juncture it is advisable for family members to seek some kind of counseling through specialized agencies so they can learn that alcoholics need freedom and families' trust, not chaperoning. Indeed, at this point family smothering, in the name of protective love, can be very threatening to newly won sobriety, and it is imperative that a recovering alcoholic strike out into a new experience, as I did with real estate, to see new faces, meet new challenges, and be occupied with something different and exciting.

Our hypersensitivity at this time; our proneness to self-pity because of our new lives without alcohol; our defensive, combative natures—all tend to get us into trouble very quickly, especially in regard to family situations which we never were able to handle before and haven't yet learned how to handle. This control will come in time, as we become emotionally stronger and more self-sufficient. Right now we are a poorly bandaged bleeding wound.

Our loneliness at this stage of sobriety is especially poignant because our ability to feel things has begun to return. Whereas we have been burying disturbing feelings, we must now experience them. We cannot scream out, "I'm not ready yet. I can't handle loneliness, isolation, and feelings of separation." Life goes on whether we are ready for it or not, and this cold realization often strikes us too late. We waste time and energy wishing everything could be different.

Although all of us look for solutions to the disturbing emotions we feel, the answers are not always complete, just as my suggestion that you learn something or be involved with something you've never done before is certainly not a complete answer to overcoming your feelings of loneliness and isolation. It will help you, but it is not the total answer. My real estate courses did not suddenly eliminate all feelings of loneliness. Many times I experienced it, even while driving to real estate classes. How many rain-soaked nights I wondered what in the world I was doing, being out in such miserable weather, driving to a place I really didn't want to be. But thank God, alcoholics are tenacious, and that helps us forge ahead.

I think that we are also romantic in that we fall easily into patterns of thinking about what once was or what might have been. One of our great faults is our striking inability to live in the present. Often our loneliness will be increased by our experiencing nostalgia from a special fragrance that revives memories of having a wonderful time at such and such a place. Or we'll hear bells ringing in the distance and be reminded of a Sunday morning in a small New England village we visited many years ago. And on and on, down memory lane. Then we feel lonesome and lonely and nostalgic, and we'll wonder why we have such a terrible urge to drink!

So in our period of recovery one of our biggest battles is this: overcoming our tendency to live in the past or the future. Both bring on feelings of separation, feelings of isolation. Is it any wonder? Life is going on around us, filled to the brim with current problems involving our job, money, everyday problems of survival, and we are drifting and dreaming, thinking we are lonely and no one understands us. After we climb out of depression and overcome our feelings of guilt and remorse, we must begin to deal with life as it is. We must move into the present and put aside the "what ifs." Center stage for us has to be the reality of the moment, no matter how painful it may be. Usually it is extremely painful, for we have avoided reality for a long time. Sobriety often reveals that we are in the middle of crises in our marriages, and this revelation makes us want to run, makes us feel nostalgic for the wonderful, happy earlier married years. Then we feel lonely and sad and nostalgic. We don't want to face the fact that our marriages are in trouble.

Recovery at this point frequently requires the services and wisdom of marriage counselors. Too often we act hastily and run to divorce lawyers, as if to excise a bothersome wart.

Obviously each marital situation is different in the first period of sobriety. In some cases, the need for a divorce is so painful to face that the alcoholic continues to drink to avoid this reality and facing the decision that needs to be made. On the other hand, in some cases the alcoholic need only stop drinking in order to remake the marriage into one of stability.

Many women alcoholics I know have discovered when they become sober that they can no longer go on with their marriages. They may have used alcohol in order to tolerate sexual relations with their husbands, and with the anesthesia of alcohol no longer available, divorces take place. But I have known just as many women who used alcohol to quell their sexual feelings because of husbands who did not fulfill their needs. The only general truth is that in this early period of recovery we must assess our marriages and act accordingly but not hastily. Marriage counseling is a very good idea, but most important, be sure the counselor is used to working with alcoholics. Otherwise, consultation could spell disaster.

We come to find that it is much more painful to live in the present rather than in the past or the future, but the more we succeed, the less time we will have to feel lonely.

I have come to know that our earthly experiences are just

about the same for all of us, even as far as the emotional stages go. Whereas I once thought we each had very different lives and that mine was especially different, I have learned the hard way that it just isn't so. Although events are different in our various lives, the feelings and emotional hang-ups are just about the same. Too often some of us are overcome and destroyed by these experiences. Others try to escape through drinking. And still others just hang in there and overcome. All experience loneliness, but only some permit it to dominate and destroy.

If we make a real effort to understand what is happening to us, and why, we can get through this period unscathed and certainly wiser. The loneliness will not miraculously go away, but we will be fighting it, and gradually it will subside and the world will finally begin to fall into place. The emotional tumult we knew will lessen, and we will start to find some control.

It is important for us to keep in mind that it has been a long time since we knew sobriety day in, day out, week in, week out, and this in itself is an uncomfortable state for us. Anxiety, fear, guilt, depression will not just suddenly go away. Nor will our loneliness and our feelings of being different and isolated from the human race. But we now know that these feelings are not unique to us, that other alcoholics and even nondrinkers experience them. We also know *why* we experience these emotions, and we have some ideas about what we can do to alleviate them.

Early sobriety is not a fun time. It may be the most painful period of our lives, but it can also be the greatest part of our lives. We won't know its greatness until much later, when we have settled comfortably into our recoveries and our new exciting lives.

Right now this early period is painful, difficult, upsetting, and hard to understand. We are highly charged and often on edge. We cannot identify ourselves because we are still trying to find out who we are. We are very volatile emotionally, for we haven't yet solved enough personal problems to know peace and contentment.

But it is important to know that with each passing day and with the determination to overcome the problems caused by alcoholism, we will get through this period. And after this stage of recovery everything gets better and better. From now on, and for the remainder of this book, we will learn how to move ourselves away from the negatives of our lives to learn affirmations that will restructure our emotions and our worlds.

CHAPTER SEVEN

THE BIG THREE-
LETTER WORD: SEX

That the woman who drinks too much is also promiscuous is part of the forklore that surrounds women alcoholics.

None of us is naïve enough not to know that many of us have had encounters with men we would not ordinarily give a second glance to, but this does not a loose woman make. Many women have been the victims of men who plied them with liquor just to get them into bed. And my survey of 603 women showed that only 2 percent drank in public places with the other 98 percent doing most of their heavy drinking in the home.

But it makes no difference where women do their drinking. The public has an image of the woman alcoholic that simply will not go away. Women alcoholics are not acceptable people, drunk or sober. For this reason women in recovery are forced to stay under cover as much as possible because society will not accept them if they "come clean."

A large part of dealing with one's drinking is acknowledging being an alcoholic, but in the case of women this is very often impossible. In fact, it often creates a whole new set of other problems. Thus women are forced to continue to deny their illness so as not to offend public sensibility and attract negative comments. How in the world can women alcoholics get around to talking about sexual problems?

In all my years of work with alcoholics and in all my speeches and appearances in public, I have found that the popular image of the woman alcoholic is so unrealistic that one finds it hard to believe. The public sees a woman in a dirty bathrobe, hair all stringy and hanging all over her face, sitting at a kitchen table at breakfast time with a whiskey bottle and a glass, looking forlorn and hung-over. What she does all day is solicit men.

I doubt if that image would fit a half of 1 percent, if that many, of us. In our organization are thousands of women whose families never even knew they drank excessively, so well hidden was their drinking.

The public idea of the alcoholic woman is so far away from the truth that we hardly know where and how to correct it, yet the complexity of women's sexual problems is always clouded by these continuing societal images.

How can these unreal social attitudes affect women alcoholics? Where do they begin?

Several years ago a fine documentary was presented by "Nova" on television, showing clearly the difference in the treatment of small girls and small boys even by those who believed themselves free of bias. What wasn't taken into consideration by these "unbiased" people was that they had been conditioned when they were children and they unconsciously reflected these attitudes. This was true even of the female teachers, some of whom were feminists.

Adults definitely transmitted different messages. Aggressive behavior was encouraged in the boys, but passivity was expected of the girls. While the boys were encouraged to learn new things on their own, like new games, the girls were helped by their mothers, delivering the message "You can't do it alone." Later, teachers encouraged boys more, while neglecting girls. Passivity in girls not only was encouraged but was the norm.

This expected passivity in girls continues into adulthood, with women being looked to as well for gentility, moral goodness, and spiritual leadership. Women have made some progress, but it is little indeed. In most social gatherings few women express strong political opinions, knowing that this kind of behavior is frowned upon in mixed groups. Such a woman would be seen as aggressive, loud-mouthed, and troublemaking. Her behavior is criticized; her views go unnoticed.

Opinionated behavior on the part of women alienates them

from men and women. A woman is permitted to speak out only on family matters or on subjects that concern her husband and her children. When I appeared before a Senate committee hearing some years ago on the issue of women and alcoholism, almost everyone who appeared brought forth this point of the conflicted gender role and the consequences suffered by women: there was a lack of recognition of women's real problems, a lack of understanding in the male treatment community, and frequent refusal to see how woman's role is perceived and how women really are, and the problems this lack of understanding creates for women, all translating into a great need for adequate treatment programs for women, which is not now being fulfilled.

At the heart of this entire matter are society's expectations of women and the way women really are. It is true that the sight of a drunken woman is ugly and difficult to tolerate, yet society must accept the unalterable fact that women drink, become alcoholics, have problems with sex, and are sometimes less than moral. For women alcoholics, the guilt produced by these societal expectations and the reality of their lives are what leads to the devastating depression so many experience and what triggers suicide in others.

When we look at the earliest experiences of women, we can see that from birth a woman receives negative messages about herself, her body and its functions, all preparing her for later negative sexual experiences. Expecting the very best in (and from) a marriage, women generally, and women alcoholics particularly, learn only too soon that their sexual lives are often a disaster, yet rarely do they understand the why of it. Women alcoholics simply drink more.

Taught early that touching, experimenting, even looking at our sexual organs are unacceptable actions, we learn a number of taboos, among them that these sexual organs are potentially "germy" and "unclean." Admonished always to wash our hands after urinating, even though our hands never touch ourselves, we have received the message that certain parts of us are to be regarded as "dirty."

We receive other negative messages just prior to menstruation. Learning that we will start to bleed, but that this will be a joyous occasion nonetheless, gives us a conflicting message that few young women understand, in light of the commercial products that urge us to buy some spray because of its strawberry or lemon scent to mask the unpleasant odor of menstruation.

So we are taught to feel unclean and that we are to make ready for marriage and sex by taking care of, and protecting, ourselves and our sexual organs, though wrapped in this air of untouchability.

Women alcoholics long for intimacy but shy away from sex, often because feelings of arousal frighten us and make us feel "strange" and "not quite nice." Passion is not a comfortable feeling for women alcoholics. It can be handled only when we are drunk, and then not too well.

Overcoming these deep-seated taboos very frequently requires professional help, but few women alcoholics seek it. Even considering it makes us feel uncomfortable. Too often the solution is to continue drinking and engaging in unremembered sex, many women believing we can handle booze and guilt better than the discomfort of facing up to the sexual problem.

Many, many women alcoholics engage in sex for the sake of intimacy, for the sake of being held, so that fears and loneliness will dissipate. Of course, it never happens, but at times sex will mute the desperate feelings of isolation.

Then, too, there are many women alcoholics stuck in marriages in which sex is distasteful. In order to fulfill spouses' desires, many women will engage in sex but first must deaden their feelings by getting drunk. Not wanting sex as often as their mates do leads thousands of women to drinking. Many women feel used each time this happens. Few have learned how to say no. Some who have tried it end up abused and battered. The story of women battering is rife with misuse of alcohol.

Perhaps it is not difficult to understand why some women alcoholics have such difficulties with sex when we know that sexual abuse and battering are well known to women who drink.

The scars of sexual abuse remain deeply hidden and may not even seem to show, except that women cannot engage in normal and joyful sex. Many carry this heavy psychological burden—the inability ever to get close to anyone, ever to be able to trust another person—having once been turned upon by family members, friends of the family, or other trusted people whose very positions of authority permitted them the chance to abuse the women who later became alcoholics with battered psyches and bruised emotions. These are the reasons for the deep depressions and the suicides among women alcoholics, suicides that go unreported as such. In just these past several years five of my acquaintances committed suicide, and not a single case was reported as alcohol-complicated, nor was it mentioned that several had been sexually abused as children.

The great tragedy is that women who are sexually abused blame themselves for its happening. Too often those in authority convey this feeling to a woman victim: that she must have done something to bring it about. And this horrendous guilt is carried for a lifetime. When the abuse is too painful for the mind to manage, it erupts into multiple personalities. When young girls are sexually abused, not understanding exactly what has happened but knowing it was not right, they remove themselves from normal play with other children, becoming aloof and distant. In adulthood these young women still shun groups, feeling different, shameful and shamed, unclean, and guilty—and very, very lonely.

Because women are frequently abused by people in authority, in later life they seem not able to respect authority and seem to defy edicts and orders and regulations that pertain to almost every activity of life. How often we see a woman crossing a lawn that has a very clearly marked sign, KEEP OFF THE GRASS. We surely know that women continue to defy the findings of the surgeon general about cancer and smoking. Not only do women continue to smoke, but many more are taking up smoking.

Perhaps if women alcoholics were able to talk about their early disrupting experiences, recovery would be more swift and rewarding. Surely if women could find a way to talk out these terrifying happenings, advanced states of depression and many suicides might be averted.

Only recently have we begun to recognize that a large part of many women alcoholics' emotional crippling is due to early sexual abuse. I first learned of sexual abuse among women alcoholics by accident in New Orleans in 1978, when I was talking to a counselor of alcoholic women, not herself an alcoholic. I was interested in knowing if this made a difference in getting the women to talk freely. Her answer was that because she wasn't an alcoholic, she had begun talking about how she was sexually abused as a child, hoping this technique would get the alcoholic women to open up about their alcoholism. Instead, what happened was startling: They talked about their own sexual abuse, which ran as high as 60 to 70 percent in some groups.

I was stunned. And from that day forward I began to test this myself when I was speaking to groups of women alcoholics. (How much one can observe from the vantage point of being behind a lectern.) As I began to discuss sexual problems known to women alcoholics, I would then tell about meeting the counselor and what had happened: that the women had talked about their own abuse. As I spoke to hundreds of women over the years, there was always a nodding acknowledgment from the audience. Because it is not a part of my history, it took years for me to learn of it, even though I am with and around women alcoholics every day. Surely this reveals how deeply hidden this subject is.

Because women alcoholics are so emotionally battered and emotionally deprived in childhood, problems in recovery are deeply ingrained and have very often been devastating before help is ever at hand. These problems include debilitating feelings about sex: shame; guilt; remorse; confusion; a sense of being unacceptable; a feeling of not being good enough.

These feelings can be dealt with only when they are brought into the open and discussed either with a therapist or with others who have had the same experiences. The real tragedy is that few women alcoholics ever have a place to discuss these feelings openly since they should never be discussed in mixed groups of men and women. If ever there needed to be a justification for women-only groups, this is it, and if there ever needed to be a reason why treatment facilities must have special programs for women alcoholics, surely this applies.

Even in our women-only groups women have extreme difficulty in discussing these feelings. Although male alcoholics are quick to say that they would not mind, nor would they be "shocked," this is simply not true. I have met a large number of women who tried to discuss aspects of their sexual lives in mixed groups, and in almost all cases the result was demeaning and unsuccessful to the degree that those women never again went back to the mixed groups.

Imagine if you will this kind of incident: A male alcoholic, after a heavy night of drinking, ended up in bed in a motel with two beautiful women, whom he discovered the next morning. His recitation of this fictional story would be met with laughter and some hearty joshing from other men. But let's suppose that a woman alcoholic were to tell a mixed audience of a night of drinking that ended up in a motel with two macho men, whom she discovered in bed with her the next morning. She would be greeted with horrified stares and shocked silence.

No, mixed groups are not the place for women alcoholics to discuss the sensitive nuances of sexual problems that confront us. And it's not as if it were just a need to discuss the conflicts of the past. Women alcoholics have many sexual adjustments to make in sobriety and recovery. Needs, wants, desires, and especially inhibitions are problems encountered in recovery.

One woman's feelings speak for the many. She wrote, "When I was drinking, I was aggressive, and my husband seemed to enjoy it, although he wanted badly for me to stop drinking. One and a half years later I am sober, but there is no sex. It is difficult for him and me to understand. I want a tender, warm companion."

Alcohol makes many women, even those who normally have problems with sex, feel desirable, beautiful, sexy, and uninhibited. One need only look at the singles' bars to know this is where to find the action, made more readily available with the seductive power of liquor.

Feeling desirable and less inhibited helps many women with sexual problems. One woman said, "While drinking, I became uninhibited and allowed myself to enjoy sex. I find enjoying and wanting sex much harder since being sober. But I'm working on it." Another woman said, "Since I've stopped drinking, I have a difficult time with sex, especially trying to relax. I have trouble reaching orgasm since I don't allow myself to, and I seem to put restrictions on my behavior."

The reason women have such difficulty with relaxing and enjoying sex in sobriety is the carry-over of guilt feelings and the belief that to enjoy sex is somehow not acceptable. The alcohol changes a woman into another person, one unfettered by feelings of shame and guilt. Having had too much to drink can erase, temporarily, negative feelings about sex.

Then, too, some men prefer the kind of behavior that results from a woman's drinking too much. "My husband really liked that other woman, and he misses her. However, he does realize that I am an alcoholic and does not want me to drink. Sometimes I think that maybe a sex therapist would help, but I am too embarrassed to work on it with outside help." And that goes for thousands of other women; feelings of embarrassment keep satisfaction and happiness from being a reality. Is this another form of self-flagellation for the woman alcoholic?

A large number of women alcoholics are married to male alcoholics, and this presents another kind of problem, especially if the husbands are still drinking. In my recent survey I found that 23 percent of the women alcoholics are married to male alcoholics who are still drinking. When the woman gets sober, she may find her spouse offensive. Wrote one: "When I am sober, I cannot and will not have sex with my husband when he is drinking, and that's most of the time. When I drank, I didn't give a damn."

Too much alcohol leads some men to believe they desire

sex, yet they are unable to follow this feeling to a conclusion. However, just before this stage of impotency, men sometimes become particularly demanding, and this often creates an area of conflict for women. Many men view marriage as a guarantee of sexual availability, and many women have given in to demands but have felt used. In recent years the women's movement has begun a long uphill fight to free women from being sexually intimidated at the males' demand. Women alcoholics often combated this problem by drinking themselves to avoid trouble. How very sad.

It is certainly safe to say that we women alcoholics have grave problems with sex while drinking and in sobriety. Despite the age of liberation in which we live, somehow these liberated feelings have not yet reached women alcoholics. The woman alcoholic with an ideal sex life is a rarity. Indeed, the woman alcoholic who is even able to discuss any part of her sex life, good or bad, is a rarity. But there could be a significant change if women alcoholics were to have a means of working through and talking about their hang-ups and problems. This means sensitive women's programs in treatment settings, and it means all-female self-help groups with a sensitivity to women's special needs and specific problems.

It seems to me that a large part of many women's adult sexual problems stems from childhood molestation and sexual abuse. There is probably not a single woman alive today who cannot recall a doctor or a dentist or a grandfather or an uncle who didn't at some time or another "have a feel," to use a vulgar expression. Disgust and shame linger long in the child and create serious hindrances for the adult woman. This violation of our persons when we are children can be described only in the ugliest terms.

Added to this violation of our person in childhood is another negative experience: that of our unclean and untouchable sexual anatomy. Mix them together, and we become women alcoholics who have severe sexual dysfunctions for a long, long time.

CHAPTER EIGHT

WHO WILL TAKE CARE
OF ME?

Is it true, as Colette Dowling says, that all women want to be taken care of? Or is it partial truth and partial myth?

It is true that we women are given mixed signals. We learn, on the one hand, that marriage will give us security and protection along with financial and emotional dependence. On the other hand, as young girls we learn a nurturing role: that we will be the strength in a family, that others, including our spouses, will depend upon us to help them grow and mature.

Although I have spoken of these issues in my workshops and speeches, it was not until I began putting this book together that I finally realized—overwhelmingly realized—why women alcoholics experience such emotional chaos in recovery. We have been kept off-balance all our lives, and suddenly, when we try to get a handle on our alcoholism, we are confronted with numerous mixed feelings, a result of the mixed messages we've received.

When our alcoholism is out of hand, we are the ones who need nurturing, yet the unfortunate fact is that we are very often alone at this time of need. Many women are separated or already divorced. Few males stay around during this period. Many leave because their nurturers have become useless and have themselves become needy. Of course, there are some men—a minority—who do stick with their alcoholic wives, and they are the real winners for it. These women recount how grateful they are for the support they received from their spouses.

There is, however, another large segment of women whose stories are quite the opposite. With them divorces occur after

101

sobriety because their marriage partners do not know how to respond to sober spouses. Sobriety strains the relationship, and the couple breaks up. Too often a man is unable to deal with a new, strong, and resilient wife. He feels threatened and overshadowed. Within self-help groups tales about the women who began to realize that their spouses wanted to keep them drunk are rife.

Conversely, as we've noted before, a male alcoholic often has the greatest amount of support during the period of recovery. The family rallies around, having learned what to say and what not to say, knowing what telltale signs to look for, having been instructed to give him love and comfort. In the workplace much the same happens. His co-workers are happy to see him back and healthy again, while most women alcoholics in the workplace are let go because they usually hold positions that can be filled by others.

In our quest for help women are sometimes handed messages of rejection even within treatment facilities. A number of studies have found that there is a negative attitude toward women alcoholics among professional people, who see them as weak, neurotic, hysterical, difficult to treat, uncooperative, too emotional, and overly excitable. This negative attitude is held by both male and female counselors, some of whom would rather deal with male alcoholics.

Unfortunately women alcoholics are crying out for nurturing, and these negative attitudes only intensify the need and deal a heavy blow to already almost nonexistent ego structures. Feelings of "I am a nothing" are intensified.

Many women turn to the doctors for nurturing. We seek our physicians' advice, support, and, most of all, nurturing. Instead of these needs' being fulfilled, the woman alcoholic very often acquires another dependence: this time on prescription drugs. Too often our physician does not recognize our alcoholism or doesn't want to deal with it because of the very unpredictable outcome.

My recent survey of 603 women alcoholics showed that almost half (46 percent) were divorced and that many others were essentially alone, even though still legally married. Looking for help, women are turned away at almost every door. There is certain legitimacy in asking, "Who will take care of me?"

Being alone at a time when help is desperately needed amplifies a woman's loss of identity since many identify themselves only through relationships to others, most especially mates. By the time women seek help, we are totally unable to outline ourselves, a condition which is expressed in our feelings of isolation from everything and everyone.

It is an irony that women alcoholics, who have been molded all our lives into a dependent role, have little or no support when it is needed the most, while men alcoholics, reared to be independent and nurtured simply because they are male, have all the help they need in recovery by all those surrounding them.

When we think of a woman alcoholic, the picture we see, the image our minds create, is a woman alone. When we think of a male alcoholic, our minds see him in a group, in the "hail fellow well met" conviviality of hearty male fellowship.

Many women who drink do so to find their nurturance in alcohol. It becomes the substitute for the intimacy of someone's holding them and saying, "There, there, everything will be all right. I'll take care of you."

Perhaps a great tragedy is that we women perceive our dependency upon men as so much stronger than they themselves are, a fallacy that needs correction in sobriety and recovery. In the early months of recovery most women cannot say of themselves, "I am competent. I am capable of doing much." This is frightening to many women. The thought of becoming independent, of standing alone, is revolutionary.

Why do we have such poor visions of ourselves? One would think that the truth, the reality, would strike us: We are women who raise families, who have been the strength of these families, we are in the workplace; we maintain households, often single-handedly. Yet we think of ourselves as nothing, as unable to be independent, and often as total failures.

Sigmund Freud, Theodor Reik, and many others saw women *only* as passive. Even today, the connotation of being female is to be in a submissive role, even though change is in the air. This belief, this assumption is as prevalent among women as among men, and that is how we women get the feeling that we must be cared for, that we can't do it alone, that our recovery can't take place without being with someone, a male. This is why many women who attend mixed self-help groups in the very beginning of sobriety so often form disastrous liaisons with men almost immediately.

The tragedy is that women must learn this tough lesson of self-realization at a time when we really need the help of others. Even many women without an alcohol problem believe that they probably are not able to care for themselves, that they need someone to depend upon to look over them and help them survive.

But what a very difficult pattern to break. As young girls we are constantly discouraged from belief in ourselves and our capabilities. We are discouraged from independent actions and feelings and thoughts. We are molded. We are discouraged from self-praise, while little boys are praised and ego is constantly reinforced. "How well you did that, Johnny," says a proud mother. To think she was once a little girl who was handed the role of nurturing, for in this role toward her son she is fulfilling the age-old passage of rites.

As I've already noted, too often in our marriages we have unconsciously adapted ourselves to being extensions of what our husbands do for a living. When a woman is asked who she is, she identifies herself as "I'm Dr. Jones's wife," and then receives just due as the wife of a physician, not as Mary Jones, bookkeeper to Smith, Smith, & Smith. If she doesn't use her husband's identification, she uses that of her children: "I'm Johnny's mother," as if that fully explained who she really is.

It is certainly indicative of our dependencies to note that the most popular adult education course for women in this country at this time is assertiveness training. We are now beginning to find ways to say what we think, what we mean, and who we are. We are learning to be persons in our own right. And this kind of learning experience should be part of every woman alcoholic's recovery program. But isn't it a sad commentary to think that we must go to class to learn how to say what we mean, to learn how to express ourselves so that we are not walked all over?

If there is anything to be said for drinking, it might be that alcohol helped us assert ourselves. In some cases, being drunk was the only time we got to say what we thought.

In almost every interview I've done one of the reasons given for drinking is that "drinking made me feel like somebody." When the time comes to give up alcohol, all that artificial bravado is gone, and we are back to square one, feeling like nobody and nothing, feeling uncared for and unwanted. Too often this is sadly true. We are unwanted at the neediest time of our lives, and we are frequently uncared for.

It is my belief, and with some evidence, that women alcoholics drink much longer than is necessary just because as women we are unequipped to seek and get help. The picture that emerges is something like this: Here is a woman who is passive, dependent, unsure of herself, who doesn't know who she is, who has little self-identity, who needs help, who is surrounded by a number of persons who ignore her for one reason or another, who leave her to struggle, and she adds to her already overflowing storchouse of negatives another one, called rejection. Thus she drinks more, gets sicker, and becomes more lost.

As a result, women alcoholics get help much farther down the line than do male alcoholics and therefore, have a much longer road back. Added to this discouraging truth is the fact that the quality of our care, if and when we get it, is usually not geared to our special needs as women. Worst of all, we are very poorly equipped with the stuff recovery is made of: a strong sense of self.

The extensive and complicated personal problems women alcoholics experience in this early period of recovery is largely due to this lack of self-knowledge. How often I have overheard women saying, "I am so mixed up. I feel like I don't know anything."

With the cessation of our drinking we are suffused with emotions that are not distinguishable to us. We feel at sea, unable to row into a safe port. We drift aimlessly.

In my own early quest for sobriety I couldn't understand why I was unable to want life, to want to go on living. I felt worthless, unloved and unlovable, completely incapable of taking care of myself, very frightened of life, totally insecure and deserted. Yet, in actuality, I had accomplished quite a deal and, to the world, appeared to be very successful.

How can our perceptions be so wrong? On the one hand, we feel:

— Totally helpless
— Afraid of life
— Overwhelmed

To the world, the one we are blinded to, we have probably:

— Raised families
— Helped our children make life choices
— Held jobs
— Been competent in all these

Where do we get our messages of helplessness?

We must take into account the time in a woman's life when alcoholism is usually at its height, middle age, often after she has given most of her adult life to marriage and motherhood.

Although mid-life is the time when a certain percentage of women begin to drink to counter their feelings of helplessness and hopelessness, the majority begins drinking much earlier. They are beginning to discover that now, in mid-life, alcohol may be a problem. But this nagging knowledge is buried for fear of disturbing the nest.

This mid-life period for most women is one of loss—loss

of youth; loss of children's earlier closeness and total dependency; loss of husbands' full interest and time at home; loss of a time to begin careers, or so they think. This is a period of disruption and severance of some very important emotional bonds, in contrast with the men of the families, whose ever-increasing self-realization and success have taken them deeper into the world outside while their wives' world has grown smaller and narrower. Suddenly something, sometimes a single incident, happens, to reveal to us in a moment of prescience that we are out of touch with the world outside our home. We begin to feel dissatisfied, lonely, left out. And these feelings spawn guilt. We tell ourselves we shouldn't be having these feelings of being neglected. After all, we have our jobs, we have our marriages, such as they are, we have our children, so why feel so left out? Suddenly we want things for ourselves, but we berate ourselves for this feeling, and our guilt intensifies. Those of us who are alcoholic just drink more to squash uncomfortable thoughts we don't know how to deal with.

And often, as men feel surer of themselves with increasing age, secure in their positions in the world of business, they experience an overpowering need for conquest, to prove themselves. How many women alcoholics have weak self-images additionally battered by rejection during this time? It is not just coincidence that many women have the worst struggle with alcohol around the age of forty.

Even worse is that our battered or nonexistent self-images make us believe that we are unable to do anything. We are deluded into thinking that we are completely dependent on others. We are unable to see ourselves as separate and autonomous. It is surely true that those whose dependency needs are not met in childhood are missing the necessary ingredients for emotional development in adulthood. This is our problem in adulthood. We are missing vital pieces. We are emotionally dependent persons, always searching for that nurturing that was absent in our childhood and sadly missing in our middle years when we were the nurturer of others.

What better way to salve the pain than to drink?

But now, after the trauma of excessive drinking and the

period of sobriety, we are into a period of learning how to live without the easement of alcohol. And it begins with our overcoming dependency needs. We must begin to think for ourselves, we must search for identity, we must learn autonomy, and above all, we must begin to have our own self-identity that includes a deep-feeling of our self-value.

It is a harsh reality to learn so late in life, but we must learn that no one will take care of us. We must do that for ourselves. We must begin now to overcome our feelings of inadequacy, and we help this happen by learning assertiveness and by taking a position in the world of business.

So often we read that women have difficulty in this phase because they have no role models, and that may be true. But we have intelligence, and this must be put to work for us, so that we see our needs and make ways to fulfill them rather than just quit and say, "What's the use?", as so many women alcoholics are prone to do. Women are not well equipped as fighters. We lack drive and stamina and motivation for the hassle of winning over great adversity because we have not been prepared for it.

But now is the time for us to learn these things. Now is the time to search for the best in us, to set goals, to take lessons from our failures and to ask the why of them. Why do we feel so like nothing? Why do we feel so defeated? Why do we feel it's all so useless?

These are the questions I hope have been answered with some suggested solutions. Here is a plan to follow:

1. Break away from dependencies.
2. Begin being your own person.
3. Know that whatever you are is up to you.
4. Know that whatever gets done in your life *you* must do.
5. Give up waiting for life to happen; always have some goal to strive for.
6. Be in charge of your thoughts, your life, your alcoholism.

PART THREE

RECOVERY

CHAPTER NINE

WHAT IS IT ALL ABOUT?

It is said that for the alcoholic there is never enough: never enough liquor, never enough love, never enough money, never enough time...

We just keep on drinking, never looking deeply into the reasons, but what we are really doing is running away from what we perceive as the emptiness of life. We are the ones who stand on the edge of the Grand Canyon, overwhelmed by its size and beauty, saying to ourselves, "But what is the meaning of life?" This is a question we must face and deal with at this stage of recovery.

There are some who seem to know the answer. I have a skepticism that plagues me at times in my sobriety, but these times have become fewer and fewer as I have found ways to approach the question and supply a few answers.

As a Christian I accept the Golden Rule, but that doesn't tell me *what* life is, merely how to live it. So I still ask: What is life? Why is life? Were we put here on earth, a continual stream of people coming and going, only to build higher buildings and pollute and plunder the earth more than those who went before? What is it all for, and for whom? What happens if no room is left? Is there a next stage? If so, what purpose did the last stage serve, the one in which humankind covered every inch of earthly space?

Is life merely to reproduce oneself, to populate? Or are we here for no reason whatever except as organisms that move through the cycles of birth, maturity, old age, death? Did we invent God because we had to?

111

Like most people, I find myself asking life's big questions in crisis situations, never in peaceful moments. It takes the night before a serious operation while one lies in a cold, strange hospital bed to set in motion the serious questioning of what it's all about. Or attending a funeral, staring at the open hole in the ground, sets off the questions about existence. These are the times of reckoning, and sometimes they arrive too late. I should have had my time of thinking much, much earlier, when thinking wasn't clouded by a crisis. But like many others, I have been a willing victim of short-range thinking.

There are some religions that see life merely as a preparation for death. Living is, in truth, merely a temporary state. As morbid as that sounds, most of us do recognize that there is something in it. When young, we don't see a scoreboard flashing the score for our conduct in the Great Race, although I can recall one of my parents' threatening me by telling me a report on all my mischievous deeds was kept somewhere in the great beyond. And as our years accumulate, most of us tend to want to be "better."

Do we mean moral? Are we searching for, hoping for accolades from others for our purity of conduct? Are we trying to "clean up our acts" just in case there really is a Judgment Day that will consider the records of all our misdeeds? The French sociologist Emile Durkheim believed moral obligation is first experienced as an external social constraint, which is only gradually interiorized as we grow older.

By looking at the end, by looking at our demise, are we discovering what life really is? Do we discover what it was meant for?

Happy are those people who can accept a life plan through an organized religion. For them life is not too problematical, nor are the questions about life too disturbing. The cocoon of organized thought is very comfortable and comforting.

Having been raised to religion in my childhood, I still went through a lengthy period of questioning when I was a graduate student in sociology at the University of Pennsylvania. I felt great joy in learning that many of the great thinkers struggled to describe life's beginning, wrestled with the question of how matter assumed shape. What is matter? Who created matter? And can we ever decide if matter was first? Is there a divine purpose for the universe? Is there a great hand directing the universe?

It became obvious to me that many people struggle with the big question of "what's it all about?" Those who are happiest are able to accept a generalization and then move on in their thinking. The reasoning is somewhat on the order of: (1) Someone or something had to create everything, even if universal accidents happened along the way; (2) for want of a better description, we call that being God, or Buddha, or Allah; (3) from that point forward it becomes a dealer's choice; (4) did God or Buddha or Allah create and then quit, or does God, Buddha, or Allah direct us on a daily and personal level?

The social organizations within which we live serve to give us the structures we require for a life of some purpose: the family, the church, our town, the clubs we belong to, and the society of humankind as a whole. The groups that we are attached to dictate our mode of behavior. We then begin to act in certain acceptable ways.

But we, the alcoholics, somehow have not seemed to fit into any of these patterns. We rebel within strictures. We feel confined, trapped; we feel demands that we cannot meet are being made upon us. And our escape from these formal patterns into drinking has brought condemnation of our behavior, which, to us, simply adds fuel to the fire. Our world is peopled with no one. Our one unshakable, dependable companion is our bottle. Yet we discover that the more and the longer we drink, the more separated we are, and then the big question is laid right before us: What's it all about?

There is always this dichotomy in us. We want to be a part of a group or groups. We long to be like others and to fit in, yet every time we try, we yearn for our privacy. Our inability to stick with groups later becomes a joke against us because some of our recovery from alcoholism will probably be achieved in self-help groups, where a code of behavior is required for participation and belonging. Indeed, it is ironic that our recovery is based largely upon doing many things we were unable or refused to do before, one of which is to participate in groups.

During our drinking lives we have seemed not to fit anywhere. We seemed to be out of the stream of things. Maybe we tried pursuing something called the good life, only to find there is just not one answer. Financial freedom has always been a part of the good life, and many alcoholics find it, only to be left feeling empty and unfulfilled.

The good life also means freedom from stress, freedom from worry of any kind. It means happiness, a sense of peace, and a sense of accomplishment. Many achieve a lot of this and still ask, "What is it all about?" If all of us were to have everything we consider to be the components of the good life, we would be bored, irritable, angry, and eventually we would erupt in some form of personal disintegration. Daily we read in the newspaper about tragedies involving people we might have described as "having everything." Yet they went off the deep end. We rationalize our own disintegration by saying, "No wonder I drank because of all my personal problems." In the days of our drinking we always wondered where and what the answer is, and in our new sobriety we are still asking.

What we really need is a purpose in life. Years ago, when I was teaching high school in a small town in Kansas, one of my pupils was a very disruptive teen-ager. Everyone in the school, including the principal, warned me about him. But I knew how to handle Floyd, even though he had already upset many of my classes and had also removed the bolts from my chair, so that I pitched face forward onto the floor.

Several days before this last episode we had started a small newspaper for the high school, and until elections were held six months hence, it was up to me to choose the students who would do the work. My moment of genius came when I appointed Floyd as the managing editor. From that day forward we never had any more trouble with him, nor could we ever have found a harderworking managing editor.

Floyd's disruptive behavior was perfectly understandable to me, for I remembered my feelings as a high school student. Unfortunately no one had appointed me managing editor so that I could learn about feeling needed and acquire a sense of purpose and direction.

Too frequently women see their children as their only reason for being. We, especially women alcoholics, make them our purpose and direction in life. We begin to smother them as we come into our sobriety, wondering how we could have been drinking all those years when we have such precious children. And now, in sobriety, we begin to overprotect, overdiscipline, and overcontrol their lives. We are trying to make up for the times we weren't around, for the times we were unable to help them because we were drunk. Now, to overcome our feelings of guilt, we become overbearing, making them into the sole purpose for our sobriety, only to find they become disruptive and rebellious in response. We have failed to realize that our children learned how to cope without their mothers during our years of drinking. They matured because they had to. They learned to take care of their daily needs without a mother's intervening. The role reversal that took place when mother's drinking got out of hand cannot be reversed. For too long our children have cared for us, cooked for us, put us to bed, made excuses for us, protected us. Although we are now sober, we are not Mother. And we can't be.

Women alcoholics, more often than men, often reach a life crisis point when the children leave home or even just grow away emotionally. Often women into sobriety for a number of years still ask, "What's it all about?" when their children leave home, only because they have made those children their sole focal point in life. Many women tend to return to drinking at this period of life. How often have we heard the descriptive phrase *empty nest syndrome?* Because women's lives tend to be smaller and narrower in scope than men's, this inevitable stage of life becomes emotionally unbearable. Life's emptiness seems to be their only preoccupation.

For men, their purpose in life and their reason for being

come more from thinking in terms of successful careers, which then lead to them being able to support families and being successful husbands and fathers. Men think more in terms of the realities of what needs to be done, whereas women think more in terms of the emotional status within the family unit.

Our new sobriety has put us into a sort of neutral zone. We stay sober in these beginning months through sheer will, our minds racing with nagging and difficult thoughts. On the days when maintenance of our sobriety is touch-and-go, we tend to fall into the "Why am I doing this?" rut, which is followed by "What in the hell is this all about?" and "Why am I here?"

The temptation to drink again at this point is very, very strong, and for this reason alone it is important to get a few things straight in our minds. We must begin to see that our lives are of value for ourselves alone and not base our reasons for living totally upon others. It is much, much better to identify several reasons for existing so that when one is removed or destroyed, there are others to help sustain us.

Always we seem to come back to "What is life?" The farther down the road we get, the more we begin to wonder where and how and when we will die. In sobriety we become extremely conscious of the finite nature of life, and the questions of when and how creep into our thinking at odd times of the day and night. We become sensitive to seeing the ages of others, as if life had gone on and made others old while we were living our lives with alcohol. It is like a bad dream come true. And just as suddenly we become extremely aware of our own physical conditions, and we wonder what kind of damage we've done to ourselves during our years of drinking. Some women begin to exercise regularly and start to take good care of themselves through physical fitness programs, although more men follow this pattern. Many take up running, walking, aerobics, as part of this getting-back-to-good-health recovery program, and nutrition becomes important.

Although we are still floundering around trying to discover just what life is all about, we begin to enjoy it in our new awareness of ourselves as physical beings. We want desperately to take care of ourselves now. We begin to wonder how we were so foolish as to let ourselves go physically during the years of drinking. We begin to notice that with each new day of sobriety we are starting to savor life. It is beginning to feel wonderful to be alive. We still have nightmares and dream that we are drinking and getting drunk, and we still feel very troubled sometimes, but we are beginning to feel a few rays of real hope at last. Instead of running from one daily chore to another, we are searching for something more meaningful than just the mundane actions of filling jobs. We still haven't gotten our acts together, but we are beginning to believe that we can.

This is a great time to learn the value of meditation. In fact, learning the art and use of meditation at this point of recovery is essential if we are to maintain that sobriety with relative calm.

Meditation need not be complicated. There are some complicated methods, if one wishes to delve into them, but the kind of meditation I found to be effective for me and others at this stage is merely to set aside twenty minutes each morning for absolute silence. That is probably the single most important part of this exercise. There must be no sound whatever. Part of the learning process is to listen to the silence.

A second must for this exercise in meditation is to sit next to a window that looks out upon something natural—a tree, a field, a bush, a garden, a lawn, whatever, so long as it is a part of nature.

The third element is to be undisturbed, even if it means sealing yourself away from the life of the house. The best time for meditation—almost the only real time for it—is in the very early morning, when no one is awake. It should be in daylight hours, at first anyway.

And the last element is for you not to have a single thing to eat or drink with you. No morning cup of coffee or anything to nibble on. Just you.

This is the time when we start to put our lives into focus. Now is the time to consider the real meanings of our lives. Now is the time to put our houses in order. Now is the time to forget the vicissitudes of life and to think of its largeness. This is the time for us to align our priorities; we must begin to see what comes first, and second, and third in the order of importance within our lives. For many of us, the Creator, the Oversoul, God, the Universal Hand, is first, and all other priorities follow. For some it may be a career, for others it may be the family, and for still others, something quite different. We may wish to put ourselves and the care of ourselves ahead of family, for if we don't care for ourselves, we won't be able to care for our families.

For the first several weeks we should have absolutely nothing with us during this period of meditative time. Later we may wish to have something inspirational to read, but at first the very best approach is to sit with only our thoughts. This is the time for us to come to grips with our disease of alcoholism; this is the time for us to see how lucky we are now that we are sober and have elevated ourselves away from the uncontrollable drinking that possessed us for so long. Now is the time for us to be able to make some intelligent observations about our alcoholism, to see how we were caught in the trap of drinking, temporary sobriety, drinking, temporary sobriety and to see how it has taken several months for us to be free from the manipulation of that compelling force. It has taken this long for our bodies and our minds to begin to be free from urges that once controlled us.

During these morning periods of total silence we will probably really get to know ourselves for the first time. There will be disturbing thoughts and many upsetting memories, but most important of all, now is the time to remind ourselves that we are in a process of cleaning up and remaking our lives, and we can put those troubling memories in their rightful place, behind us.

In the very early days of meditation most people feel uncomfortable. The first time I tried it I was a clock watcher. I simply couldn't wait until the time was over. Somewhere I had read about the value of meditation, and then I went to a class to learn about it, only to hear about mantras and "ommmmmmm," and they just weren't for me. But I did make a pact with myself that I would try some form of meditation, and I began with setting a certain amount of time aside. Of course, I hadn't yet learned the art of meditation. I only sat in a chair, watching a clock, hoping the twenty minutes would soon be over. My mind ranged from what I had to do that day to disturbing thoughts that I pushed away from me.

How long a time, how many weeks it was before I began to come to my senses about what I was doing—or, rather, what I wasn't doing—I don't know, but I wasted a significant amount of time. I had learned nothing about myself except that I was just as impatient with mediation as I was with almost everything else in my life. Finally, because these periods produced no magic in my life, I decided to examine what I was doing and what I should be doing. In the first periods of my meditation I wasn't successful, but I never gave up.

By now, all these years later, I think I have learned how to practice a form of meditation that is almost foolproof in the results it can produce. It requires strict adherence to the rules set out earlier. Eventually you begin to experience something you have never known before: yourself. But it takes a great deal of practice in the very beginning to keep your mind from straying. I never realized before how jumbled my thoughts really were, nor had I known how my mind flits from one thought to another. Then, too, the silence is overpowering and threatening. After a few false starts I began simply to listen to the silence, and that began to be productive, for it helped stop the endless flow of disjointed thoughts. After a few days of forcing myself to listen to the silence and to empty my mind of other thoughts, I found that I was able to meditate.

Once meditation is mastered, you will discover that a great peace takes over. At least, that is what happened to me, and I have heard others remark on experiencing exactly the same sensation.

For most of us it has been a long time since we have spent constructive time with ourselves, and learning to meditate as a part of daily life is a very big step toward learning control of ourselves and knowing some peaceful moments. My knowledge of alcoholics, including myself, shows that our thoughts literally race through our minds. We often speak very quickly, and we come forth with many impractical plans. We are often restless and edgy, wanting always to be doing something but not knowing what it is we want to do.

Meditation will probably be the most difficult of all the exercises we master in sobriety, but it is also the most valuable technique in learning the basis for the new lives we must learn to live.

Meditation every morning helps us start the day on the right foot and it helps us overcome our normal restlessness of thought. It helps us get our "ducks in a row," it provides the time for us to be grateful for our new lives, and it leads us to see the events in our lives in true perspective. We are able to see which events are more important than others, and we can acknowledge the value of life itself. These early-morning periods help us put our alcoholism in its rightful place as an illness we must deal with physically and mentally.

Without adding meditation to our lives in recovery, we tend to lose sight of the proper order of things in our life. Our normal tendency is to let our minds be concerned with the mundane things of life: getting gas for the car, picking up the cleaning, making certain of appointments with so-and-so, and on and on. The details of everyday living corrupt our vision of the wholeness of life. We become preoccupied with the vicissitudes of each twenty-four hours and fail to see the long range of our lives. We are blinded by the everydayness that made us drink excessively in the months and years before, yet now, in our new sobriety, we tend to forget the externals that led us so easily into drinking. We lose sight of our relationship to eternity and our primary purpose of life: emotional and spiritual growth.

The time for running away from life's realities ended the day we stopped drinking. We are now faced with learning to know, and to cope, with ourselves in a wholly different but more peaceful way. Finally we come to grips with the truth of our not being able to escape wrestling with the big questions of life, with our lives. The time of pushing aside the big questions is over. The time of endless tomorrows is coming to an end, and we are staring maturity in the face. Even the meaning of life is changing for us, now that our views of life are not clouded. We know that we are on a search for life's meaning, despite the anguish we are experiencing, anguish we used to bury in drinking. We are faced with the pain of reality, with the realness of life now complicated with sober thinking.

Too often newly sober people stumble at this point in recovery because it is a painful time of realizations. We are on the threshold of meeting truths we put aside for our drinking years, but we are now again face-to-face with them. In our pursuit of lasting sobriety this juncture is probably the one of most importance. Getting through this stage of thinking about our lives and life's meaning is the fundamental first step toward positive living.

George Bernard Shaw's famous observation of its being a pity that youth is wasted on the young merely bolsters the truth of time's fleeting essence. When young, we see life as a marvelous adventure, stretching before us with colorful rainbows arching over our path. We know that nothing can go wrong. Every day is filled with sunshine, and we are exuberant, powered by self-starting energy, ready to conquer the world surrounding us.

And then we wake up and find that reality has come into our world, and we shrink from it with glasses in our hands. Many alcoholics I have known never do get over this hurdle of accepting the truth about life—that it isn't dreamland—and many alcoholics stay stuck in this mire of disbelief.

We who have come back to the real world can accept the painful parts of life as soon as we learn a confidence in ourselves and our abilities to handle any situation because of our new inner strength. And this begins to happen as we learn to know ourselves through meditation.

CHAPTER TEN

TAKING CARE OF NUMBER ONE

For too long it has been generally believed that alcoholism is a result of the physical environment within which a person lives, that attitudes, cultural and otherwise, are its cause. Many studies, but not nearly enough professional acceptance, show the physiological reasons for the development of alcoholism in individuals, and these must be recognized if the alcoholic is to be helped.

Too often we mouth the words *Alcoholism is a disease,* but then we go on and talk about it, and treat it, as a moral weakness. It is certainly true that people who turn to the use of alcohol in crises need to learn other coping mechanisms, but this habit of using alcohol does not create the disease of alcoholism. Other physiological factors must be present, and we must treat alcoholism with physiological solutions. That means we must establish a nutritional program to repair the physical damage.

Just to stop drinking does not solve the problem. The alcoholic is nutritionally deprived, has experienced major cell damage, and must devote sober time to providing care for and repair of this severe metabolic crisis.

Having spent a lifetime studying alcoholics, alcoholism, and the effects of alcohol, Dr. Roger Williams, at the University of Texas, sees the derangement of the appetite mechanism located in the hypothalamus of the brain as the most serious toxic effect of alcohol, one that seems to be singularly overlooked by most professionals who try to help the alcoholic.

As a drinking person loses appetite for food, more drinking occurs and food becomes totally repulsive. Thus good nutrition and heavy drinking are totally antagonistic to each other. When drinking ends, the alcoholic must begin a program of good nutrition and care of the physical body.

As we drink, we eat less and less. The crucial nutrients are then missing, and that is when cellular damage occurs. Dr. Williams makes the point that not only are brain cells damaged from the excessive use of alcohol combined with the cessation of eating, but cells in every organ and tissue are severely affected. Biochemical impairment is the effect of alcohol; severe cellular damage is the result.

Obviously a large part of our recovery from alcoholism must include a serious consideration of how we care for our bodies, and we must adopt proper habits in the very beginning. During the first days and weeks of getting off alcohol, we go through a very bad time. Of course, the degree of difficulty to which any of us suffers is in definite proportion to the amount we drank and the length of time we drank. For some, perhaps detoxification is necessary, but for the majority it is not. Instead, we must endure days and weeks of discomfort. There is one great advantage: We gradually begin to feel better physically than before, and we are able to return to eating in a normal way. Headaches sometimes persist for a while, and we will experience great anxiety, sometimes feeling as if we were about to jump out of our skins. We will be nervous and not know what to do with ourselves. And time will hang heavy.

In this early period proper eating and the taking of vitamins can lessen these uncomfortable feelings, so let's take a look at this subject.

NUTRITIONAL RULE 1: NO MATTER WHAT ANYONE TELLS YOU ABOUT EATING CANDY, AVOID IT LIKE THE PLAGUE. EAT NO CANDY, NO SUGAR, NO ICE CREAM, NO HONEY.

One big no-no is candy, almost always a big temptation for the recovering alcoholic. Sugar at this time simply plays havoc with blood sugar and will aggravate mood swings, in addition to everything else that is going on in your body. Some old schools of thought claim an alcoholic should eat candy whenever there is an urge to drink, but this is very, very poor advice in light of what modern medical science tells us. *Anything* is better than candy!

There is a great controversy about whether or not alcoholics are hypoglycemic. Some physicians see *all* alcoholics as hypoglycemic, while others believe this to be untrue. In any case, whether or not we are hypoglycemic, there is no question about all of us having to be very careful about our diets and keeping free from excessive amounts of sugar. Even small amounts of sugar can create problems for the newly recovering alcoholic.

When we permit our blood sugar levels to drop, we will experience cravings for alcohol and sugar. To prevent this, we should eat six small meals a day and follow a high-protein, low-carbohydrate diet. This regimen will minimize excessive feelings of anxiety and headaches and also helps keep depression at arm's length. By avoiding the ups and downs of a seesawing blood sugar level, we will do away with the cravings for a drink and for sugar.

NUTRITIONAL RULE 2: DO NOT BECOME ADDICTED TO COFFEE, TEA, OR COLA. USE IN MODERATION, IF AT ALL.

And what about coffee?

Long seen as the great friend of the alcoholic in a myth perpetuated by Alcoholics Anonymous, drinking coffee is probably the most destructive habitual pattern an alcoholic can establish in sobriety. Like candy, coffee can postpone sobriety by the very effect it has on the body. Caffeine is an addictive drug. How can we be recovered if we merely substitute another drug for the one we've just given up?

Alcoholics who wish to drink coffee should always use the decaffeinated type, yet I have almost never seen an alcoholic do this—and I include myself. Perhaps my one redeeming feature is that I have now reduced my coffee intake to about one cup a day.

However, I have seen alcoholics make the drinking of coffee

throughout the day into a ceremonial rite, fervently believing they are "taking care" of their alcoholism.

Let us always remember that the less we make a big deal out of our alcoholism, the sooner we will recover from it. We must not spend each day, each minute, each hour concentrating on it and taking care of it by looking for a cup of coffee. We must not become professional alcoholics, believing that nothing else in life has any importance. As one woman once said aptly, "Alcoholism is my illness, not my identity." Those with heart disease, diabetes, or MS do not spend entire days thinking and talking about their conditions to the exclusion of almost everything else.

Many alcoholics—the professional alcoholics—drink coffee in the same way they drank alcohol, merely substituting the beverage. That is surely not a change in habit, and they are hanging on to a pattern of behavior that serves only an inferior purpose. They continue to perpetuate the habit of drinking and the patterns of drinking. Truly recovered alcoholics do not have cups of coffee as if they were alcoholic drinks. I have been with alcoholics who go into restaurants and, before ordering meals, insist on having coffee first. This is the behavior of a professional alcoholic.

In the early stages of my sobriety I kept reaching for a drink, so finally I tried seltzer water and found it satisfied my need to have a drink close by. Eventually it was no longer necessary to have it always at hand, but that was several months later.

New sobriety is the time to break all addictions and not to substitute new ones, such as coffee, tobacco, etc. This applies to tea, cocoa, and other caffeine-containing drinks, too.

Have you substituted a new drug for the old one, caffeine for alcohol?

NUTRITIONAL RULE 3: EAT A BALANCED DIET AND A VARIETY OF FOODS, ESPECIALLY THOSE HIGH IN PROTEIN.

Alcoholics are always in very run-down conditions when their drinking ends, and there is now more and more agreement that the poor physical condition of the alcoholic has a lot to do with the cravings experienced in sobriety. Each day there is more evidence that the dry-drunk behavior some alcoholics display in sobriety is induced by the excessive use of coffee and candy. Since we have already explored the dangers of these substances, let us now move on to just exactly what we *should* be eating.

We definitely need protein at this point and should eat foods such as:

ITEM	GRAMS OF PROTEIN
1 cup cottage cheese	40
4 ounces lean beef	22
4 ounces chicken	18
4 ounces codfish	16
4 ounces scallops	16
1 slice Swiss cheese	10
1 egg	9
1 cup milk	9
2 tablespoons peanut butter	8
1 cup cooked peas	8
1 cup yogurt	8
1 slice bread	2

Destructive thinking can demolish our normal supply of energy. In these early days of sobriety we often expend our total selves in anger, hostility, and negativity. We actually devour our energy packages—minimal to start with—and cripple ourselves for normal behavior.

The excessive fatigue we experience in early sobriety may come from a protein deficiency. Because we have eaten so poorly and so erratically while drinking, we sometimes continue to eat unbalanced meals when we finally stop, and the protein deficiencies cause extreme fatigue and irritability. Our unbalanced diets leave us sometimes with severe headaches and feeling nauseated, slightly dizzy, and somewhat light-headed. Many years ago, when I was in graduate school and drinking, I was experiencing these feelings. When I called my doctor and described my symptoms, he said only, "Go out and eat a big steak dinner." I couldn't believe I was hearing correctly. Somehow I thought I had some very serious illness, which would take medical science much effort to diagnose. But I did as he suggested, and within an hour I felt wonderful.

Too often we are not aware of the degree nutrition plays in our lives. Our bodies are screaming for the proper nutrients, but we, especially those of us who have been drinking over the years, starve ourselves of them.

There is much controversy about how much protein we need daily, but for women the figure generally agreed upon by most nutritionists is fifty-five grams. However, I have seen estimates ranging from forty to seventy-five grams.

Most of us never come close to the latter figure. In fact, probably very few of us actually get the fifty-five grams daily that we need for cell repair. Our diets are frequently made up of sugar, white flour, junk foods, fast foods, and soft drinks. This kind of diet, low in protein, will certainly make us tired, fatigued, and depressed and will lead us to a craving for a drink.

Certainly consuming enough protein is a way to combat that tired, let-down feeling experienced early in sobriety. Our recovery from alcoholism is greatly affected by the way we feel. Many times the early days of sobriety are filled with hours of feeling anxious, restless, unsatisfied, nervous, depressed. These feelings are enhanced by poor eating habits.

Doctors have now learned that hyperactive children may be helped by the removal from their diets of certain food additives. Alcoholics are the same way. A diet high in junk food may make us hyperactive, nervous, and restless, filled with a sense of impending doom and disaster. And as we are beginning our recovery, these feelings are precisely what we do *not* need.

We must be certain to eat a variety of foods and try to eat them in a balanced way. The food groups we should choose from each day are as follows:

CATEGORY	FOODS	CONTAINS
Meat and meat substitutes	Lean meats, poultry, fish, eggs,	Protein, iron, B vitamins

	nuts, peanut butter, dried beans	
Vegetables and fruits	All vegetables and fruits	Carbohydrates, iron, vitamin A, vitamin C
Milk Products	Milk (all forms), cheese, yogurt, cottage cheese	Protein, calcium, phosphorus
Grains and cereals	Whole grain cereals and breads	Carbohydrates, B vitamins and fiber

NUTRITIONAL RULE 4: USE VITAMIN, MINERAL, AND AMINO ACID SUPPLEMENTS.

This is a controversial area in the treatment of alcoholism, but my belief is that vitamins and minerals are of the first order for attaining and maintaining sobriety.

Which vitamins to take? For alcoholics the most important are the B vitamins, but we should really take a super one-a-day type of vitamin supplement, especially heavy in the B vitamins. We should also add to our supplements glutamine, an amino acid the use of which Dr. Roger Williams has pioneered for alcoholics. Glutamine (not glutamic acid, which is a relative) will inhibit the craving to drink, some studies seem to indicate.

Minerals are equally important because they help make the vitamins effective. Most formulas of high potency include small amounts of necessary minerals, and usually these are enough. Make certain, however, that whatever formulation you choose includes the minerals.

Obviously a long discussion on minerals, vitamins, and amino acids could follow, but suffice it to say that recovery can be helped immeasurably by their use in conjunction with a proper diet.

HEALTH RULE : BREAK THE SMOKING HABIT.

In our pursuit of health and recovery perhaps the most

important no-no for women alcoholics is smoking.

It is very difficult to understand why women have *increased* their smoking ever since the surgeon general's report on its deleterious effects. Is it because women simply want to ignore the facts and want to act as if nothing would happen to them? Surely it displays a great weakness of character since most women alcoholics to whom I have spoken even refuse to attempt to stop smoking. Even worse, many women alcoholics will say, "Well, I gave up drinking, and I just can't give up everything at once." This may still be said two and three years after sobriety.

Of course, the easiest thing in this world is to turn to other addictions after having given up one. In my own case I was able to give up prescribed drugs, street drugs, alcohol, smoking, and, eventually, excessive amounts of coffee only then to have problems with binge eating. Overeating also has ill effects, but certainly nothing at all like those we get from smoking. Overeating does not have the same terminal prognosis.

It is true that *some* women gain weight after giving up smoking, but surely a slight increase is a lot better than lung or throat cancer. There are some women who have gained as much as fifteen pounds after giving up a pack of cigarettes a day. But after the body has adjusted to being without cigarettes, without nicotine, and the habit of smoking has been broken, then the weight gain can be attacked. *Of course, that gain does not have to take place. It is not inevitable.* It is only something that happens some of the time.

Smoking is both a filthy and an unhealthy habit. Cigarette smoke contains a large number of compounds, which include nicotine, tars, and carbon monoxide. The constituents of tar are known to cause cancer and bronchial disorders. At the rate of about fifteen milligrams of tar per cigarette, an average of almost four ounces of tar is deposited in the lungs of a pack-a-day smoker every year.

The short-term effects of smoking are:
1. Increased pulse rate
2. Rise in blood pressure
3. Drop in skin temperature

4. Increased acid in the stomach
5. Reduced urine formation
6. Stimulation, then reduction of the brain and nervous system
7. Loss of appetite and physical endurance

Long-term effects, mostly in the bronchopulmonary and cardiovascular systems, are:

1. Hardening (narrowing) of blood vessels in the heart and brain
2. Shortness of breath; coughing
3. More respiratory infection in the form of colds and pneumonia
4. Chronic bronchitis and emphysema
5. Risk of cancer of the lungs, mouth, larynx, esophagus, bladder, kidneys, and pancreas
6. Stomach ulcers
7. Risk of thrombosis in users of birth control pills

Women who smoke often have smaller babies and very frequently have more premature births; there is also a greater occurrence of miscarriages and stillbirths among them than in women who do not smoke.

According to the Royal College of Physicians of Great Britain every cigarette cuts six minutes from the smoker's life. Isn't it time you quit?

In recovery, let's not trade an addiction to alcohol for an addiction to other drugs, such as caffeine and nicotine.

Your goal in recovery is to be the healthiest you can be, and to help you with this, it is a good idea to subscribe to a health magazine, which will provide an incentive to aid your recovery. Magazines such as *Today's Health* or *Let's Live* or even *Weight Watchers Magazine* although you may not have a weight problem, focus on fitness and good eating habits plus healthful living styles. And that is what we are striving for.

CHAPTER ELEVEN

SELF-ESTEEM: THE MAGIC BUILDING BLOCK

Our forays into meditation and nutrition are the first steps into the process of learning about ourselves in a positive way, without the baggage of the old negative feelings we once carried into every situation in our lives. We are ready to pursue the acquisition of positive feelings about ourselves, beginning with the feelings of self-esteem necessary to help us with all our re- lationships—with ourselves and with others, in love and in sexual relationships.

When I first began to study the process of recovery, I mis- guidedly believed that self-esteem came first, but actually we need to find a road to feelings of self-worth, because this precedes our eventual feeling of self-esteem. Perhaps the difference is minor, but it is certainly there.

The majority of us have never experienced any real feelings of self-worth. Indeed, this is at the basis of our poor relationships, sexual and nonsexual. The way we feel about ourselves is really the way others will feel about us. The way we "love" is dependent on our opinions, beliefs, and feelings about ourselves and our sense of self.

From observations of myself and other women alcoholics I have known, it is evident that as the process of self-discovery takes place and feelings of self-value grow, so, too, the capacity to love (and accept love) develops. It definitely seems that one is in correlation with the other: The better we think of ourselves, the less we suffer from feeling unloved or rejected. We have a buffer that protects us from demoralizing emotions. We are not totally devastated. We do not feel betrayed and alone. Healthier egos allow us to say the heck with any rejection and to walk away from the situation.

When we do not possess any feelings of self-worth, we short-change first ourselves and then others. We are indeed our own worst enemies, and much of these feelings of self-condemnation were at the base of our drinking. Our poor ego structures made us use alcohol to help us feel abler to meet life. Too often the alcohol pushed us over to the other side, and we appeared to be outgoing, strong, self-confident, and totally in charge of ourselves. However, any rejection quickly shattered this false image, and we toppled over.

Our feelings about ourselves account for our success or failure with life and with others in our life. Unfortunately few of us learn this until we go through something as traumatic as alcoholism.

The reason we can be successful in a love relationship when we feel good about ourselves is that the other person is reaffirming what we know about ourselves, that we are somebody worthwhile. Yet, if we do not have that sense of self-value, we are likely to feel threatened when others say to us, "I love you." Our first reaction is to wonder what they want from us since we are certain that they can't possibly really love us.

We ascribe to others our feelings about ourselves. More than that, as much as we want to believe it when others say, "I love you," we back away because we are frightened that very soon they will learn the real truth about us: that we are not at all what they think we are, that we are not worthy of their love, that we have somehow misguided them. So we draw back into our shells and have another drink.

In the early years when I tried to get my alcoholism under control, I spent a great deal of time trying to unravel myself and my emotions about myself. It was necessary for me to try to understand *why* I was punishing myself. I began to see that I was using alcohol to beat myself to death. It was a method I had chosen to commit suicide at a slow rate. I knew I couldn't handle alcohol, yet I continued to use it to punish myself. For what, I didn't know, but I knew I had to keep on asking myself.

In the early days there were times when I was able to maintain sobriety for ten days to two weeks but then I was back into drinking heavily and not understanding why. Eventually it began to be obvious to me that I started my drinking sprees on days on which I felt very self-destructive and that these feelings of self-destruction came from my extreme dislike of myself and my life. There was not a single thing I liked about my world, neither what I was doing nor myself and what I was or wasn't. And I also discovered that in these times, experiencing these emotions, I tore apart all my relationships. I destroyed everything, picking arguments, saying horrible, unforgivable things to those I loved.

All this was followed by utter remorse, terrible feelings of guilt, more self-flagellation for being this world's greatest fool, black periods of depression, and hundreds of promises of what I would do to change *my drinking*.

Although our problem is alcoholism, and that we can no longer drink, the deeper and more realistic problem is why we turned to alcohol in the first place, and therein lies how we will maintain sobriety, by making the necessary basic corrections.

Every time I ended up in a liquor store in those early days of trying to stay sober, I discovered, after my drinking spree, that I was in a self-destructive period which had been fostered by my severe negative feelings about myself.

After having tried and failed so many times to stop drinking with various programs, I decided to begin with understanding myself and, in that way, find a way out of the morass. Obviously I had a severe drinking problem. At that juncture I wasn't able to call myself an alcoholic. But I could see, and accept, that I had problems with handling alcohol. And I could accept the disease concept of alcoholism, for I knew that each year my drinking was worse; I knew that once I began, I couldn't stop, and I knew I was experiencing all the other elements that make up alcoholism— blackouts, to name just one. All this I could accept. But it was the why of the whole nasty business that I had to discover. Why did I want to obliterate myself? Why did I continue to turn to alcohol when I knew that it was devastating me and ruining my life?

The answer became very clear when I took the whole puzzle apart. I turned to alcohol because I knew it would destroy me, and that is what I wanted to do. One step deeper into the mystery showed that I wanted to destroy myself because I felt unworthy, unloved, incapable, like a loser. The chorus of my life was "I am nobody, I am nothing, nobody will ever love me, and no one cares now."

For those with very poor opinions of themselves life is a jungle of unsolvable problems. Failure is an inevitable result of any attempted action, which serves only to reinforce the weak self-imagery.

With my discovery of what was at the basis of my alcohol use, it became clear what I had to do. The how still eluded me, but I began to think about breaking the habit of always feeling I couldn't do something. Daily I began to work at getting rid of these negative thoughts by replacing them with positive thoughts, forcing myself into seeing that I was a capable person if I let myself be. At the very heart of my recovery was to change the "I am nobody and nobody loves me" person to a someone who could say truthfully, "I am a capable person whom most people can, and will, like. Some will even love me."

Saying, and writing, these words about myself became part of an exercise I did every day first thing in the morning after my period of meditation. This time I spent in creating a positive self-image became the aftermath of my meditative period. Sometimes I spoke the words and found that I felt extremely uncomfortable. I was much more at ease with the old negative thoughts about myself. There were times when I just couldn't speak the words, so I began to write them on a piece of paper, over and over. Then, during the day, I began to say them silently, letting them be a litany in my mind as I worked at other things: "I am a competent woman."

It's surprising how we condition ourselves all the time without even knowing it. As I started this exercise to change the old feelings, I became very conscious of how much of a sponge our minds are to the thoughts that flit in and out, usually willy-nilly.

Now, with a conscious effort, I was changing the atmosphere of my mind by changing my thoughts, which eventually would change my actions! I became conscious of watching people to see if I could discern their feelings about themselves, and I found this not at all difficult. Many times I've spent hours in airport terminals, watching others, and without my ever speaking to them, it is obvious to me and the world what their feelings are about their self-images. Taking note of this, I began to walk differently, feeling as if nothing in this world could overtake me, that I was capable of handling whatever came my way. Strangely enough, thinking it made it become a significant part of my life.

Because our recent past has included such negative feelings about ourselves as the result of our drinking, trying to feel good about ourselves is very difficult for alcoholics to do. Our drinking days threw us into extremely negative circumstances. We were constantly involved in denials—about our drinking to others and about our alcoholism to ourselves—and now we learn that our recovery is dependent on our becoming positive persons with strong positive self-images. Immediately we begin to think it won't work; it's too far-fetched; it's not for us.

We begin to see that we are again back into those negative feelings, even about how to help ourselves.

Sometimes the beginning of a positive self-image comes from feeling some pride in being sober. This is a good beginning. It represents changing a habit, the old habit of thinking only negative and destructive things about ourselves, the old habit of believing ourselves incapable. Now, of course, we are embarked on establishing a new habit, one of automatically feeling good about ourselves.

Much of the time we talk about how hard it is to break a habit, and it is, but we forget to consider that creating a new habit is equally hard. In the case of remaking ourselves, we must do both: break a habit and create a new one.

One difficulty in changing ourselves is remembering to do it. The method of thinking about, writing about, and verbalizing the image we want to create for ourselves is sound, but the results are dependent on our carrying out these processes. We must work very hard at canceling the old images, even though most of us fight change and still feel extremely uncomfortable about saying anything reasonably nice about ourselves. Self-loathing is easier. We will have to overcome the awkwardness and embarrassment we feel when we say or think, "I am a capable woman," yet this is what we must do. Convincing ourselves that this is true is another goal we must move toward, and we should take great pride in our new sobriety as an example of our being able to do something positive.

Some recovery programs stress that alcoholics must focus upon remembrance of past degradation in an effort to remain sober, but this approach defies all logic for remaining sober and effective in rebuilding our lives into forceful, meaningful, and productive ones. Women already feel degraded, and our whole focus must be to overcome these feelings to combat our strong feelings of helplessness and powerlessness.

There is sobriety, and there is recovery. One is merely a cessation of drinking, and the other includes emotional and spiritual growth. We can put our pasts behind us, or we can keep them alive by reliving our humiliations, by recalling and retelling them, and become what I term professional alcoholics.

Our quest for self-respect starts with self-acceptance, which must begin with our forgiveness of our actions, especially those that were not socially acceptable. Self-reproach must be put behind us. Not a single thing can be gained from it, and we stand to lose everything if it continues. Let us never forget that continuing self-reproach has led, and leads, many alcoholics to the act of suicide, the rate of which for alcoholics, as we've noted, is far higher than for the general population. These suicides occur when we are both drinking and not drinking, and they are a result of our continuing self-reproach and our living in the past, never climbing out of those deep negative, depressive states of mind.

We *must* forgive our faults. Too often we have tended to put the emphasis on the worst moments of our lives. We have permitted the darkness of those moments and actions to overshadow the better and more redeeming moments and actions of our lives.

In order to change the old habit of self-condemnation, we must work very hard at the establishment of new thought patterns. We must get to work with a piece of paper and a pencil, as childish as that appears. Indeed, we will feel ridiculous and uncomfortable at first, hoping no one sees us and what we are doing. And our first exercise is to examine and write down the things we do to determine which are self-destructive and which are not. Usually this is a startling revelation. Examine every action for the past seven days, and note how many were not favorable to emotional growth.

After you examine your actions, the next step is to draw a stick figure to represent yourself. Beneath this figure write anything positive about yourself that comes to mind. When I first did this, I wrote: "I am a capable, competent, and caring woman. I believe in myself and all that I do. I am a positive person, filled with productive ideas for advancement, and I am a loving and dynamic person."

After the period of feeling foolish and self-conscious, we will begin to find that this exercise is a great way to start each day. Let us never forget that behind us are years and years of negativity that will resist change. We are in the difficult process of breaking old habits and creating new ones, and it definitely takes determination and self-application to do this. However, positive self-image building is the most powerful force available to us, and our ultimate and total recovery is based on our achieving success in this particular step forward.

Creating a new self must become a daily habit. The best results will happen if you write about yourself after your daily meditation. What you are writing about yourself is being imprinted onto your conscious and subconscious minds.

When I first started writing about myself, I not only felt uncomfortable but experienced a number of disturbing guilt feelings. And I have spoken to others who felt the same way. All of them were women who felt as if they were not worthy of feeling good about themselves. For women this is a major problem.

Perhaps this is a reflection of our experience of having had others tell us we were no good during our drinking years. Deep down in the storage closet of most women alcoholics lies this belief of being no good, not acceptable, not nearly the same as others. We feel like social rejects and oftentimes act that way.

How often is it said that no one is all good and no one is all bad. It would serve us well to remember that. Indeed, so many times we are much better than we think we are. And the saving grace is that the part which is not really great can be changed by our spending some time in changing it.

Don't feel foolish doing these exercises, for they are the answer to future happiness and self-satisfaction. Without them, we cannot ever really recover. Having seen many try these exercises, I can only say that those who practiced them faithfully became very happy and well-adjusted people, while those who did not bother to do them and put up mental roadblocks ended up with continuing and plaguing thoughts about drinking again.

We can think about those in recovery in three ways. First there is the person who no longer drinks but who does nothing to change herself; then there is the person who no longer drinks but spends much time talking about the drinking years; and finally there is the person who follows much the best road of no longer drinking and spending considerable time learning new and different thought patterns.

All our actions are a product of our self-conception. The less well we think of ourselves, the more necessary it is for us to hurt others. Correspondingly, the better we think of ourselves, the more generous we can be in our acceptance and outgoing feelings toward others, and the more accepting we are of the faults of others.

When we do not have a good sense of self-esteem or it is badly battered, we try to find it elsewhere, as we did with alcohol. Drinking helped us fill in that void. We were able to brag about ourselves, and if not that, we were able to fool ourselves by creating a state of amnesia for a short period of time. We could wallow in our nothingness.

Yet always there was the next morning and the days thereafter, in which we again felt like nobodies. This, of course, was reflected in our poor relationships with others—our families, our employers, our friends, our children, and our spouses.

Feelings of self-esteem must be based upon images of ourselves, and my experience has shown that most women have little concept of themselves. That which most do have is as a caretaker, as a wife and mother, the image most often given to little girls rather than that of an astronaut or a surgeon. Males on the whole have much better self-images since they as children were given stronger and more precise outlines to follow in life's adventure.

There is also the social conditioning, mentioned earlier, to which all of us were subjected as children. To most little boys goes encouragement from the elders, words such as "Go ahead, Tommy, you can do it," while passivity is urged upon little girls. In adulthood women take far fewer chances than do men. Women fear failure, but most of all, they also fear adventuring. Few things are invented by women or conceived of by women in an original form. Venturing into strange waters does not even come to mind. When women think about themselves, it is very, very rarely in a role that is strongly individual or novel or adventuresome.

Correspondingly, men rarely see themselves primarily as husbands. Rather, they see themselves as firemen, policemen, surgeons, explorers. The role and image of husband come lower down on their lists.

Women often drink to get a sense of person for themselves, while men often drink because their sense of person is a failure, because they have not succeeded as they expected to succeed.

Perhaps one of the most interesting aspects of finding out who we are and establishing a sense of self-value is that what we begin to perceive of ourselves is not anything close to how others perceive us. Many times there is a vast discrepancy, and we think far worse of ourselves than others do. Obviously this is not always the case. Sometimes family members, who have been hurt by our drinking escapades, see us as cruel, vindictive, angry, destructive, and totally without feeling. Acting in these ways may well have been true during episodes of drinking, but they are not the real core of ourselves. It was the person we became because of our alcoholism.

Ever since I've been sober, I have been extremely aware of how people talk to me and deal with me. And it is not always the same. There are times I have been able to feel the respect others have for me because of my now being on top of my drinking problem. Some, however, still feel a contempt for me that has carried over from my years of drinking. When speaking to those in the first group, I feel ten feet tall, I feel proud of myself, and I am ready to conquer all problems. But when I am faced with the other people, those who remember only my past mistakes, I feel very uneasy and disgruntled—and angry.

These emotions are not conducive to a happy recovery. They certainly do not help us with building self-acceptance, self-value, and self-esteem.

It is an unfortunate fact of life that we are often conditioned by what others think about us and transmit to us through their words or their actions. We respond to them. We take these transmitted opinions onto ourselves as if they were absolute fact. Right now I could probably think of at least fifteen to twenty things said to me that were crushing, that cut me into small pieces by their very devastation of my fragile feelings about myself. More than likely I deserved the words and the opinions but they tore through me as nothing else could. Of course, I can also think of hundreds of things I have said in anger, purposely, to destroy others' strong, confident feeling about themselves.

It is easy for us to see how what is said to us and what we say to others determine the way they think about themselves, even if they or we recognize that only a kernel of truth lies in the words expressed. Is it any wonder we have such difficulty in finding a sense of self-worth?

It becomes ever clearer to us that we must really get to the basics about ourselves and try not to be too influenced by what others say of us. Only we can determine our honesty, our decency, the code of ethics we live by, our motives, our true value as persons. Too often our last few years have led us into devious behavior patterns and deceptions with other people, almost always centering on our use of alcohol and our patterns of drinking.

The years of our drinking must be put into the past and we must search for our true selves. We must also begin with feeling a sense of pride about ending our drinking years. We must see this as one of our finest hours. By starting at this point, we will also keep before us our new sobriety and why we are maintaining it.

Early sobriety is a very difficult time for us to establish new thinking patterns because this period is made complicated by words of advice from those surrounding us. Frequently they want to direct us, many times suggesting that what we are doing is much too dramatic and that we aren't really alcoholics, but only drank too much most of the time. This early period will be filled with unasked-for and unwarranted advice, most of it worthless and some of it upsetting.

For a woman this period is most particularly difficult if a marriage is intact. Too often a husband is ashamed of his wife's abstinence, believing that it calls attention to them in social gatherings and that she should take at least one drink to maintain a certain social posture.

Male alcoholics feel the pressure of social posturing when out with business acquaintances, most of whom expect to imbibe in jovial good fellowship and with an old-boy camaraderie. This is a period of downfall for both men and women—because of the social pressures put on us by our peers.

In my early days of sobriety I attended a dinner, at the home of a doctor no less, and it was a disaster for me and the others. The cocktail hour went on from 4:00 P.M. to 10:00 P.M. while the dinner hour was postponed for hours. Meanwhile, I had consumed enough tomato juice to last a lifetime. More important, however, I saw how changed all these people became as the evening wore on, and I was enlightened in a way that could never have been possible except for the fact that I was not drinking but was watching behavioral disintegration. Never before had I known just what others must have witnessed in my behavior while I was drinking. I am certain I experienced all the emotions once experienced by others about me. It is impossible for me to describe the disgust I felt in seeing these normally intelligent professional people speaking and acting like spoiled children.

That awful dinner party etched on my mind a picture of drunken behavior so indelible that today it is as sharp as it was that night. My disgust is just as keen. The tragedy is that I spent almost half of my lifetime exactly that way, hurting and embarrassing so many others.

Our recoveries can move forward only if we put the recollection of these repeated drunken incidents away from our present thoughts. Who among us will ever forget those humiliations? Constant and repeated recollection can only impede what we must do, which is to build ourselves into new and strong characters.

Other problems that often need additional professional help are those of self-destructive behavior arising from sexual inadequacy. Until these are erased, we will not be able to move forward in our pursuit of feeling good about ourselves. The severity of some of our sexual problems were only masked by our drinking. Too often, in fact, our sexual problems prompted our drinking. In sobriety the most frequently ignored area of discussion is that of sexual complexities, and a Band-Aid approach through self-help therapy merely postpones the ultimate need for professional help. Frequently our new feelings of freedom from hangovers and headaches lure us into the belief that all our other problems will quickly disappear. For a few this is true, but unfortunately the majority of recovering women who had sexual problems in the past continue to have sexual problems in the present when they are sober. To postpone getting help is only to jeopardize their new sobriety. Sobriety can be maintained only so long as we begin to eliminate our problems, and moving from being negative persons to a positive person requires more than just a change of thought patterns. It is true that many of our sexual problems have to do with our thinking processes, but professional help provides the answers in a way no other avenue could.

The more problems we have had and carry into sobriety, the more our chances of being successful in our new life are threatened. And so are the new feelings of self-esteem we are trying to build for ourselves. All our past failures, whether sexual or otherwise, have weakened our feelings about ourselves. If we have failed in business, sexual union, or relationships such as marriage, we are walking shattered egos unable to experience feelings of self-value and self-esteem. We feel like total failures. We feel defeated; we feel down; we feel crushed in every possible way. We can see no hope of ever getting out of the holes we are in. Our thinking is all negative.

It is obvious to everyone that with thoughts such as these no one could ever successfully recover from alcoholism. And it certainly shows with clarity why we continued to drink. Feelings of failure are turned into self-destruction.

We should now see that the basic building block of our sobriety is the development of positive attitudes about ourselves, beginning with the pursuit first of feelings of self-acceptance, then of feelings of self-worth, all of which lead to much-needed feelings of self-esteem. This is the crux of recovery. It is also the beginning of us as nice persons rather than the losers we once were. We will no longer be helpless.

There is a power deep in us that we have never before touched. We have never taken the time to find it, even if we knew it was there. Now we are going to find it and use it. This is the power of our mind and the power of our thoughts, through the use of which we can significantly change our lives.

CHAPTER TWELVE

SIX KEYS TO A LIFETIME RECOVERY

By now we understand that we must excise our negative thoughts about ourselves and must learn self-acceptance, self-worth, and, finally, some feelings of self-esteem. Our new way of life needs structure, and this is our final approach to our successful recovery for a lifetime.

The six-point program is merely a map, a plan, a guide to a new way of organized thinking about ourselves and our lives. These keys should be learned and used every day, until they are so much a part of our thinking that they dominate and force out all our old negative thoughts.

These six key thoughts are:

1. Problems bother me only to the degree I permit them to.
2. Negative emotions destroy only myself.
3. I am what I think.
4. The past is gone forever.
5. Love can change the course of my world.
6. The fundamental object of life is emotional and spiritual growth.

All these statements seem obvious, yet few of us live by them. Living by them is now our goal.

PROBLEMS BOTHER ME ONLY TO THE DEGREE I PERMIT THEM TO

The premise that problems bother us only to the degree we permit them to is sometimes difficult to accept at first. However, we will begin to feel a great sense of relief when we *do* accept it and learn to trust it, and this comes about through testing it.

When I first heard this concept, I didn't believe it until I started practicing it. My problems arose because I was still not aware of the power of my thought patterns or the control my thoughts had on my life. Somehow I simply never correlated my thoughts with resulting actions or feelings. I especially remember the time of deep depression in the very earliest days of my sobriety when I came upon this idea. I tested it, and it worked. My depression was a feeling. I was experiencing it only to the degree I permitted it to affect me, and I was permitting it to affect me totally. So the statement became "I am depressed, but this feeling of depression can disturb and disrupt me only *to the degree I permit it to disrupt me.*"

Immediately I was startled by this realization. When I learned that I could control the depression rather than have it control me, it made a world of difference thereafter in my life. At times, when overwhelmed by the death of someone close to me, I managed to overcome the grief and sadness by letting my mind know that I was permitting myself to experience it to an extreme and I wanted to change the degree of intensity.

There are some emotions that we should experience and then be rid of. Grief is one of these; anger, too. But to be a victim of emotions that continue for long periods, believing them to be beyond our control, is certainly not necessary.

Our lives are filled with problems of all sorts, mostly revolving around relationships or money. Are there any other kinds? Of course, there are, but it does seem as if life were mostly made up of problems in these two areas.

Again, we will find that we can control the degree of concern and control our emotions. If I worry about bills that are unpaid, I am disturbed to a degree that affects everything else I do. In fact, I just may not be able to do anything else. My job may be in jeopardy because I am inattentive and nonfunctioning. And were I to lose my job, my unpaid bills would increase.

Too often we believe that there is absolutely nothing we can do about this type of situation. And for us in early recovery coming back to the world of reality we have so long ignored, having unpaid bills is a very real problem. However, we can, and must, control the way we think about them. "Problems (bills, depression, anger, grief) bother me only to the degree I permit them to." We are in charge of our thoughts. We may never have approached life this way, but now we are going to see how wrong we were and how we can now take control of what does and does not bother us.

Control is a major element in an alcoholic's life. When we are drinking, we try to control everyone surrounding us. We are heavy-handed and obnoxious. When we become sober, however, we have difficulty with taking control of our lives. We are at the other end of the spectrum. We feel incapable, almost helpless, easily overcome by the toughness of life. We shrink from problems. We turn away from responsibilities. There are times when we believe that being sober is enough, and we inform others to that effect: that they shouldn't expect anything more from us. We have enough to do just not drinking. We are self-righteous and berate them for making demands on us, like paying our bills, getting back to work, facing domestic problems.

But the more we let our problems slide by, the more we are berated, and the more we move toward upsetting the whole applecart by saying, "Well that did it. You pushed me just far enough. I warned you!" And out we go to buy a bottle. We're going to *show them!*

In certain ways it is ideal if an alcoholic can go to a treatment facility for the first twenty-eight days of recovery because she is then away from the immediacy of family, problems, and arguments, from the environment in which there is friction and in which she acts out destructive patterns. Unfortunately this luxury treatment can be enjoyed by very few because of the cost, but it certainly is ideal.

However it is possible to get through this period without the help of a treatment facility and the segregation of the alcoholic from the troublesome environment. Just practice the new things we are learning about ourselves. Every morning, we must set aside the learning period that we've already discussed, beginning with meditation and then moving into a period of working on our self-images. During this period of self-reflection we can study how we have always reacted to other people. Not only will we be able to see how we have created problems in our lives, but it will also become obvious that we have run away from problems in our lives by just drinking more.

Starting to recognize and face problems is not easy in this early period, and that is why this statement "Problems bother us only to the degree we permit them to" is helpful to us at this time. It puts us squarely between two extremes. Either we used to ignore our problems and ran away from them, or we recognized them and made them larger than life, both reactions giving us another weak reason to drink.

Our goal now is to recognize our problems and to put them into a proper perspective: accepting that we have them and they must be solved but not letting them take us over. This new middle-of-the-road way of life will be very unfamiliar, since we have mostly lived with go-for-broke, self-destructive attitudes much of the time.

Alcoholics are often reactive people, all or nothing. Unfortunately this has not served us well but has always created problems for us, some very serious ones. And when they became serious, we ran from them. It will be difficult for us now to come to grips with problems and not to be thrown by them.

Learning this way of not letting problems bother us without our permission is a new habit we must develop. It is not easy, for we must also break the old habit of letting everything rock our boats, but it can be learned with constant practice.

I have known alcoholics who have found use of this statement and remembering to use it every day to be the most important part of their recovery.

NEGATIVE EMOTIONS DESTROY ONLY MYSELF

There are many who believe that whatever we exude, that is what we will attract more of, and sometimes this seems to be true. It certainly is true that if we meet unsmiling people, smiles from us trigger smiles in response.

Can we go further and say that if we are negative persons we attract more negativity?

As women we should be expert in this area and know the answer. We have generally been pessimistic, complaining, negative, self-destructive, defensive, and argumentative. How much more negative can one get?

Perhaps of the six statements we will learn for our successful recovery, this one is the most difficult because we have to break old and ingrained emotional patterns. We have been the very essence of what negativity is all about. We are the original negators: "Why bother? It won't work." Does that sound familiar?

How much of our time did we use negativisms to give us reasons to drink? Indeed, we looked for things to fail, not to work, to go awry, to be impossible so that we could justify having just one more. We were at times jubilant that we had good cause for our hangovers and headaches.

To make our recovery successful, we must remove the negativities from our lives, for they were our justifications for drinking. At first it will seem very strange to experience tribulations without a drink. In my own recovery I found this to be most difficult. When all things fail, when something goes wrong in the job, when someone disappoints us, when we wish we were somewhere else than where we are, we used all these events as excuses for drinking. Now we experience these occurrences and have no actual way to act out our disappointments.

I felt lost. It had been so many years since I was without

the chance to drink that I didn't know how to handle negative happenings. My old way had been to come up with a corresponding negative emotion of my own—and a drink to help me over the rough spot.

When new in sobriety, you will find this part of recovery very strange and certainly uncomfortable.

Of course, the realization that you are a negative person is not the place to stop. It is the beginning, for the next step is to move ahead and realize that the negativity can be ended only by being replaced with positives.

This is a great time to reexamine the past year of your life. Write down the negative events that happened in the past twelve months, and record your reactions to them. From this you will be able to tell if your reactions spawned further negative events. Let us make up a script: A vacation trip you and your spouse have planned must be canceled because your mother-in-law is coming for a visit. Now that in itself is probably bad news. So you begin to drink as your way of accepting bad news. But your drinking is very upsetting to the family, and you and your spouse have a terrible fight. This additional bad scene leads you to drink more, and this leads to more scenes.

Here we can see how one negative event and a negative reaction to it have created additional negative situations. We continue to react to a negative stimulus that by itself was enough bad news without more being added to it.

Our sobriety must be protected from this type of chain reaction—that is, if we are serious about staying sober. We must be able to identify negative situations right away, and we must learn to counter them with some positive actions. And if we cannot come up with some positive actions—such as (1) taking the mother-in-law along, or (2) asking her to visit at another time, or (3) letting her bring a friend to the house to stay with her while you go on your vacation anyway—then we must accept, without negative reactions, the situation as it is and know that the world will not come to an end. We must know that any, and all, negative emotions destroy only us. Our negative emotions will do nothing to our mothers-in-law but will only be cancers within ourselves to which we will react. Therefore, we *must* assert ourselves.

It is surely evident that negative emotions destroy only ourselves, but they also do something else: They create a chain of negative reactions. Too long have we women felt helpless in the face of negative situations. Now we must learn to act.

Removing negative reactions from our lives is tough. Old patterns and inclinations are hard to deal with. They resist new ideas, new methods. Only our persistent desire to have a successful recovery from the devastation of alcoholism can give us the drive to overcome negativism. To do it requires constant vigilance. I find that there are times, even now after twelve years of sobriety, I still fall into the trap of "It can't be done" or "What's the use?" Of course, I no longer think of counteracting with a drinking episode, but sometimes I still have negative reactions, and I have to be constantly on guard against them.

I AM WHAT I THINK

Of all the new ideas we are trying to put into practice, this one is the most important. "I am what I think" is based upon a certain view of the world. It accepts the belief that what we create in our minds as ideas or thoughts will become fact. That is to say, if we believe that we are attractive, our actions will transmit this belief to others. Our actions will be those of attractive people, and the message will be relayed to those who view us.

We act out what we think of ourselves. When we think of ourselves as nothing and nobodies, we will act this way. Others will perceive us this way because this is the message we are giving them, and they will treat us in the way we present ourselves to them.

I never write about this that I don't think about a perfect illustration. Many years ago a friend of our family, a rather ordinary man, during World War I worked his way up to the temporary wartime commission of colonel. From the time of his separation from the army when the war was over, he chose to retain his rank and was thereafter called Colonel. What was the most interesting thing about this was that he went back to his very ordinary job in a factory, and everyone just always called him Colonel because that was what he chose. But he also acted like a colonel, and all his friends over the next thirty years and all the acquaintances he made during that time treated him with deference.

He thought of himself as a colonel, and he acted that way for all the rest of his life. He was what he thought he was, a high-ranking officer in the U.S. Army, even though he really wasn't. Perhaps the strangest part of this whole thing was that no one ever questioned him and everyone addressed him as he wished to be addressed even though almost everyone knew his had been a temporary commission in a war a very long time ago.

We are exactly what we think we are. We create that image in our thoughts, and our actions reflect these thoughts, this image. Women have an especially hard time with this, for we think little about thinking good thoughts about ourselves. It is an extremely difficult thing for most women to think anything at all, especially something very positive, about themselves. In fact, women rarely view themselves individually, thinking of themselves as Johnny's wife or Tommy's mother, as mentioned earlier. Women tend not to have a thinking image, and for women alcoholics trying to recover, this is devastating. When women alcoholics think of themselves, they think more often than not, *I am nothing. I am no good. I am unworthy.* In learning how to maintain sobriety, I found this to be my biggest problem. I had been able to figure out what prompted my drinking episodes—these very negative feelings about myself—but changing them and finding a positive image were the hardest part of all. When I tried to think an image, I was lost.

In working with alcoholics, I have found that men are able to restore acceptable images of themselves, their drinking having only bloodied their working images of self, whereas few women have ever had images of themselves. Perhaps men grow up wanting to be strong, "in charge," capable, able to take over any situation, while these feelings are totally foreign to most women. In widowhood few women display a capability for taking over or taking charge of the situation, even though most have run households for many years. Women tend to feel unable to do it, that they haven't the strength of character or the know-how. Women tend to feel helpless in this situation and display helplessness largely because of having talked themselves into it. In truth, the potential of capability for men and women is about the same. The difference is in the thoughts about it, the images each works from. Men *know* they can do it. Women *are sure* they can't.

In both cases, however, we are dealing with our mind's thoughts and oftentimes conflicting emotions. We might be able to put the positive image thoughts in our minds, but our emotions will be saying, "It's not true. I am a nothing."

We can see clearly that our biggest battle is to *feel* capable and to *feel* like a colonel.

At all times we must recognize that the basic reason we drank was that we didn't face up to situations in life or we didn't care about facing up to situations in our lives. We abdicated, we eluded, we tried to escape, only to be trapped by alcoholism. And at the basis of this entire structure were our feelings of inferiority and inability, our feelings of not being capable translated into feelings of "I don't really give a damn."

Even in this we "proved" the premise "I am what I think" with our thoughts of total incapability, total failure, total inferiority. We thought it, and we became that way. We made ourselves that way, fulfilling our self-images. These thoughts kept us trapped in our alcoholism, our need to go on drinking, no matter what the price. Some of us paid a very high price, and some continue to pay the high price. No wonder we kicked, hollered, screamed, ranted and raved when everyone attempted to take our alcohol from us. How could we live? How could we manage?

I suppose the tragedy is that we should have had to go through this charade, because in reality, we are just as capable as the next person and many of us are much more capable than the average nondrinker.

Perhaps an even greater tragedy is that we don't know it, and many never know it.

Now is the time to grab hold of your life, and this can be made possible by grabbing hold of your thoughts. Master your thoughts and thinking process. Take charge, and know that this is the way to overcoming alcoholism and all the personal problems that have been haunting you. Your personal problems will be solvable because you will bring confidence and thought to them. You will be acting out of a new knowledge that you are a capable person, able to handle all the knots of your life without alcohol.

Say it a hundred times a day: "I am what I think." Then make up several sentences to be repeated after that. Tell yourself with every breath, "I am a capable person." In addition to thinking it, begin to know it. This is not making up a false picture. This is coming to know the *real* you. You are a capable person. You probably always have been but have defeated yourself in everything you ever attempted before ever getting started.

We cannot produce a positive person out of negative thoughts. We learned earlier that negative thoughts destroy only ourselves, and the negative thoughts we have about ourselves destroy only our whole lives. Negativity to an alcoholic is as destructive as the alcohol itself.

The time to ensure our recovery is now. And this is the most important of all things for us to learn and put into practice: feeling genuinely good about ourselves and knowing that what we think about ourselves is the way we will be. Keep uppermost the story of the colonel.

This is the time to think about the planting season; flowers never come from a garden of weeds.

THE PAST IS GONE FOREVER

As true as we know these words to be, we still have a strong tendency to live in the past, to pull forward past failures, to sift through memories, usually only those that are painful, and to react to these feelings by feeling sorry for ourselves.

Of all groups of people, alcoholics seem to spend an inordinate amount of time living and reliving the past, good or bad. Many believe that recovery from alcoholism can be effected by living in the past, by recounting drinking histories, no matter how gruesome they are. This may keep the fear of drinking alive, but it does little else. For some it even triggers additional drinking episodes. For a woman there is little value in constantly keeping her drinking past alive. Who among us needs constant reminding that we acted like fools, that we embarrassed ourselves and our families, that we were obnoxious, acted in exceedingly disgusting ways on many occasions, were loud-mouthed, insulting, rude, overbearing, humiliating, immodest, immoral, and just plain ugly?

Lasting sobriety and true recovery cannot be based upon the kindling and rekindling of these emotions in us. Quite the opposite. They serve only to make us feel anxious, and we want to run away and hide. We want to scream, to be free, to be let off the hook; we want peace of mind. Instead, the constant reminding makes us think about drinking again. We wonder, *What's the use?*

No, this is not the road to true and comfortable recovery. The road to recovery is an upward climb, moving away from those old misdeeds, and changing ourselves into new people.

Who has ever found value in "what if"? Thinking and talking about the past very often lead us to ask, "What if ... ?" and we take ourselves right back into feelings of remorse, guilt, anger, anxiety, and depression. What a way to recover!

It is true that millions of alcoholics do find sobriety and stay sober with a method of recall and retelling of their alcoholic drinking days with their peers, but this does not really constitute recovery. It is sobriety through recall and fear. It does not allow for upward mobility and change, for it links the alcoholic irretrievably to the past and keeping the past alive.

Successful recovery can be achieved by our putting the past behind us, there always to be tapped, if needed, for pleasant memories, but kept where it belongs.

We alcoholics must learn to live in the immediate present.

When drinking, either we drank because of the good old days and nostalgia for a time that cannot ever again be, or we drank to the possibilities of the future, usually based upon some hare-brained scheme that had no chance of success. Or we drank to the future because it was going to be better . . . somehow. How it would be better we really didn't know. But it would be better, so we drank to it.

Living in the present has always been a problem for us because we are unhappy, unfulfilled, anxious, filled with fear, depressed, angry, and without hope. We have felt helpless to change.

Our drinking made time pass rapidly. One of the first things we notice when we sober up is how long time is. An hour seems like a day. A week seems like forever. And this should be a reminder to us of how we threw away time, how we made time pass because of our boredom and our depression alternately.

We must learn how to live in the present. We must learn to live today. As we begin to move away from our negative period of depression, loneliness, overcoming guilt, we will begin to cherish each day and our sobriety and our new feelings of good health. We will begin to have energy that we haven't had recently. We will begin to have some enthusiasm as we come into a period of self-knowledge.

All these good feelings come to us as we recognize the futility of reacting to our past, which is over and done and must be put where it belongs, behind us. There is not a single thing we can change about our past except the way we think about it: that it is over and we are changing.

For years I had been haunted by my past misdeeds, especially how I hurt my family. We are able to forgive ourselves, sometimes, because we acted while drugged. But those we hurt make us ache to change it all, to go back and do everything differently. We fall into the "if only" frame of mind, and then we are finished. Our sobriety stands threatened.

Since we cannot change anything, we must give up this foolish exercise. In order to change ourselves into normal, productive drug-free persons, we must recognize futility. The past is gone forever. We goofed. But we can change.

Perhaps we should take a lesson from the very old in our society. When men and women in their eighties gather together, they often talk about the past. They do this because they believe there is no more future for them. In believing this, they have given in to no more future. But we—we have futures. For many of us decades spread before us. We have the opportunity of whole new lifetimes, beginning now, in the present. And the best part of this new adventure is the discovery of ourselves and exactly what we can do with our drug-free lives.

Not only are we going to put the actions of our past behind us, but we are also putting aside our old patterns of thinking. There is very little we wish to carry into our new lives from our pasts. There may be some very good memories, but even these are of relative use to us in our new lives of learning. Our pasts are always with us, but the constant reliving of it or not reliving it is within our control.

Our pasts, of course, are never severed from our lives' biography, but we should learn that we live in our minds. Whatever our thoughts are, that is where we live, where we are, where our beings are. If our thoughts are about the past, then that is where we are. Living with these thoughts, bringing them forward into our conscious minds over and over, we are bound to play the "what if" game. And then we are finished. Too many "what ifs" will endanger our recovery and can lead us back to the old drinking ways.

Even though we have trouble with living in the present and feel scared about life and the reality of our responsibilities, we must recognize that these feelings are so much better than the "what if" or the "if only" feelings. Our recovery must be centered in now.

LOVE CAN CHANGE THE COURSE OF MY WORLD

At first you may ask what love has to do with recovery. I could be glib and say, "Everything." It may not be *everything,* but love and learning about love are another big hurdle in the process of getting turned around.

Many people, including myself now, believe that a law of compensation is at work. That is to say, we get back what we give out. If we are mean and bitter, we will attract those qualities. If we are outgoing, loving, and giving, we will attract those traits from others. As already mentioned, this can be easily evidenced by our seeing unsmiling people break into smiles when we first smile at them.

Naturally the question is, Why would we want to be loving and outgoing? I suppose the easy answer is, Because it is a positive feeling and keeps us in the positive mode of behaving. That, however, seems only skin-deep. What we really want to acquire are genuine loving attitudes. This possibility will exist as soon as we become positive people and are rid of our bitterness and anguish.

Most of us are often extremely critical, frequently irritable, and usually impatient. These attitudes are known to us because we are out of sync with ourselves. In my own recovery I continue to struggle with these attitudes. However, on enough occasions and for certain long periods I have been able to be free of them and have been able to feel and express love in a very heartwarming and genuine way. There is definitely a relationship between our being able to know love and our attitudes. During all those years of drinking I believed I was "in love" many times only to learn that what I experienced was as far removed from love as the North Pole is from the South Pole. And in sobriety being in love and loving are two related feelings but are still different from each other. In retrospect, I can now see that some people were truly in love with me, but I certainly ended that quickly by my childish and self-defeating behavior. During those years I knew absolutely nothing about love, of any kind. I was far too deeply into self-centeredness for anything like genuine feelings of love to penetrate. To love and to experience love, we must first be sensitive and receptive. And that I wasn't, although I deluded myself on enough occasions to believe myself to be the most loving of souls. I was sensitive, but in all the wrong ways.

Of course, part of the ability to love comes from being able to give something away for which we might not get any return. For most alcoholics, male and female, loving is very difficult and a very new experience.

Being in love is an even greater problem since this is a relationship, and women like me have been real washouts in relationships. A relationship is usually based on a feeling, a mutual feeling of love, an ingredient most women seem not to be able to give during the drinking years. Yet as alcoholic patterns intensify, women hunger for more love. It is this irony that accounts for the terrible isolation we women experience. We are aware of our unlovability, yet we yearn for love. Without recognizing it, we yearn to *be loved*, not being aware of our inability *to love*.

Sobriety is a difficult enough time without all these other complications, but it is a period in which we must come face-to-face with our inadequacies, one of which is our not knowing how to love because we still haven't learned how to give of ourselves. We really haven't enough to give anything away because we still do not have much for ourselves. And this is both the problem and the answer. Too often we feel used and abused. Often we are.

In order to receive love, we must give love. That can happen only when we have good feelings about ourselves. And that's where we fall apart.

Surely we can see that our entire recovery, and its success, are based on our need to build feelings of self-value. We always come back to that, don't we? Our success in love and in relationships is in direct proportion to our good feelings about ourselves. Almost all of us have been in disruptive relationships and have had disastrous sexual associations. Too often we have looked for love in meaningless sexual relationships only to come away from them with deep feelings of disgust for ourselves and with greater needs to drink to try and forget our feelings of humiliation.

Our needs for decent relationships are imperative to our happiness. We know that as the process of self-discovery and the emergence of feelings of self-worth take place, so the capacity to love, and accept love, grows. The direct correlation of one with the other is: The better we think of ourselves, the less we suffer from feeling unloved or rejected. We have a buffer that protects us from demoralizing emotions.

The reason we will be successful in love relationships when we feel good about ourselves is that the other people will be reaffirming what we know about ourselves: that we are worthwhile. It always comes right back to the fact that we reflect what we feel about ourselves and it is those people, those reflections that others respond to.

Being able to love others and receiving their love are almost a second stage in our recovery process. Usually right at first we are not ready for relationships, not serious relationships. I have seen a newly sober person move right into a relationship before learning much about self, and it is always a disaster. The alcoholic has had insufficient time for self-repair and, whether consciously or not, is really looking to the relationship for it, believing that the relationship will expedite recovery and that she will not have to do it personally. Very often this leads the alcoholic right back into a drinking situation.

There is just no way around what needs to be done by us to have loving relationships. We must first repair ourselves, and then we will be able to love others and to receive love in an adult and mature way. We will not be suspicious of the love but will be trusting, something new to us. We will be able to be trusting because we will feel a strength within ourselves that we can depend upon. It's called self-confidence.

THE FUNDAMENTAL OBJECT OF LIFE IS EMOTIONAL AND SPIRITUAL GROWTH

This is the kind of statement about life that we should keep handy for reference. It is meant to remind us that life isn't just bills and doctors' appointments and slogging away at dead-end jobs or whatever. It is to remind us that there are more important things in life than the immediate annoyances. Of course, the immediate annoyances are very real, but we are in the process of learning a new way of looking at them, such as "Problems bother me only to the degree I permit them to."

More than that, life is larger than the negatives. For us, emotional growth, such as being able to accept the annoyances without reacting by getting drunk, is one of our objectives.

Emotional growth comes from frequent introspection, with an eye toward changing for the better. It also comes from the extractions of useful self-knowledge from traumatic situations and even from ordinary, boring situations. Emotional growth for us is not reacting to every little thing. As a group alcoholics are often written about as reactive individuals. Although I hate to admit it, it is true in my life. I did react to everything, good, bad, or indifferent. No matter what the situation, I reacted. Even now, twelve years into sobriety, I still have a tendency toward this, but I have learned to take a sit-back-and-wait attitude and to see things in perspective. What once appeared very large and overwhelming really assumes its proper shape and size and importance if I relate it to seeing that the most important thing in life is emotional and spiritual development, not the immediate annoyance, no matter how big or threatening it may appear at that moment.

Certainly one aspect of emotional growth is to take things in stride and not be thrown by them. Another is to know who we are so that we are not always reacting from various roles we may be playing—the affronted wife, the martyr, the ailing alcoholic, the guilt-ridden wife, and so on. Because we have played so many roles during our drinking years, it is very difficult for us to sort out who we really are. This is part of the reason we feel like nobodies when we first quit drinking. We really do not know who we are in those first months. We have been stripped not only of the alcohol but of all the many faces it has helped us hide behind. It is as if there had been a death in the family, for when we stop drinking, we have lost something very close to us: alcohol. For us alcohol was everything, and when without it we go through a period of first grief, next anger because it was taken away, then depression from the letdown before we finally begin to see the light: that it is gone forever. This is the point at which emotional growth can begin, or we can stay in that rut and become a professional alcoholic, forever talking about what we did when we were drinking, our exploits and how funny so many incidents were when in actuality they were only disgusting. We can, at this point, use our alcoholism to create histories for ourselves. Some even turn the stories of their alcoholism into epics that grow larger with each year's telling.

This is the make-it-or-get-stuck point. Not going forward into a period of self-discovery and self-realization is the difference between just being sober and true recovery. Recovery does not mean that there can be a return to drinking. Recovery means the acceptance of a life of abstinence and the acknowledgment of a need to change, a need to learn self so that first emotional and then spiritual growth can take place.

Emotional growth means overcoming helplessness and dependency and worry, anxiety, and depression. It means a search for the strength within ourselves that we can depend on to see us through situations. Emotional growth is knowing that we cannot mend without changing our thought patterns. It means that we are on a wonderfully exciting quest to discover harmony within ourselves, to find the internal peace that has for so long eluded us. Indeed, for us emotional growth is just knowing that this is a possibility, that we needn't spend our lives being upset, filled with fears and anxieties, always feeling hostile and defensive and helpless.

Emotional growth occurs when we are finally able to make decisions about our life on the basis of our real desires rather than in reaction to people, things, and events. Emotional growth has happened when we have control over ourselves, when we are in charge, when we are operating the mechanism known as us, rather than being driven by our emotions. It is the triumph of reason over reactive emotions. Good feelings about ourselves end decision-making out of fear, worry, and anxiety. Time has shown that the more we do with what we have, the less likely we are to have feelings of inferiority and anxiety because we are beginning to find that inner core of strength, long buried in us. We are starting to learn about our capabilities and how to use them.

Emotional growth is not always a happy time. The results will please us, but getting the results is sometimes unnerving. My struggle with guilt lasted for a very long time, and guilt still appears every once in a while. Then I go through the reasoning: There is absolutely nothing I can do about it now. Everything is over and done with. I can change things only by the way I think about them, which means to accept the happenings and to know I acted unforgivably during many bouts with my alcoholism. That person was someone other than the real me. This is true for us. Knowing that none of this can be changed now and no longer reacting to these past circumstances in a negative way are part of emotional growth.

With that growth we usually are moved toward some kind of spiritual awareness. Perhaps this aspect doesn't take place for years, and that's all right. Many recovering alcoholics seem extremely disturbed if they do not become spiritually involved at a certain time. But this is not anything to be put into a time scheme. Spiritual awareness happens to all of us at differing periods. Recovery is not mandated by it, although it seems that when it does occur, the recovering alcoholic is more at peace with life and self.

Continued emotional growth will serve to prevent our former intense unhappiness because we will be learning how to handle the negatives that caused our unhappiness. It will also provide us with a course of life to be pursued. It leads us to emotional peace and calm. We will have learned self-control and certainly self-understanding, which is the ultimate sign of emotional growth.

Spiritual awareness is a part of our recovery. Our time of sobriety becomes a time when we become more and more aware of our spiritual nature, our reason for existing.

Earlier we considered the question "What's it all about?" As our period of sobriety lengthens, we must seriously deal with this at some point. Indeed, as we grow emotionally, we will find this to be an inevitable next step as well as the final step to our moving out of and away from the negatives of alcoholism and the reasons we were so enmeshed in it.

Our spiritual awareness shows us our reasons for being, our reasons for existing. It is the essence of our lives. It is knowing that all we take with us when we leave this earth is what we have become, and it is our knowing that we must use our period on earth to refine ourselves to our fullest capabilities.

Spiritual growth is complicated because it moves into soul involvement. It is more assimilated than emotional growth. It is a step beyond emotional growth, but it follows as night the day. Spiritual awareness is knowing our place in the scheme of the universe. It is the feeling of a relationship to all things and to something greater than ourselves.

There is a point at which we become aware of being alone in the universe. No matter how many or what kinds of relationships we have or are involved in, we are unalterably alone. The realization of this during our drinking days led us to ask, "What is it all about? What's the meaning?" Knowing we were alone, having no answers, and feeling isolated and frightened, we drank more.

It is obvious that successful recovery is based on our asking, "What's it all about?" and knowing the answer, which is the quest for self-refinement, the fulfillment of the golden rule, the shaping of ourselves into the best we have to offer and then offering it to others. It is the discovery of self-realization to its highest degree, which is emotional and spiritual growth and evolvement.

Knowing our aloneness in this world, yet feeling the need

for a relationship, we can turn to a higher authority, supreme being, God, Buddha, a universal soul. For some it may be Nature. We may feel our oneness, our joining with some other force when we see a sunset, or a sunrise, or dawn or a thunderstorm or a volcano or a lovely golden spring flower that shoots up through the snow. Or as an eighteenth-century poet noted, to see the world in a grain of sand is our recognition of universality. This is the microcosm representing the macrocosm just as surely as we represent the world.

Spiritual growth is an end to self-inflicted pain, an end to self-destruction, an end to devastating negativisms and bad trips. Spiritual growth removes us from the destruction of self-flagellation.

CHAPTER THIRTEEN

MIND CONTROL FOR LIFE CONTROL

Our entire process thus far has been a step-by-step method of moving away from the kinds of personality we were, women who used alcohol in every conceivable way to avoid facing the issues in our lives. We drank because we were happy and wanted to celebrate; we drank because we were sad and wanted temporary escape; we drank because we got raises; we drank because we didn't want to go to funerals, to dentist's appointments, or to PTA meetings, or we didn't want to take out the garbage; we drank because we were upset; we drank because we were worried about paying bills; we drank because we were sometimes afraid; we often drank because we were lonely; we drank to the "good old days," and we drank to the rosy future that seemed to lie before us. Sometimes we drank just because we couldn't help ourselves. We gave up having excuses.

When the alcohol caught up with us, we finally learned that our drinking was a result of alcoholism, which is what created the compulsive craving every time we drank. Because of this condition of alcoholism, we lost control of our drinking, and we learned that the only solution was to give up alcohol altogether. At first we didn't think this was ever possible. When I first was told that I could never drink again, I was disbelieving. I knew there was no way I could live without alcohol in my life. I just knew it.

All of us feel like this in the beginning. We have for so long depended on the use of alcohol in our lives that we deny its importance. We all know how we hid it and sneaked drinks, so

165

that no one ever knew how dependent we were. We even had to deny it to ourselves. Many times, when we first sober up, we are amazed at how much we once drank. We ourselves can't believe how great our needs had been. And we want to continue to convince ourselves that we drank only because we wanted to and not that we couldn't stop most of the time. We'd also like to think that once we quit drinking, all our problems are solved. It is not easy for us to see that we have a long road of learning ahead of us.

In the long run, actually stopping the drinking was the easiest part of the whole recovery process. Our changing into different kinds of people, our remaking of ourselves, is the harder part, but it is such a worthwhile part. It will turn us into very happy and well-adjusted people.

There are a number of ways to recover from alcoholism. All of them are based on the first must: giving up alcohol for the rest of our lives. Once we can understand this and accept it, then we are ready to go to work on ourselves.

We can get sober in a treatment facility or in a self-help group or with private counseling or any combination of the above. There are even some people who never use any of those methods and still recover. However, we can rush the process if we use one of the methods of self-help, counseling, or treatment facility.

It is important to learn and to know forever that *we must change if we are to be fully recovered and happy*. There are many ways to get sober, but they do not always include a new philosophy of life. This book is aimed at doing just that, providing us with an entire philosophy for living; it is a new way of looking at life that can be applied to the whole of each of our lives. It is a method of thinking, a way of seeing the place where we live. It is a metaphysical approach to living. The philosopher Plato saw ideas as real, while all else is not. And it is this we wish to work from. We will see that our ideas will translate into actions, into what we will know as our reality.

We can change our lives radically by believing that thoughts are everything. What we think happens. What we say also happens. We must realize that our thoughts create our worlds for us. We saw earlier that we created our own negative worlds: We thought that we were no good, were nothing, that no one could love us, that life was terrible, and so was everything in it. We had dark moods and negative feelings most of the time. In truth, that was the world we lived in. What we didn't then recognize was that we ourselves had created that negative world. We were unwilling to accept responsibility for our own lives or for creating the negative worlds we were in. We tended to put the blame on others or on circumstances. We did not then know what we are now learning: that the worlds we live in we create. Life itself does not beat us down; we do it to ourselves. We do not just inherit tremendous problems; many we create. Those that we don't create we can change by our attitudes toward them.

Every thought that crosses our minds will somehow be translated into realities. Anytime we want to, we can change our view of our lives, of our worlds. We may not always be able to change the people surrounding us or the circumstances in which we live, but we can change the way we think about them, and in that way we change *our* worlds, for our worlds are our thoughts.

We live in our minds. Whatever our thoughts are, that's where we are. We can sit in a chair in Albany, New York, but think about the Bahamas, and we are really in the Bahamas because that is where our awareness is. We have the faculty of being able to transport ourselves where our minds take us. How many of us have been present at a boring lecture or a boring sermon and transported ourselves to some other place, closing out the droning voice of the speaker?

We will find that just as our thoughts are, that is the way our worlds will become. If we think positive thoughts and project these, we will attract positive persons to us. Negative persons will disappear, and our worlds will gradually change into positive, productive places where we will discover the best of ourselves.

This new adventure in thinking and in living is hard for us at first, for we have too long been negative old bears, difficult to be around, grumping about everything, and finding life stultifying. It is almost too much to suppose that such a person can be changed into the positive person pictured in this ideal sobriety.

But it *can* happen with your cooperation and participation. Obviously, without these, nothing will happen. You may be able to stay sober, but you will probably be your old grumpy self much of the time.

Try this new way of thinking. Learn the six statements to change your life, and practice them each day. Put them to the test, remembering always that mind control is life control. Remember, as you permit thoughts, that is how your life will be. Think happy thoughts, and you will be happy and will act happy. If you see someone not smiling, give him or her a smile and you'll get a smile back. Think positive thoughts about your new life of sobriety, and you will be happy about it and feel that you have, at last, found the right road.

Over the years I have probably met several thousand alcoholics, and I am always startled when I meet those who still resent their inability to drink, as if that were some great wonderful pastime taken away from them.

We should see our sobriety as rescue from a life-threatening terminal illness. This is a truth not to be toyed with. And it is something we should think about often. We should see our sobriety as a happy event and as a time when we can discover the best in ourselves since we have for too long seen the worst in ourselves.

We begin our new worlds and our new lives by cleaning out the negativisms from our thoughts and then molding new thoughts. Our thoughts are our lives. Our thoughts are everything. Our thoughts are a new power we have never tapped. Now is the time of self-discovery and self-responsibility. We must work very hard at learning that we are in charge of our lives and responsible for everything in them. For some people assuming this new responsibility for self is extremely difficult. However, it is a very necessary step in recovery. In order to put the negatives aside, we must take charge of our entire lives, not just a part. We cannot keep old thoughts that hold blame or go on believing that part of our problems are due to others. Believing this will only impede our progress and emotional growth. Again we must know that our thoughts control us, and if we keep any of these old thoughts, we are really only sinking our own ship.

HOW WE WERE—FILLED WITH:

Worry
Fear
Guilt
Feelings of helplessness and powerlessness
Excessive feelings of dependency
Self-condemnation
Self-destructiveness
Loneliness
Isolation
Depression

WHAT WE ARE BECOMING:

Understanding of ourselves and our alcoholism
Thankful that we finally know the truth
New persons through learning new ways to view
   life
Meditative, happy, and self-developing
Proud of our sobriety
Independent and self-confident

We may not become these new women overnight. It takes time to break old thought patterns and create new ones. But it can be accomplished with repeated attempts and with our periods of morning meditation when we put our lives and our thoughts into a proper perspective for each day. In our morning time to ourselves, we can fill our minds with positive thoughts that will carry every situation that day. Our morning meditations give us the opportunity to realize the futility of the negative thought. We will acknowledge that conditions don't hurt us but thoughts do.

Let us never forget in our new lives that we live in our minds, and whatever our thoughts are, that is the kind of world we create. We are indeed what we think. Our worlds are indeed what we make them. And we can think about only one thing at a time.

In our new worlds we want also to fulfill our very highest potentials of achievement. We want to find ourselves and to learn what we can do. We want to set goals for ourselves and find an excitement in life that we were always looking for in the bottom of a glass. We want to think about success, not about failures.

This is a new lease on life for us. It is a time of opportunity and a time of discovery. It is a time of loving and giving, a time of new relationships and a time of new and positive feelings about ourselves. It is a time for us to feel pride and to know that we have finally made it out of the cellar.

We create our life through our thoughts. We are responsible for who we are.

As Lily Tomlin's Edith Ann says, "And that's the truth."

APPENDIX

Interviews with Three Women

THE NUN

I am a woman religious in the Catholic Church. I am fifty-six years old, and was born in the Midwest, in the city of Detroit. I've lived here most of my life, except for sixteen years when I was sent to various parts of the country by my religious community.

I had four sisters; there were no boys in my family. I was the youngest. My oldest sister is dead. She died at the age of forty-one after having a massive stroke and being in a coma for two days. She's been dead now for twenty-seven years.

At the time of her death I was stationed in Washington. In those days we were not permitted to return home if we were so far away, and we were also not permitted to go to the funeral of a sister or brother. My family did not know that part of it, but they knew that I could not come because of the distance, and I let it go at that.

I don't really know how to describe my feelings when she died except that it was a great loss. I was very close to my oldest sister, and losing her was a tragedy. Then, not being able to be home with my mother—my father was dead—was very difficult. It wasn't until I was in counseling, about three years ago, that I found out I had never properly said goodbye to my sister because she died when I was so far away. It awakened a lot of feelings in me that I guess I had never dealt with. After this I went to the cemetery and said my goodbye.

Later I was stationed in Detroit, and then my brother-in-law died. He was an alcoholic, and after my sister died, he drank

173

himself to death. He left two children whose lives were devastated by the loss of both parents. Today my nephew, who is in his thirties, is an alcoholic. Most of the time we don't know where he is. He goes underground and then surfaces again. I understand he is also on drugs. I have tried to contact him but to no avail, and it has hurt me greatly because I often wonder if he's sick somewhere. I would like my dead sister to look down on me and feel that I am doing my best for her children, but that's not to be.

Both my parents are dead now. My father has been dead for a long time; my mother, for three years. She died in a nursing home, and I have horrendous feelings about that.

I am presently a member of a religious community, a teaching order. However, we do many types of diversified works, different types of ministry. I taught school, for twenty-one years, mainly primary grades. The last few years of my teaching career I taught fourth grade, and I liked that better than all the other grades I taught.

Before I stopped teaching, I had serious back surgery. After that I had a job running the bookstore in one of our high schools. I had that job for a year and a half. Then I asked permission to go back to working in an office—I had worked in an office before I became a sister—and that's what I've been doing ever since. I've worked at three different places during this time, and that is my ministry: the business world.

Three years ago I left the convent living area and moved into an apartment on my own. I requested this move for my health and for personal reasons, and it has been very beneficial to me. It has been a slow process for me to be doing things on my own and to get away from institutional living that was bogging me down.

I don't remember when I had my first drink. I come from a Polish family, Polish-Americans. Beer was in our home all the time. We were all raised on it! I can still see beer being put in a little spoon and given to a baby in our family. Wine was in the house during the winter months. The Christmas fruit cake was always wrapped in wine-soaked cloth. On some occasions my father would have his schnapps, but that was not very often. It was always beer.

My father had a feeling about drinking, a very strong feeling. It was "You will learn to drink under my roof so that you will not go out and make a fool of yourself, and you will learn to control your drinking." Because he had this attitude, it was impressed very strongly on us that this is what we would do.

I can remember that when any of us had cramps, my mother would say to my father, "I think we need something; one of the girls needs something." If he didn't have wine in the house, he would go to the tavern for it.

Sometimes we used to walk my married sister home. Her husband was working nights, and she would come and visit us. We would take her and the baby in the little buggy and walk her home, my mother, my father, and my other sister. After we got her settled at home, we often stopped in the local liquor store on the way back, and all of us would get a glass of wine. I remember I always gulped mine down. Both my parents would ask, "Why do you do that?" I never answered, but I know now that I did it for effect. I liked to gulp it down, and I was always hoping I'd get a second one. I never did, but I also never gave up hope.

Alcohol was always there, and it was a cultural ritual with us because every night, automatically, at nine o'clock, no matter what we were doing, we would all go to the kitchen, and my father would bring out the quart of beer. Sometimes we had cheese and crackers, and sometimes we would just drink beer. We would all sit and talk. This was a time to share, and it was done with beer. I also remember that if we were out on dates, when we came home, we automatically went to the icebox and got ourselves a glass of beer before we went to bed.

I don't recall when I first drank as part of an evening out. When I went on a date, I did not drink because I was always afraid that the guy would take advantage of me. I drank soda instead.

My father felt the way he did about alcohol because his youngest brother was an alcoholic. This uncle lived on the South Side of Detroit and we lived on the North Side, and it was like two different countries. We never traveled to the South Side. My uncle would come visit my grandmother, who lived across the street from us, and he would get money from her which he used for drink. My father was always very angry with my grandmother for giving him the money because he knew the family would never get it back.

My aunt had a very unhappy life, yet she stayed with him all of her life. My father always felt sorry for the children. There were two boys and a girl. The girl is a year younger than I am, and she is an alcoholic. She now attends AA. Her husband divorced her, but she has remarried, someone she met in AA. The youngest boy in that family is also an alcoholic. A year ago I confronted him about his alcoholism, offering help, but I have not heard from him since.

My father's sister, my aunt, became an alcoholic. Her husband was a problem drinker, and periodically he would get very drunk. He'd go on these binges and always ended up at our house. He would be crying and carrying on all the way down the street. My feelings were not of anger. I felt very sorry for him. It was after his death that my aunt became an alcoholic. I don't think my family wanted to admit that she was. There were no treatment centers at that time, so my other aunt had her committed to a mental institution. She died there. They never did tell me that my aunt was an alcoholic. They were protecting me, as they always did. Facing the reality about my aunt later was a shock to me. I really thought she suffered from a mental condition.

My own drinking in those days occasionally got out of hand. Before I entered the community, one of the women where I worked got married. I went to her wedding with some of the other women from the office, and I had a lot to drink—more than I should have had. I remember being very silly. That was the first occasion when I had too much. I also remember that as a teen-ager I could be very funny when I had too much to drink.

At the end of the Second World War, when I was sixteen, we were in southern Illinois visiting relatives. We were so happy and excited. We went in celebration from one relative's house to another, and everyone was drinking beer, naturally, and I drank far more than I ever had before. We got back to the house where we were staying, my sister and I. When we got in bed, all of a sudden I said to her, "Oh, Mary, I am so sick." I was so drunk I didn't know what I was doing.

The next morning was a holy day, and we all went to the parish church for mass. I had a hangover, and I was still very sick. I had to leave church. My father came out with me, and I was terrified because I felt very guilty. I knew that I had been drunk the night before. I was afraid what my father would say to me because he had strong feelings about people who could not control their drinking.

I remember he walked with me, but I can't recall that we talked. I'm sure that if he did, I would remember it. I had a lot of guilt and fear about what my father would think of me because I was always concerned with his opinion of me. My mother always used to say that I worried too much about what others thought of me, and I have carried that trait all through my life.

When I entered the religious community, my drinking was cut off. There were no alcoholic beverages available while I was in noviceship, and there were no opportunities.

After two and a half years I went out to teach. The superiors always locked the liquor they had in a cupboard. They would ask the priest to give them liquor for the sisters when we had a cold or something else. When you had a cold, you could ask the superior for some wine or whiskey, and she would give it to you. I don't recall in those early years ever getting whiskey. I always got wine. I do recall one year having a terrible cold and the superior made a hot toddy for me. That really threw me. I had to get up and go to the washroom, and when I attempted to get up, I couldn't make it. That happened to me several other times when superiors made hot toddies that were really strong. But those were the only times I had whiskey. And I didn't like it.

Eight years later, when I was stationed in Washington, we had picnics every Friday in the summertime. We all stayed at one of our high schools. It was a boarding school during the school year, and we stayed there in the summertime and went to summer school. All of us would come from different schools in the area to this one location.

Different groups volunteered to help with our picnics. This one night we had a Gay Nineties theme and had gotten permission from the superior to have beer. This was the first time I'd had beer in seven or eight years, and when I saw it, I was delighted. I offered to help with the serving, and in between I was sneaking cans of beer to drink. I got very dizzy, and when I got in bed, the whole room was going around because I had more than I should have had. This time I had feelings of fear, not guilt.

In the morning I went to chapel, but I got sick and had to leave. *Then* I had a lot of guilt feelings. I was afraid the sisters would put two and two together and know that I'd had too much to drink, although I don't know how they could have done because no one saw me sneak those other cans. However, I was afraid, so at the table I made up a fictitious reason for my illness. This was when I began lying about my drinking.

In Washington there was a parishioner who owned a restaurant. He was an Italian, and he gave us a lot of wine. We could never have this at table; that was not done in community. It all was all locked up and used for medicinal purposes. But our superior gave us wine on Friday nights. There were times when she put the bottle and glasses on a little table outside her bedroom door for us to take. There was even one occasion when she had so much wine she gave each of us a bottle. She could have gotten into a tremendous amount of trouble from the mother house if it had been reported.

Later, when I was back in the Midwest, I would ask for wine if I had a cold or if I was having pain in my back. But I always found that just one glass stimulated me and I couldn't sleep.

In the 1960s there were many changes in the church. Things

became more lenient. What had been locked up was now opened. We didn't have superiors anymore. We were responsible for ourselves. A sister was put in charge. She was called a community representative. Actually she was not in charge; she was a go-between between the pastor and the sisters. She really had no authority.

For years I had been suffering with a severe back problem. I had this problem before I became a sister, but it accelerated through the years. At the time of the changes in the church it was decided that the liquor cabinet would be left unlocked, and the sister who was treasurer in the house decided she would buy a big bottle of whiskey and leave it in the medicine cabinet. When my back was hurting, I'd take some whiskey and lie down right away, so I wouldn't be sick. I wasn't used to whiskey, but I found that it killed the pain and I relaxed.

So I began using whiskey for medicinal purposes. And that's how my problems *really* started.

My mother lived with my oldest sister and her husband. She stayed on after my sister died to help with the children. And then my brother-in-law died, and she went to live with my other sister and her husband. The changes in the church allowed me to visit my mother and family. We were in the same parish. When my mother became sick and had to go into the hospital (my brother-in-law was also in the hospital), it turned out that I had to take over the responsibility. Thank God for the changes in the church because I was now able to do that. Five years earlier I wouldn't have been able to. My sister would have just had to cope.

So I took over the responsibility for my mother, and it was a big step in my life. I was under a lot of tension and was still having trouble with my back. Eventually my mother had to be put in a nursing home, and this was the hardest thing I ever had to do in my life. But there was nothing else to do. I had no choice. And my mother had no money. When my father died, he left her nothing. I wasn't there when he died, but I was told that his dying words were "Who's going to take care of Mom?"

I had to try to get her public aid, and that was a very
humiliating experience for me. The woman behind the desk was
screaming at everybody. She took the form I had filled out and
tore it up in front of me, yelling, "This is not done properly." I
remember coming out of there and leaning against a building and
just crying. I was in full habit at that time. Here I was, thirty-
six years old, and I wasn't prepared for this. I had entered the
community at the age of eighteen and had led such a sheltered
life. This emotional turmoil devastated me. And I was so concerned for my mother. She did not lay guilt on me for this. She
was very noble, taking it, accepting it, but I was nevertheless so
guilt-ridden. Oh, God, I was guilt-ridden! And it was then I began
increasing the amounts of liquor I drank.

When my mother first went into the nursing home, I didn't
have trouble with the bureaucracy because the people in charge
were very nice and my mother seemed happy. But after a while
there were problems with nurses, problems with aides, and problems with the administration. I would come home from dealing
with that situation so emotionally upset and filled with so much
guilt I would take liquor. What started out as a medicinal means
to get rid of back pain now became my way of meeting emotional
stress.

I became a real controller of my mother. I controlled her,
and she submitted to it. There were times when she would get
very angry with me, but 90 percent of the time she allowed me
to control her life. There was the alcoholism there, making her
dependent upon me, having to control all situations. And I drove
myself into the ground with the guilt I felt. I hated myself. I felt
I was a bad daughter because I put my mother in a public nursing
home. I drank every single night to drown those feelings of hatred
for myself. I drank and drank and drank.

I remember going to my family doctor and saying that I
didn't know what was wrong with me. I told him I had gotten
up in the night to go to the washroom and the whole floor rose
to meet me. He thought it strange and asked if it had happened
before, and I said, "No, never before." And, to be honest, I was

not aware that it was my drinking that did this. I remember one night I vomited all over my bedding and I had to go down to the laundry in the middle of the night to wash it. I was very upset over it and hoped nobody would find me in the laundry room. There probably was also a tinge of guilt.

Then all kinds of things happened to me. There was a sister principal with whom I had never gotten along; there had been a power struggle between us from noviceship days. Now she was my principal, and we never did see eye to eye on a lot of things. I bucked her at meetings, and she resented me and I resented her. Towards the end of the school year she did not recommend me for rehiring. She had me kicked out of teaching. She went to the supervisor of schools and claimed that because of my back, I shouldn't be in the classroom. That was devastating to me, but the supervisor went along with it.

My drinking didn't have anything to do with this particular occurrence. It was a personality conflict of long standing, and she had the upper hand, she had the authority. I was terror-stricken because I didn't know what I was going to do. I didn't want to go away for retraining because I never liked being a student and I never was a good one.

So the whole bottom of my world fell out, and it was then that my back again created problems. The doctor I was seeing at the University of Chicago orthopedic department decided on surgery. This possibility had been hanging in the air for some time.

The young intern who interviewed me before the surgery asked me questions, one of them being "Do you drink?" and I lied and said, "Oh, I have an occasional beer." But I'm sure they found out the alcohol content in my blood test.

I had the back surgery, and I was in recovery five or six hours. I was in shock, and my blood pressure had dropped drastically. They had all kinds of blankets on me, and I was shaking all over.

But I survived. I was in a body cast from my neck to my knees for three months. In the hospital, once they had wine on my tray, just once. Then I was put on Valium, and the wine was stopped. My doctor said he thought I seemed very upset, but I didn't tell him I had all this hanging over my head. I had been bumped from the classroom, and I'll never forget the day I signed my resignation—twenty-one years of teaching and it was just like it was for nothing. Well, I didn't tell him what was going on in my life, and I went home with the Valium. When I had pain, I took Valium and I took some whiskey. The whiskey was still down in the medicine cabinet, and although the treasurer remarked about it going down fast, she bought a large bottle. While I was in my body cast, I was returned to the convent for the last month, and I was drinking whiskey and taking Valium. When I think of it now, I know I could have killed myself.

When I was taken out of the body cast, I was offered a position as head of a bookstore at a high school. I wanted to stay at the convent where I was presently living and commute back and forth, but permission was refused. So I went to live in the convent attached to the school where I was going to work. It was a very large house; there were forty high school nuns. They were of a different caliber than grade school nuns, and during the ten years I lived there, I became more unhappy every year. I had a very hard time adjusting to the convent and the people in it. And I was drinking. I found excuses. I told the sister I was having back pain and needed some whiskey. She fell for the story and gave it to me. (It was locked up in this house.)

I was very unhappy. There were times when it was difficult for me to get a car to visit my mother. I was meeting a lot of opposition all the way around. On Sundays I often had free time since I no longer had class papers to correct, and I didn't have anything to do. So I would take my monthly allowance—about forty dollars, out of which we had to buy our clothes and other personal items—and I would go to Walgreen's and get myself a bottle of wine. I'd sit and watch TV and drink a quart in an afternoon. Instead of going to the library and getting a book to read, I would drink. And I had terrible feelings of loneliness. I didn't seem able to identify or talk with the people there. We all lived together but, we really didn't care about or know each other. I didn't trust some of them—most of them.

After about a year and a half in the bookstore I was bored. I had organized and straightened out everything. Then a laywoman was hired to replace the sister principal. She was an exnun but not of our order. She didn't like the way I ran the bookstore and wanted it changed. She was a humdinger, and she scared me. I was afraid, and I was angry at her. It got to the point where I was walking squares in my bedroom and couldn't sleep at night. I talked to my provincial supervisor, who suggested I get professional help.

I went to a psychologist, and he helped me, although I didn't tell him about my drinking. He asked if I liked beer, and when I said yes, he said, "Well, why don't you get yourself a can of beer once in a while to relax?" Little did he know that I needed this encouragement like I needed a hole in my head. And I was beyond beer.

It was through him that I decided to get another job. I couldn't handle the bookstore anymore, so I got permission from my provincial superiors to go job hunting. It was a risk because I had led a sheltered life. Now I was going out on interviews and was trying to sell myself and my skills.

It was really a big thing in my life. The feelings of anxiety left me, and I got a job as a secretary to a marketing director downtown. I was still seeing my psychologist.

As I had to get up early in the morning, I would go to bed early. I was drinking then because we had a community representative who felt the wine should be put out at night for the sisters. At first I started with a nice small glass, then it got to be bigger and bigger amounts. Remarks were made at house meetings about how fast the wine disappeared, but I'd say, "Well, what do you expect with a large house of forty people."

At my new job downtown I had a private office, and there was also a room with some files in it. There were various bottles of different kinds of liquor in there. I don't know what they were used for because they never had a party. There were occasions when I told myself I had a headache or a back pain and needed something, so I'd sneak in and open a bottle. I finished a couple and left the empty bottles there.

At times, when I was tense, I went to a bar in a building down the street. I didn't sit. I just leant against a barstool, and then I didn't consider myself sitting at a bar! I would order a shot of whiskey and swallow it down, and that was that. I would go back to work with the smell on my breath.

After I'd been there six months, we got a new vice-president—and everybody quit! I was one of the last ones to quit but finally I got a job in the suburbs, and the community furnished me a convent car to get to work. It was a small company, and I did production typing. I liked it a lot, and I liked the people.

Meanwhile, things were becoming bad at the nursing home. The building was sold, and the condition of the home was deteriorating. It had been beautiful when my mother first went into it.

I was drinking more and more. Then the wine was stopped because we were using too much of it, so I used to ask for it, saying I had pains in my stomach. I was vomiting a lot at night, and I had many feelings of guilt and self-disgust. In the morning I would look in the mirror and I would say to myself, "You're disgusting." And I would tell God, "Please, I'm not going to do this again." But I did. Over and over again.

Even though the wine was no longer out all the time, we were still having it at table. When anyone didn't want it, I would always take their share. I would always go back for more.

About this time the office manager, whom I liked very much, was killed in an automobile accident. I was promoted to her position, and the responsibility added stress to my life. To make matters worse, my boss did not back me up. He expected me to do everything but didn't stand behind me as he had for the woman before me. I became hostile and aggressive. At noontime I would go to a liquor store, buy miniature bottles of liquor, and drink one. I didn't do it all the time because most of my drinking was done at night in my bedroom. I was taking the money allotted me for lunch and buying liquor—not whiskey anymore; I was now drinking brandy.

There were some nights when I could hardly wait to get to the store, to get that bottle and get home to have a drink. I drank about a pint a night. I was still living in the convent, and before going down to supper, I'd open the bottle and have a swig. This was an appetizer. After I ate, I'd go to my room, sit in my easy chair, and watch television. At every commercial I would get up and have a drink, and by the time the evening was over, I was pretty much into the bag. Then I'd go to bed but couldn't sleep, so I'd have to get up and have more and more.

One night I fell and cracked my ribs. I went to emergency and said I'd tripped over something. Another time I fell and hit my face. I remember that when I fell, I didn't know, later, how I got back to bed. This began to frighten me. I was having blackouts and feared that maybe I had met with another sister and didn't remember. What did I do? What did I say?

I was having feelings that I wanted to end it all. I knew I was getting sicker and sicker. I prayed to God to take care of me until my mother died. Then I planned that I would drink myself into oblivion until I killed myself because life wasn't worth a dime. I hated living.

About three years before this a sister from another community, a recovered alcoholic who had become an alcoholism counselor, came and talked to our community about alcoholism among sisters. While she talked, all I was thinking was *This is me!* I was terror-stricken because I realized that I had problems. She told about a three-week program at Lutheran General Hospital, and I stood up and asked if they had an outpatient program. She said no. I said to myself, "Well, there goes that for me because I just can't get away from work for three weeks to get that help." And I had my responsibility to my mother. I decided I'd have to lick this thing myself.

Well, I wasn't able to lick it.

One day my provincial supervisor summoned me about a

matter she wanted to discuss with me. In the course of our conversation we talked about people seeking help when they had emotional problems. I said, "I admire people who feel they have an alcohol problem and seek help."

With that she said to me, "There's something I'd like to ask you."

And I said, "What is it?"

She seemed extremely nervous, and I wondered what in the world it was she wanted to ask me. She said, "There's a couple of sisters you live with who think you have a drinking problem. How do you feel about that?"

It was like the whole world had opened up when she spoke. I felt such relief. I guess what I had said about people seeking help was really a cry for help for myself. I had been falling, having blackouts, and the amounts I was drinking were increasing. I just couldn't live without alcohol. I *had* to have it every day.

When she asked how I felt, I said, "I do have a problem. I don't know what to do about it."

She asked, "Would you like to talk to the sister who gave us a talk several years ago?"

I agreed, and my superior went with me for an evaluation. Sister Theresa asked me all kinds of questions about my drinking, and I was crying all of the time this was going on. I kept saying, "I'm so ashamed, so ashamed." And I was. I felt I had betrayed my father because he always said, "You're going to learn to drink under my roof without making a fool of yourself." I felt that I had betrayed my community, that I was a bad person, that sisters don't do this. And I said, "With all my religious training I should be able to control this thing."

She said, "Can you cure diarrhea with self-control? You must go into treatment."

I said, "There is no way, absolutely no way. I've got to take care of my mother; I do her laundry, and I go to see her all of the time. And I've got my job—" I had all of this denial.

Sister Theresa said, "If I were a doctor and told you that you had to go in for treatment, what would you do?"

I said, "Why, I'd go in."

Then she said, "Well, you have a terminal illness, comparable to cancer, and you must go for treatment."

I went on crying and saying, "I can't, I can't."

Then the provincial supervisor came over to me and said, "I can't tell you what to do. It's your decision. But I really feel that you need to go into treatment while you still have your dignity."

My dignity. That was the thing that clinched it for me. What people thought about me was very important. So I agreed to go into treatment.

I was told that I should tell my family, but I refused to tell my mother, who was eighty-four years old. I did go to my sister, and when I told her, she was shocked. I began crying, and she threw her arms around me. I began again, "I'm so ashamed, I'm so ashamed," and she said, "It's okay, you're not an alcoholic." I kept saying, "Yes, I am. I am so ashamed."

I made her swear that she would not tell my brother-in-law, but after I was in treatment several days, I said she could tell him but not the children. "What if they found out their aunt, the nun, is an alcoholic?"

During the first three weeks of treatment I think I cried every day. I also said I would not tell my boss, but after I'd been there a week, I decided I would tell him the truth. I called him. He was very kind and understanding. He was willing to have me back and said he hadn't known about my alcoholism because it had not affected my work.

But I refused to tell the sisters I was living with. Every time I passed one of them in the hall I wondered if she was the one who told on me. I could have wrung their necks. I was so angry. And I did not feel that they were a group of people who would support me if they knew. I really threatened the woman in charge, saying she was the only one who knew and, if it got out, I'd know who told.

I had one good friend. We had entered Community together and had been friends through the years. We were very close. She had the bedroom next to me, but she did not know that I was alcoholic or had even been having problems with drinking. She knew I liked to drink but didn't think it was a problem.

When I first went into the treatment center, during the couple of days when I was in detoxification, I looked around at all those people who were so sick, and all I kept saying was "I don't belong here. Why am I here?" But it wasn't until I got into the lectures and the films and the group therapy that I realized that I *did* belong there. And I needed help.

I came out of treatment and went to AA, and I tried very hard. I went to several different meetings, and it was hard for me to find a place where I felt at home because they were all large groups and I couldn't share much. I couldn't talk. I finally found a small group, but it was mostly men. I was often the only woman at meetings. We were only six or seven sometimes.

Some of these men were really helpful to me, very supportive, very encouraging. I know that it was the support of these men that helped me stay sober. But all through this I was unable to get over my terrible depression and the awful feelings I had about myself. I kept thinking, *I'm an alcoholic, and I'm a bad person.* And I also had this tremendous guilt about my mother, about the fact that she was in a nursing home. Occasionally I would bring up this feeling of guilt at the meetings, but I couldn't get any help from the men because they simply didn't understand. They tried, but they just couldn't. They'd say, "How can you feel guilty? You're lucky she's in a home. Just walk away from it." But I couldn't.

One day I found a brochure put out by Blue Cross/Blue Shield, and it told about Women For Sobriety. About four months later I wrote to find where there was a group, and eventually I went to my first meeting. The day I went to the first meeting was the day I walked out on my job. I had just had it. Things had been going from bad to worse with my boss and his wife, my stress was mounting, and I had the feeling that if I continued, I'd go back to drinking. And that was the time I recognized how full of anger I was. It was during treatment that I had realized that I was a woman seething with anger. I had kept in my anger for so many things, and anger had played a tremendous part in my life.

I went to Women For Sobriety, and I've been going ever since. Even at these women's meetings it was hard at first for me to share, but eventually I began to talk, and I'm now able to express myself and share with others. I found that I had submerged my anger. In the religious life you are told in your noviceship that you cannot show your feelings; in fact, I was reprimanded many times in the early days for showing my feelings. One time I was told I didn't have to say anything; it was written all over my face. So, for many years, I squashed all anger: anger about the fact that my mother got so sick; anger because I had to put her into a nursing home; anger because I was a bad person; anger because of my drinking; anger at my sister because she didn't share the responsibility for the care of our mother. I was just angry at everything. Angry at work, angry at the way I was being put upon, that I had allowed myself to do a lot of things around the office—janitorial work—and that after doing it voluntarily, I was being ordered to do it. And I walked out. When I got in the car, I banged on the seat, and that was the best thing I could have done; I let it out.

There have been occasions in my religious life where my rebellion against authority created problems. On two occasions a superior almost destroyed me. The first time was when I was kicked out of the classroom. The other came after I'd had two years of sobriety. I was extremely happy, and I was getting much support and help from my WFS group. I remember it was my second anniversary and they had given me a necklace. Anyway, I got a call from a provincial superior who wanted to talk to me. I certainly wasn't prepared for what she said. She wanted me to get out of the convent I was living in because I was not attending prayers and I was not attending house meetings. I tried to explain to her that there was no way I could attend the house meetings or prayers because I was up every night until midnight doing laundry for my mother. I was going right from work to the nursing home, caring for my mother, coming home late, and then doing her laundry because my mother was allergic to the soap they used at the home. There was no way I was going to get up at four-thirty or five in the morning so that I could get down for six or six-thirty prayers. And I did not get home in time for evening prayers. I reminded her that since the Vatican changes in the 1960s, formal prayer was a choice for us. One could choose to go to formal prayer, or one could pray on one's own, privately. I told her it wasn't right for her to question my prayer life, and as far as going to the house meetings, I wasn't there because I was at the nursing home. One night a week my sister went to the nursing home, and that's the night I went to my Women For Sobriety meetings. Of course, the sisters didn't know I was a recovered alcoholic, and they did not know about those meetings.

I could not believe what was happening to me. In fact, I sat in my chair and just wondered about it all. I felt that I just couldn't take any more. I already had so much stress.

I did get myself together, and with help from two sisters, one of my own order and the other from another order who worked in career counseling, I learned assertiveness skills.

So I confronted the provincial superior. We had battle after battle, not in an aggressive way but in an assertive way. Since I had to leave the convent where I was (they had given me two months) and I refused to go to the convent she named, I told her I would like to go into an apartment. I had wanted to do this for some time, but she said there was no way I could do this, that I had responsibilities to my religious community and I couldn't leave. Actually the people I lived with cared nothing about me. The only reason they wanted me with them was because I should be toeing the line. I was free, and they weren't. They wanted me shackled with them.

I looked for apartments, and when I found one, I made a down payment and let her know. She was ready to cut me into pieces. She told me I should get my money back. Well, we had another, final, confrontation. I was very calm, but inside, I was like a volcano ready to erupt. She continued to say I could not move into an apartment, and I got up to leave, telling her I was going to the superior general, who was a psychologist and from whom I felt that I would get fair treatment.

Because this provincial superior was forcing me into a bind, I had to go over her head, and it infuriated her. To tell you the truth, I thought she was going to have a stroke right there in the corridor. She began screaming at me when I told her what I had done. It turned out that the superior general was very understanding and gave me permission. I later found out that the one I had so much battle with left the community and ran off with an ex-priest.

I am in my apartment now and have been able to renew this permission a year at a time.

But there have been struggles. I'd say the present coprovincials have been very nice on the whole, but I've had a little trouble with them also. I wanted a copy of my records from the treatment center, and one of them didn't want to give it to me. She felt I didn't have a right to it. I eventually won out, but she was very angry with me. I needed those records. They are no one's business. They belong to me.

I also had a slight confrontation with the other coprovincial. I talked to her about a sabbatical so I could finish my schooling next year. I think she's going to come back to me with the canon. We shall see.

My sister was concerned about my going into the apartment. I think she feared that I might start to drink again. I moved into the apartment on August 1, and my mother died October 4. In that last year I positively lived my mother's life. I was constantly running, running, running, taking care of, doing, being attentive, fighting the establishment, fighting with nurses, fighting with the administrator, seeing to it that she got the best possible care.

And I wanted so hard to have my own life. About a week before my mother died, I was in my apartment, and now my chores included grocery shopping, cooking, and all those things. I remember saying to myself, "I can't do it anymore. I think I'm going to die. I just can't do it." And I firmly believe, as I look

back, that if God had not taken my mother at that point, and had
I continued on the treadmill I was on, I would have died. I had
reached my peak physically, emotionally, psychologically. I was
the baby in our family, and I was spoiled. I resented the fact that
I had to pay the price. Because I was not married and didn't have
a family, I was to do it all. But I had a religious community, which
was my family. So there were lots of feelings, most of them guilt.

My mother had two massive strokes, and she was paralyzed
from her neck down. She was that way for a whole year, and she
did not speak. She just stared. There were times when she managed a word or two, but that was all. A whole year she was that
way, and I'll never forget it as long as I live. It was horrid. I went
every single night to the nursing home. It was an hour's drive
one way. I took care of her and tried to do everything possible.

It was my Women For Sobriety and AA meetings that kept
me sober because if anybody would have taken to the bottle, I
certainly could have during this time. It was terrible. It was hard
to see her like that. And the worst part is that the night she died
my sister and I had been with her into the wee hours of the
morning and had gone home as the nurse told us to do. Then we
called and were told she'd taken a turn for the worse. I think she
was dead at the time, but that was the message they gave us.
They were to have called us if her condition worsened, which
they didn't do.

When we got there, she was dead. The door was closed,
and I thought it was closed to give her some privacy, but there
was a sheet over her. I made the mistake of pulling down the
sheet, and the look on her face was horrible. I'll never forget it.
Earlier she had said something about dying to me, and I promised
her I'd be with her. When I saw her with the sheet over her, I
felt so much guilt. I had promised her. I had been there every
day, and I wasn't there when I should have been. She was in the
nursing home for thirteen years, and I had been beating myself
with liquor.

She was a strong-willed person, and I admired her for the

way she accepted being put into the nursing home. I considered her a noble woman, a strong woman. And I think I'm a lot like her. I know I'm a lot like her in my alcoholism.

My mother had a problem with alcohol. I believe it started when she was going through her change of life. Sometimes when I came home from school, I could tell by her face. She looked different. Although she was an extremely affectionate woman, she was more so at these times. I remember my father sometimes saying that so much wine was gone. I don't recall her response to that. I remember my middle sister screaming and yelling at my mother about her drinking. I was angry at this. I do remember my father having words with my mother. He stormed out of the house and slammed the door. I remember being frightened and afraid he wouldn't come back.

For a time the problem drinking stopped. But I remember one time when I was in the eighth grade and my mother and father had gone to some kind of a party. When we got up the next morning, we found my mother had fallen down a whole flight of stairs and cut open her shinbone and her glasses had cut into her cheek so deep she needed stitches. For a while there was concern about possibly having to amputate her leg. It finally healed, but she had a big scar for the rest of her life.

I had been in the community about six years when my father died. Then my mother *really* began drinking. She just couldn't adjust to his death. She was very dependent upon him, and I think he made her that way. At his death he said, "Who's going to take care of Mom?" He left her nothing.

She was living alone and drinking. Eventually she moved in with my oldest sister and her husband. He was an alcoholic, so she had a drinking companion. When my sister died, my brother-in-law asked her to stay, and then, when he died a year and a half later, my mother moved in with my other sister, the one who used to yell at her for her drinking.

A couple of years later she went into a psychiatric ward after having a nervous breakdown. She admitted herself. She had shock treatments. Although she got out of the hospital, she went back in later. She was on all kinds of tranquilizers and was dependent upon them the rest of her life.

I don't think my mother had a mental problem. The root of the whole thing was her alcoholism.

I never told my mother I was in treatment for alcoholism. If she had been younger, I would have told her, and I know she would have supported me, certainly would have understood.

My relationship with my father was very good. My father really wanted to make something of himself. He was a cigar maker and owned his own store but eventually lost it. He had a lot of failures in his life. My mother had gotten money from her parents at their death. She wanted to buy a house, but my father put the money in stocks. And then came the crash, and they lost everything. My mother never, never threw it up at him.

My father and I were close. He was a quiet man. He was not what you'd call a real popular man. He had the last word in the house, always. He was not a violent man, and I rarely saw him angry. He had a terrific sense of humor. He teased a lot.

I was a tomboy. Many times I heard my mother say, "You know, your father always wanted a son, and each time he hoped for a son, and then you came along, the last one. . . ." So I tried to be a boy. He was determined to make me a softball pitcher on a girl's team, and he would practice with me. I would get out of doing the dishes in the summertime so that he and I could practice throwing and catching.

Sometimes I'd feel inadequate because I wasn't that boy he wanted. All my life I tried to please and be what he wanted me to be. Then there came the time in my life when I decided that I wanted to be a sister, a nun. I thought about it seriously and prayed about it. And I decided this was what I wanted. My oldest sister was married and had a little girl, and another sister was going to be married the following September. This was October. And I wanted to go to Community in the summer. My father opposed this. He was alarmed that I wanted to leave home and join the convent. I was seventeen when I broached the subject, and I wanted to leave right after graduation. To my surprise he said, "Absolutely not."

I dropped the subject, but I was a religious person and I went to church a lot. It got to the point where he was telling me I couldn't go every day but could just go to mass on Sunday. He was really giving me a hard time. I told my parents that I wanted to go to Community and I would go with or without their permission.

The next class was in February, and my father didn't talk to me for the next four months. This tore me to pieces. I think he did it because he thought I'd change my mind, but I didn't. This hurt him very much because he felt that I didn't want to be at home, that he was going to lose me. He was devastated by the whole thing, and it severed our close relationship.

He was like a raving maniac the day I got my obedience. He was at the mother house, down in southern Indiana, to visit when I took my first vows. My mother told him to pull himself together, that this was my life and there's not a thing he could do. Then he began to act half-decently.

The second year, when I was in Indianapolis, he and my mother visited me, and he saw my classroom and visited with the sisters in the convent where I was living, and he began to resign himself to the fact that I was happy. But he never once said to me, "It's okay, it's your decision, and you have my blessing." And the following year he died.

That has always hurt me deeply, this deep severance in our relationship.

I entered the religious life of my own free will, and nobody forced me to stay. In fact, some were sent home who were considered unfit. I was very happy in my religious life.

Those friends that I had, those girl friends who are now women friends, always stayed in touch. They sent me pictures of their weddings and their children, and we'd get together periodically. They have always remembered me at Christmas, always had me to their homes. I'm just as close to their husbands as I am to them. I've had a great deal of love from all of them.

When I was in Catholic high school, I used to go to the dances they sponsored—not often because I was not popular. I did date, but not a lot. There was one young man I went with who I liked a lot. He studied to be a brother in a missionary order, and he left. He was wanting to be more affectionate than I cared to be. I was kind of cold. I was like my father, who was affectionate but not demonstrative. And that's the way I am. I can feel very strongly about a person, and I can be extremely loving toward a person within myself, but I don't show it. I find it hard to hug. Women For Sobriety has helped me to do more hugging than I've ever done in my life.

My community will never replace my family of origin, my love relationships. Never. Nothing can undo that, and I wouldn't want it to. It's a different kind of relationship. But I was happy. I had a lot of friends, and I was going to school. I had entered a teaching order. In the back of my mind I was hoping to be a missionary and go to China. But my ideas changed the longer I was in community. Physically I could never have gone to China, and I have no desire to be a missionary anymore.

I loved my community a lot, but it seems that when we enter community, they put a tag on us: the haves and the have-nots. If they consider you a have, they push you and put you into positions you are not qualified for. And if you're a have-not, what qualities or talents you have will be submerged, and you are going nowhere under the guise of "You should be more humble."

I expressed my opinions about a lot of things, and I was put down. I was told I was not humble. It wasn't until the 1960s, when Pope John XXIII opened the windows of the church and we began to be liberated, that I was able to express just how I felt about things.

I had stayed in Community under the old system because I wanted to be a sister, but I resented the rules. Some were outrageous. Many of them punished our parents. We weren't allowed to go home; we were allowed to write only twice a year. If our parents came to visit us, we were not permitted to eat in front of them. We were always put in another room. We even had to ask permission to go upstairs to our bedrooms to wash our faces!

This system kept us as little children, and it kept us dependent upon the authority figures who had this tremendous power over us. So I had a lot of resentment. I wanted to make my own decisions, and I wanted to be responsible for my own life. But I wanted to be a good sister and wanted my life to be a striving towards a perfection, and because we entered the religious community, we allowed them to have this power over us. So all of my religious life I've had problems with my religious superiors. Always. Authority figures have always been a problem for me.

I have been sober now for ten years and have made a tremendous amount of progress in my life. I have made a lot of choices and changes, especially in the last three years. The first two years of my sobriety I white-knuckled it. I was sober, but it was very hard. I was very depressed. I still have trouble with my self-esteem, and I resent being put down. I get extremely angry at work, and I get extremely hostile when I am put down, especially by a man. But I am definitely on the defensive with them. I feel I have been used by men in the working world. But in my religious community I have been used by women much more than I've been used by men. And I think that's something I ought to look at good and hard.

My feelings of guilt are still there. They keep cropping up. And my feelings of shame. I don't really think I hurt anybody while I was drinking, just myself.

I have problems when I smell alcohol, when people around me are drinking. I try to get away from it. We had what we called Province Day a few years ago, and they had wine at every table. The wine bottle was next to me, and sitting next to me was one of the coprovincials who knows about my alcoholism. And some of my friends who know about it were sitting at the table. At one part wine was poured into everyone's glass, and these were supposed to be held up and a prayer said. As they started pouring the wine, I knew the coprovincial was not going to pour any for me. Just then one of my friends said to me, "Would you like me to get you a 7-Up?"

I said, "Yes, please, I can't get out."

Well, she got the 7-Up, and it was put into my glass, which I held up when the others held up their wineglasses. But I resented it. This was the first time something like this happened. I was angry because I felt that my anonymity was put on the line. There were many sisters who, I'm sure, were under medication and should not be drinking wine. And there was a sister at my table who had three or four glasses within an hour's time, and she was driving.

When I was drinking and living in the convent, the craving for alcohol was tremendous. I had to have it. At night, after everybody was asleep, I would go down to the kitchen and search the cabinets for cooking alcohol—anything. There was some crème de menthe that one of the sisters liked to use on her ice cream. I drank that and finished it. I finished all the old liquors that people had given us. I drained all of them. Other wine and liquors were locked up, but through soft-talking the sister in charge, I found out where the key was kept. One time I got the altar wine that was used in mass.

I didn't feel any qualms about the fact that I was stealing. I rationalized by saying I was entitled to it, that I was a nun in this order and I should have it.

The biggest revelations of my sobriety were getting to know myself. In religious life, through meditation and prayer, we try to get to know ourselves. We try to be better and strive toward perfection. But I never felt I *really* knew myself until I became a recovering alcoholic. Now I've taken many courses, gone to seminars on effective living, I've taken assertiveness classes, taken a workshop on anger, one on stress, and I've done a lot of reading for the alcoholism courses I'm taking to be certified as an alcoholism counselor.

I have had personal counseling for two years and have gone to AA and Women For Sobriety. During this last summer I went to a morning breakfast meeting at AA that I hadn't been to for a number of years. The friends I once knew who attended this meeting weren't there, and I sat by myself. I did not get any positive vibes. I felt very depressed. I felt like this organization was tearing me down again and wanting me to think badly of myself. I came out of the meeting saying, "I can't handle this." And I don't need it. That's my opinion of AA. For those who want it, fine.

Several sisters and myself often get together and talk about how we might get other sisters into alcoholism treatment. Since we have been helped by Women For Sobriety and AA, we would like others to have the help they so desperately need. We wish we could do more. We meet every month in the Detroit area and we have an AA meeting. I can handle this meeting. Not too well, but I manage. I really don't work the AA program.

Anyway, we have been meeting at one another's apartments. We take turns. Those who are in the convent do not have the meeting. I guess they feel that even though the sisters they are living with know that they are alcoholic, they will be saying, "We don't want these alcoholics in our house."

There are sisters on this task force with me who are members of my community who are recovering alcoholics, but I don't get on with them at all. They are always putting themselves down. I get very upset, and we don't share with one another. I speak up at meetings and say things they don't want to hear. At one recent meeting it was about our attitude toward sisters who repeatedly have been in treatment but refuse to go anymore and continue to get drunk. Some said, "We think we should kick them out of the community. We should tell them to shape up or ship out." This attitude appals me because we are dealing with women who are sick. They have a disease; they are not women who can control their lives. To kick them out of their community is, to me, unchristian.

We had what we call a corporate reflection, where the whole community meets once or twice a year and reflects upon a certain subject. For discussion, they talked about chemical dependencies, especially alcoholism, as being demonic forces within us. I resented this very much. Can you believe—talking about demons in us and making this illness a religious thing! I confronted the superior in charge with a letter. (Here we go with the power play again!) We had various confrontations, but she would not give up.

This past summer the task force met with the provincials from all of the provinces, and I wanted to speak up about what I felt was very wrong about intervention. I asked God to give me the courage to speak up, and He did. I know that the women on the task force were disturbed with me, but I wanted to get across to the provincials that it is very wrong for the women in a community to confront a sister with a drinking problem. You must have people who love her do this: family members, her friends. They may even be friends in the community where she is living, but you don't have the whole house do this because their confrontation of her about her drinking problem can be very destructive especially if they don't like her. And there are plenty of people we live with that don't like us, that we don't get along with. Nuns are no different than other women. We have the same feelings and the same thoughts. We are striving for perfection, but the human is with us. And we can be as unchristian as anybody else. We can be just as nasty.

When I came out of that meeting, I felt good about myself because I had had the courage to stand up and to express how I felt about the way an alcoholic sister should be dealt with. I feel that the authority figures do not have a right to bring in the canon and use it against a sister who is sick. It should be just the opposite. We should give her all the support we can. It is very dangerous to create a crisis in the life of a sister by confrontation in her community. There are not too many outlets for us, and I think that when we are backed into a corner, it can trigger suicide. I'm not saying I felt that way when I was backed into a corner in my community. I came out fighting like a lion. But that's my nature, my personality. And the crisis created for me was not about my drinking but about moving into an apartment. If they had assembled me into the community room and faced me with my alcoholism, I do believe that that humiliation would have tipped the scales for me. And I believe I might have committed suicide. My dignity and my reputation, my good name, are very important to me, and I could not stand being judged by a group of people who don't really know me, whom I live with but whose only relationship to me is passing in the hall and saying "Hi."

Let's face it. We're living in a convent with people who are not blood relatives. The intimacy of blood relationships and the intimacy of sex is about comparable. But when you are living with people in a religious community, they are supposed to be family, but there isn't that love, there isn't sexual intimacy, there isn't closeness. There can be a closeness of friendship, but that happens only with a few persons with whom you live. You're not that way with everyone you live with. And there are jealousies, resentments, and people try to do others in because we are human. There is little that is binding.

The sisters in the community are not the right people to confront another sister with her drinking problem. It must come from those who are close to her. And that's what I wanted to say, and I did say.

At our monthly meetings in our apartments you can see, in the new sisters that come in, their low self-esteem. But as they get more into sobriety and into AA, they grow, and AA seems to work well for them. But there are some that don't come back. I never shared with them that I don't go to AA, but they know that I go to Women For Sobriety. I think they feel they have to go to AA and that their religious superiors are checking up on them. No one has checked up on me.

Women For Sobriety has been so very helpful to me. It has saved my life because I was going nowhere with AA. Had I kept going, I would have only gone down, and I think I would have ended up drinking again because of the rebellion in me. I couldn't handle the suppression I feel in the AA program.

I hope that I can do a great deal for women alcoholics and women religious. That's the field I wish to work in. I've always been called to the service of others. That's why I joined the religious community. I think that's why I am always discontented with working in an office because I have this call to service. I am attracted to helping women religious and I hope that my future lies there. It is what I am striving for.

RITA: THE LESBIAN

My name is Rita. I am forty-five years old. I was born in New York but was raised in the Midwest, where I lived until I was twenty-one. I lived in the same house the whole time I was there, with one brother, who is two years older than myself, my mother and father. My father has been dead about fifteen years, and my mother still lives in the Midwest. My brother lives in the same state and teaches in a small town.

Both my brother and I were adopted. I think that is very significant and has a lot to do with my alcoholism. My adoptive parents did not drink. Oh, maybe one occasionally at their bridge club, but that was it.

When I was about twelve years old, I had my first drink at a neighbors' house. One of their children was getting married. It was Danish beer. It looked very expensive and very good. A friend of mine said, "Come on, Rita, let's drink one of these beers just for fun." I watched her guzzle one down, turn red, and almost throw up. I was very scared. I knew that was something I wasn't supposed to do. So I had a sip, and that was all.

Two years later, when I was in Catholic junior high school, I remember going to a party one night. It was a picnic. Most of my girl friends were several years older than I and fixed me up with guys their age. Anyway, this was the first time I got very, very drunk. My girl friends had to help me get into the car, and I don't remember going home. At home I was very sick in the bathroom, and it woke up my mother and dad. My father was very, very upset. He yelled and screamed a lot and made me stay

203

home for something like ten days. I wasn't allowed to go any-where.

I probably didn't drink for a while after that because it scared me that he knew. Up to that time I'd led a pretty normal life for a kid. I was very outgoing with my classmates, and I made friends easily. They were always welcome in our home. My folks were good about that; I could always bring anyone home.

One thing I remember about this time. I was really becoming rebellious. I had a very hard time with my father. He idolized me, but I had to do everything he said I should. You could never tell my father he was wrong. One time I got out a book to prove him wrong, and that was the worst thing I could have done, so I gave up and I became rebellious.

I started to drink quite a lot in high school. I thought my parents were strict, but as I look back on it, maybe they weren't as strict as I thought.

Public high school was very different for me. In Catholic school we were all in one classroom all the time, and we were very close. I had grown up with just about everybody in my class through the eighth grade. In high school I hung around with boys and girls who were several years older than myself.

When I was sixteen, I had a blind date with a young man of twenty-two—quite a difference in our ages. We drank a whole lot that night and got very, very drunk, and I went to bed with this guy.

As a teen-ager I wanted to try everything. Unfortunately the first time I went to bed with a man, I became pregnant. I knew nothing at all about sex. I had no idea how you got pregnant or how you had babies. This was 1956, and sex just wasn't talked about in a good Catholic family. I wasn't sure what to do. I remember hiding in my closet and crying for weeks. I was also getting very sick, and it was hard to hide this. I was sick a lot in school in the morning, and I was pretty miserable. Anyhow, I told my best friend, who lived across the alley, and her mother found out, and my mother finally found out. She came to me and asked, "Are you pregnant?" And I just started to cry and cry. It was hard for me to talk about it. So she took me to the doctor, and sure enough, I was pregnant.

This was a real critical time with my father; it seemed to be the end of our relationship. He called me every name in the book, and he had absolutely no sympathy whatever. He just couldn't believe his little baby daughter was pregnant. I guess it was really very hard on him because my mother talked about it a lot many years later. I ended up finishing my junior year in high school, and by then I was five months pregnant. That was also terribly hard on me. Everybody knew I was pregnant. It was pretty obvious. I was really miserable and really scared. I always remember, as a little kid, I never wanted to have kids because I thought it would be very painful and I wasn't that crazy about kids period. The ironic thing is that I ended up pregnant at a really young age.

My parents decided to put me in a home. They didn't know what else to do. I couldn't stay at home in those days. They sent me to a Catholic home for unwed mothers in another city and went to great lengths to deceive my friends about where I was, like having me write letters to my friends, sending them to my aunt in another state and having her mail them. I actually spent three months in this home. I went right back to school as soon as I got home, and I was able to finish my senior year. That was also very hard. A lot of people called me names, and I remember one guy was making a whole lot of fun of me the first week I was back in school. It made me very angry, and one day I slammed him across the hall into a locker. After that day nobody ever said one word to me, but it seemed like my girl friends had no respect for me anymore. And I felt like I'd grown up about twenty years.

My mother and father came to visit me every Sunday in the home. My dad never spoke to me. Many years later my mother told me that every time they left, he would go home and cry. I don't think they had any idea what I was going through. The home was a good place, run by nuns. They taught us how to have a baby in the most natural way, so I wasn't afraid when I finally went to deliver. I didn't want anyone to know. I didn't let my mother and dad know until a day after I had my baby. It was a boy. I got to see him in the hospital through glass. I never could touch my baby. I never wanted to give up my child. Of course, he was beautiful because he was my baby. They kept the babies at the home until they were ready to go to the parents who were adopting them. When my father came to take me home, he demanded to see my baby, right in front of me. Several nuns told him they never did that; it was just never permitted. But my father insisted, and so they finally gave in to him and brought my baby to him. My father cooed and cuddled my baby in front of me and said how cute he was and how much he wished we could take him home, but of course, we couldn't do that. Then he gave the baby back to the nun who was in charge of the nursery and said to me, "Well, let's go now." And it was like that was the end of that and I shouldn't even think about it or have any feelings. He could have torn the skin off my body and it wouldn't have been as painful as that whole scene was. I will never forget it as long as I live. Several weeks later I went to the basement of some courthouse, where everything was hush-hush and it was very dark and I remember a lot of women crying, and I had to sign my baby away. I was told that I would never, ever be able to find out where he went, and that the records were sealed, and that I would never know anything else about my son.

I went back to school, and it was hard for me to finish that last year. I hated high school. I couldn't wait to get out. Somehow I managed to get on a work program in high school, so I only had to go half a day, and I worked in an insurance company, as a typist, which was something else I really hated. But I took a business course because my father wanted me to do that. That's what I was supposed to be, so that's what I did.

There were several incidents in high school. I remember now that I got drunk before I was pregnant. Even in high school I was drinking at lunch or going out and drinking and coming back in drunk. In fact, I got kicked out of high school several times for being drunk. Something else that was happening in my life was that I was becoming more aware that I liked women instead of men. It was really hard to deal with that, too. I know I drank a lot for that reason. I could hardly deal with my feelings about it because of course, I was raised to think and know that was just about one of the worst things you could ever be—a homosexual. My father was terribly, terribly bigoted and prejudiced, and those are some of the other things I really rebelled against.

After I finished high school, I had a full-time job. I resented that a lot because all my other friends were going to college. Just about every single one of my friends was going to college, and I felt kind of left out. I really didn't like doing what I was doing, being a secretary for the rest of my life. I was already losing the battle as far as drinking was concerned.

I remember going to a party when I was about nineteen with some women from work. Another woman and I were talking in a bathroom, and she told me how much she missed her boyfriend and I said, "Why don't you pretend like I'm him?" and I remember kissing her. About a week later the police came to my mother and dad's house and said, very quietly, "Would you like to come with us? You're under arrest for rude and indecent conduct." So I quietly went away with the police, and I was kept in jail for three days. It was humiliating, to say the least, and of course, there were only obviously alcoholic women in the jail. I remember thinking it was like a zoo, worse than a zoo . . . women wetting all over the floor, throwing up, screaming and yelling for their booze. It was pretty bad.

I went to court and they assigned me a woman who was something like a public defender. One of the first things she said was "This girl comes from a really good family. She's well educated from an upper-middle-class family, and her mother and dad are here in the courtroom." Then they started to read about the whole incident at this party, which I think was totally ridiculous. Actually I didn't give a damn. I was to the point where I really hated my parents. I hated just about everything.

I got out of going to jail because of my parents. I was put on probation for a year at that time. And it wasn't long after that

that I think a real significant thing happened. I belonged to a health club, and on the way home from there was a bar that was a favorite hangout. I started going in bars long before I was twenty-one, and of course, I had a fake ID—everybody did. Anyhow, this particular night I don't remember having what I thought was more than three drinks at the very most. I borrowed a friend's car when I left there, and I believe it was my very first blackout because I remember nothing. The story went that I was driving down a very busy main street, and I drove up on a boulevard, and it was snowing. Snow was piled up about three feet high in the middle of this divider. Somebody remarked that I looked like a snowplow going down the middle of it. At the end was a signal light, which I hit and broke in two. I totaled the car, and when I woke up, there was somebody in the front seat asking if I was okay. My mouth was bleeding, and they took me away in an ambulance. I was obviously drunk, but I didn't get thrown in jail because I was hurt, and they took me to the hospital instead. I did get a ticket for drunk driving and reckless driving. About this time I moved out of my parents' home. I could no longer stand living in that house. My father and I hadn't talked for about a year. I was sitting in the courtroom, and my dad came behind me and said, "Here's a hundred and fifty dollars. This is how much it's going to cost to get you out of this." That was the only thing he said. He gave me the money and walked out of the courtroom. So I paid the fine and left. My father also paid to buy my friend a new car, paid for the stoplight that I wrecked, and it cost him a lot of money. He bailed me out—which he also did an awful lot in later years.

His answer to everything was "Send her to a psychiatrist." I had already seen a whole lot [of doctors] through my high school years. This time I think he also sent me to another psychiatrist as well as a medical doctor. I remember having an EEG—an electroencephalogram—and the results of that were really interesting. This was way back in 1959. My father told me the results. The doctors didn't communicate with me; they communicated with the people that sent you to them—in this case, my father. So my father told me the doctor told him that I was the type of person who was on the verge of being an epileptic, that I was extremely allergic to alcohol, and I should never, ever drink alcohol because it could really be a disastrous thing in my life. I've already said how I felt about my father: I never believed a word he said. I totally ignored everything he told me, and I continued to drink.

I got fired from my job because of the incident with the "rude and indecent conduct." My mother would get me out of bed every morning and say, "Get out of the house; look for a job; you're not going to lay around here." So every morning I would get up and go downtown—and, at that time, you had to get dressed up in dresses and heels and gloves and really look your best; I mean, that's just the way everybody dressed. Sometimes it was hard to do that. I started going into bars really quite early in the morning—maybe around ten o'clock. I remember I had a savings account that was dwindling away fast. Every week I was drawing money out of it to drink when my parents thought I was downtown looking for a job. I was really sitting in bars, sometimes getting drunk twice in a day. I made friends with a bartender who would let me sleep off my morning drunk in the back room, and then I'd get up and go back to the bar and start drinking all over again. Then I'd usually pick up a man because I was running out of money and let him buy me drinks, and I usually ended up leaving with this man—whoever it might be—and sleeping with him. In the back of my mind I really wanted to have another baby; only this time it was going to be my way: I was going to keep that baby. No matter what I had to do, I was never going to let anybody take another child away from me. I wasn't doing much with women at this time. I knew I had to be drunk to sleep with a man, and I did a lot of that. Fortunately, and I do mean fortunately, I never did get pregnant again. I guess God was really watching out for me because God only knows what I would have done in the horrible, horrible alcoholic years that were in front of me.

In the neighborhood where I grew up there were nine kids

across the alley, eight of them boys. Across the other way from us between the four corners there were twenty-five kids just in those four homes. I think some of the reasons for my sexual behavior may have been caused by some things I didn't remember until years later. At the age of three and a half when we first moved into this neighborhood, the guy next door, who was a teenager at the time, used to take me in his car in the garage and force me to have oral sex with him. With the eight boys on the other side of me I remember more than one time when their folks weren't home and they turned out all the lights and dragged me into the bathroom and took all my clothes off and kissed my body all over. I probably wasn't even six or seven.

I was always trying to protect my brother, and he was quite a loner, a skinny little kid who most of the other boys in the neighborhood made fun of. I always stood up for him. He's still a loner. My brother's never married. He lives alone to this day, but he does love kids, and he's really good with them—at least from what my mother tells me anyhow. I'm sure he is. He's taught in the same school for fifteen years. But I guess we were both pretty strange kids when you get right down to it. My brother, I think, probably hated my dad more than I did. To this day he says that he's really glad he wasn't related to him, and my feelings are pretty much the same about that.

I was very athletic, participated in a lot of team sports, and I think that's why my dad initially favored me. I was really like the boy in the family. He played ball with me, came to my ball games, took me fishing, and we did all sorts of things that I guess he would have normally done with his son. I don't remember what my brother did. It just seemed that he was there, but they'd say to him, "Why can't you be more like your sister? Look at all the friends she has." And then they'd say to me, "It's too bad you can't be more like your brother—look how smart he is," especially in math and those areas which I wasn't that good in, although I was an honor student through most of my school years, at least up until high school. Things started to go downhill in high school.

Another incident happened when I was nineteen. I was on my way to a party at a friend's one night alone, and I was already drunk. When I got there, I knocked on the door and there didn't seem to be anybody home. I noticed there were about five guys that followed me up in the elevator and were supposedly coming to the same party. So, when no one answered the door, I got in the elevator and went down with them, and they offered me a ride to wherever I was going. When I got into the car, they all turned into a bunch of animals, and three of them jumped on top of me in the back seat, and they were all going to have sex with me—which they tried real hard to do. I didn't really fight a lot, but I made it hard for them to do that, and needless to say, it was hard anyhow in the back seat with four people. What they ended up doing eventually was throwing me out of the car, and I was very thankful. I remember lying on the ground thinking, *Thank God, I would rather break every bone in my body than be raped or touched one more time by those animals.* I never told a soul because I thought it was my fault because I was drinking. I think I really started to hate men about this time. I managed to get a cab and go right to another bar and do more drinking that night. I really knew I had a problem already when I was nineteen. In fact, I was having a terrible time getting a job. Being fired from my very first job was awful, especially the reason I was fired.

I was going to an employment agency a lot and still drinking lunch just about every day. One day I thought, *The hell with it, I've had it, I just don't care anymore.* The employment agency was on the fifth or sixth floor of this building, and I opened one of the windows down the hallway and sat out on the ledge. I thought I would jump out of the window. I think I was dealing with a lot of my feelings about my homosexuality because I remember I had a crush on the woman who I was seeing at the employment agency. I wanted to get her attention any way I could. Anyhow, I don't remember who saw me sitting out on the ledge, but I know she had something to do with it because some men from AA came and they pulled me off the ledge, so I guess I wasn't that serious about killing myself. They took me to an AA club, and I remember them giving me a questionnaire and having me fill it out. When I started to sober up, I couldn't wait to get the hell out of there and start drinking again. About this time I found a girl friend of mine, and I found out she was willing to admit that she was a lesbian, a word which, of course, at that time, was never used; I didn't know what it meant. She told me there was a bar where other lesbian women went, and I couldn't quite believe it. I thought, *There really are other women like me,* which I hadn't thought there were, although I'd had several affairs with women even in high school, and I had a very heavy affair with a woman when I was nineteen. I know it was the first affair of that type for her, and it certainly was for me. It was real interesting because her father was an alcoholic and he went to AA all the time. He was always leaving the house, and of course, they never talked about it. Then one day I asked her, "Where does your dad go every night?" She said, "He's an alcoholic, only he doesn't drink anymore, but he goes to these meetings all the time." And I thought, *Hmmm.* And we drank a lot, both of us, and pretty soon she couldn't deal with my drinking either. So our relationship kind of ended then.

It was also about that time that I realized I didn't want to live in Minneapolis anymore; I needed to get away from my folks altogether. I knew I was a lesbian. About that time I was getting questions from my father like "How come you don't go out on dates anymore? Who are all these strange women calling the house?" It was getting to the point where I knew I had to get away totally. I'd always wanted to go to the West Coast, to California, so that's what I set out to do.

As for my relationship with my mother, I never felt really close to her either. I ran away a lot when I was twelve, thirteen, and fourteen, and I remember one time, when I came back, she was sitting on the edge of my bed. She put her arm around me and said, "You know, we really do love you." I guess I never felt that a whole lot. She sided with my dad, whether they were her own feelings or she was doing it out of terror of him. He yelled and screamed at all of us and a lot at her. Many years later my mother told me she thought of leaving him, but she never would have because of the kids—us, my brother and I. I got a lot of things from her that I got from my dad, only she was more understanding, but we were never that close.

I've never been married. I came close to getting married a couple of times, also to appease my father. Thank God I never did. In fact, one of the guys I was engaged to was an alcoholic. He gave me a ring. And in the few weeks after he gave me the ring, I remember I had to bail him out of jail for drunk driving. It was really obvious to me that I didn't want to marry him or anyone else, actually, and I gave him back the ring, and that was the last time I really thought of getting married.

So I left for California, and I lived there for thirteen years, and I drank the whole time I lived there. I had a million different jobs. I remember going for a job interview one time, and it said to list the places that you've lived in the last five years. Well, I counted twenty-three and decided I'd better lie on the application. I was still incredibly naïve, but I made up my mind that I definitely was a lesbian and so those are the kind of women that I sought out. I did make some good friends at the beginning. I was only twenty-two when I moved there. Actually there were some really good times, and I still have friends from those days.

But for the most part it was quite a nightmare. There were years that I don't even remember being in California. It's a wonder I ever survived some of the things I went through there. My father was still bailing me out for many years after I got to California. I was picked up for drunk driving at least five times before they took away my license. For five years I was never allowed to own a car in the state of California. When I did get my license back, I had to pay a horrendous amount of liability insurance. It seemed for several of those years I ended up in jail almost every weekend. I did some absolutely horrendous things. I stole money, embezzled money from one place I worked in order to have enough money to drink. I really believe I was becoming quite insane because of my alcoholism. But in my younger years nobody really seemed to notice that I had a drinking problem—just that I drank a lot. I had numerous relationships, and most of them ended because of my drinking.

My years in California aren't very memorable. I also got into heavy drugs there, including heroin. I had some really terrible reactions to that and ended up in the hospital one time with a tumor on my uterus the size of a volleyball. It scared the hell out of me, and I just knew that it was drugs that caused it. So I gave up the drugs, but I continued to drink. I had some bad years with drugs. I don't really remember a whole lot between 1965 and 1970, I moved around so much.

I had many jobs. There was almost a year that I absolutely couldn't work. Fortunately I found a woman who was willing to take care of me during that time. I always seemed to find a woman to take care of me—somebody who would feed me booze and give me money for cigarettes. I woke up every day planning my whole life around drinking and how I was going to do it, when and where. I lived with this woman for five years, and about the fourth year things really went downhill with us. My alcoholism was totally out of control. I had a job, but it was hard for me ever to get there, and we started arguing and fighting over that a lot. She also drank, but she didn't seem to have any of the problems that I had. The horrible last year I really didn't get to work a whole lot. But I also gained tons of weight. I'm a short person—I'm only five feet two and a half inches tall—but I'd gone up to one hundred sixty pounds. I always seemed to have money for food and booze, and I guess that's where it all went. All I really thought about was dying. I was hopeless. I had driven everybody away. I had one friend in California. She did my hair and became a really good friend. And I never looked bad. I had a really clean home, and I dressed well. I always made sure my home was in order before I started to drink. Things were always neat and tidy. People used to say, "You can eat off Rita's floors." This hairdresser friend of mine came over to our house, and she had some material in her hand that was AA stuff, and she took me aside and said, "Rita, did you ever think that you might have a really bad drinking problem?" It made me furious that she said that, but she gave me these things and said, "Here, read these later." I remember shoving the literature in the bottom drawer of the dresser, and I didn't pull it out for months, although I did look at it, and I remember thinking, *Yeah, you really are an alcoholic, you're a hopeless alcoholic . . . you might as well kill yourself. . . .* I never believed, ever in my entire life, that there would be anything else for me but alcohol or could be. I just didn't realize there was a place for alcoholics to get help, I had no idea whatsoever.

The woman who I lived with had a really neat family. She had five sisters and a brother, and they all lived in the LA area. At first they all liked me a whole lot, and their kids liked me, but I even drove them away. There was even a time when I thought of killing her mother and her and myself. I was really, really insane . . . really insane. But anyhow, one evening I had a bottle of Valium—about fifty of them—and a bottle of scotch, and I took the whole bottle of Valium and drank the bottle of scotch. And I called the only friend I had left in LA that would even talk to me. I don't remember calling her, but I said, "I just want to say goodbye 'cause I just died." And I guess I hung up the phone. And she immediately called the paramedics and they came to my house and broke down the door and dragged me out to the hospital and pumped my stomach and saved my life. When I woke up, I was really furious that I was still alive.

That was probably the low, low bottom of my alcoholism. It was definitely one of the lowest times of my drinking days. My lover came back to the house and said to me, "You're gonna have to leave. I don't care where you go, but you're gonna have to get out of here." I had wanted for quite a long time to go to New Mexico. I had visited there earlier, and I had two friends who were willing to let me stay with them until I could get a place of my own and a job. And I really didn't have much choice. She put me on a train. I had two suitcases, fifty dollars in my pocket, and my two cats. And we left California.

I came to New Mexico. Immediately I loved being there. It was a very good feeling. However, I was still drinking. There weren't a whole lot of jobs here, and all I could find were waitress jobs. And of course, I got waitress jobs that were usually in bars. And in a period of three months I already lost several jobs because of my drinking. Also, the two women that I was staying with had already asked me to leave. They couldn't put up with my drinking anymore. I had bought a car which one of them had cosigned for, and I almost drove it in a ditch. It was laying up against the bridge; it was another miracle that I wasn't dead. We towed my car out of there and...well...my drinking really wasn't any better at all here. I still was drinking. I ended up in jail about three times in the small town I lived in. It was really, really bad.

Needless to say, I didn't have very many friends. My one friend from California, however, had moved here; she was the only one who seemed to stick by me. She didn't like me very much, but she still talked to me because she, too, was new to New Mexico and didn't have many friends. I continued to work from bar to bar and I was running out of bars to work in because it was a small town. I was getting really desperate. Actually, I was living in my car pretty much at this time. I didn't really have anywhere else to live. I was able to get a motel once in a while because I still had my two cats who I was dragging around in my car, and I felt it was really hard on them.

Finally my car blew up on me, too, so I stayed in a motel and took cabs back and forth. I made a few friends, who would pick me up. And then one day I met a guy in a bar who told me about a house that was empty, but the owners wanted somebody to stay in it. So I moved into this house. It didn't have any furniture, but it was really beautiful. And I felt that was sort of my saving grace because I'd contemplated many times already going back to LA because I didn't think I was going to make it here. And then also about that time I got a lump sum of unemployment money from California which kind of saved my life. I knew I would probably be able to stay here and forgot about all the thoughts I had about going back to LA, where I almost died, and really didn't want to go back at all.

Then one night I got very drunk—of course, that's what I was still doing every night—and I ended up at a woman's house who I didn't know very well, but she seemed to have a real insight [in]to me or to really be tuned in on where I was coming from. I remember laying on this couch, and I heard her say that "She cannot stay here because I don't want her to die in my house." And then she came out into the room and said, "You can either ...I will call you a cab to go home"—which was about twenty-five miles away—"or I'm gonna take you to the hospital because I think you're really sick."

And this was definitely the ... really the significant part and the beginning of my recovery. She ended up taking me to the hospital that night. And she left me there, and they wanted to keep me. I had pneumonia; I was suffering from terrible malnutrition; I was really a very sick person. I had acute alcohol poisoning. I was very bloated, and I was really, really a mess. I don't remember anything much for the first couple of days in there. I remember waking up with lots of IVs in my arms. And I remember crying a lot.

I listened for the first couple of days to this really neat woman who was the head nurse on the floor. They always had the curtain around my bed pulled—I shared the room with another woman who had a stroke and had lost her memory. I remember listening to this head nurse talk to her and thinking what an incredible woman she must be to have that kind of personality and to be able to do what she did. No one seemed to be paying much attention to me, but I knew I was really sick. I started crying a lot, and one day the head nurse came to my bed and she said, "What's wrong? Is there something I can help you with, or is there something you want to talk about?" And I told her I thought that I had to do something about my drinking, that I thought I really had a problem with it, and it was then I realized I didn't want to die a drunk. For some reason I just really didn't want to die a drunk. And she proceeded to tell me about a woman my age who earlier that week had died of cirrhosis of the liver, and what a horrendous, horrible death it was, and that she bled from every opening in her body, and her skin even burst open and she bled through her skin and died . . . in her own blood. And it just sounded pretty horrendous. She started to really care about me, and later on she told me she was so interested in me because we were the exact same age, only when they brought me in, she had thought I was a sixty-year-old woman because of how horrible I looked. I remember how bloated I was and how puffy my cheeks were and how sick a person I really was. But I realized I really did want to and I needed to do something about it, and I didn't have any idea what I could do.

So this neat, wonderful woman started to look into treatment centers for me, and she kept coming every day and saying, "Hey, I've talked to some really neat people. There's a treatment center right her in Santa Fe, and when you're well enough to leave the hospital, I'd be happy to take you there and show you around. You don't have to stay there, but why don't you at least come and look at it and talk to the people?" So I ended up staying in that hospital for about twenty-five days, and I was really feeling good. I remember it was the fourth of July, and, of course, I lied to the doctors most of the time I was there about my drinking. They kept asking me how much I drank. In the meantime, they had done millions of tests, and they thought I had all sorts of diseases like Hodgkin's disease, Parkinson's disease, and when I left the hospital, they were treating me for lupus. They really thought I had lupus, so they were treating me with cortisones and all sorts of horrible things that I really didn't need. They also had done a liver biopsy and found out I had at least the beginnings of cirrhosis and some scarring on my liver. The doctor said to me when he let me go, "I know you're feeling really good now, that you've dried out this long, and you're dying to get out there and have a drink. But I'll tell you something, and I'm not kidding: If you go out there and start drinking again the way you did, you'll be lucky to live for a year—a year and a half at the very most. You'd better really think about it." And that hit me really pretty hard.

So I did go look into the treatment center. Helen, the head nurse at the hospital, helped me an awful lot. I met some really nice people. I became involved in a group of newly recovering alcoholics—men and women—that was being run by a psychologist and a social worker. This woman who was a social worker ended up helping me tremendously also in my rehabilitation and my sobriety, as also did the woman psychologist who was running the group. I knew I had to do something, so I was pretty desperate, and I was willing to listen to people and willing to do the things that they were telling me I should do. I spent two weeks there, and I realize now how fuzzy the whole thing was and how sick I really was. I heard a lot of what they said to me in the lectures, but I also see a lot of it didn't get through at all. I was really a sick person—mentally and physically.

They took us to AA meetings. I had a real hard time with that, only I went because we had to go. I didn't quite understand what those people were all about, and I thought they were a lot of religious fanatics. But I cried a lot there because I realized there were a lot of other people like me, and I could relate to that and that's about all, and it made me cry because it made me sad. It made me see what a mess my life really was, I guess.

I left the treatment center feeling really good physically— probably better than I had felt in years. So, of course, I felt so good I knew I could go have a drink. And that very week out of treatment I got really drunk. I was supposedly on the way to someone's house for dinner. I don't even remember getting in my car. I drove about 100 miles, and I don't remember a thing, except I was stopped by the state police and it took four state policemen to get me out of the car and arrest me. I spent five days in jail, and some nice AA people helped get the charges reduced, and I went right back into that same treatment center for two more weeks. Actually that was the only way I could get out of all the charges that were being filed against me.

After that I lived alone, and I think that made it a lot more difficult because it was easy for me to think I could still drink and nobody would know. I did continue to go to the group, and that helped a lot. It was a place where I could go talk about how I was feeling, and mostly that was really quite good. I realized that physically feeling good was really important to me. My head was beginning to clear up some. The social worker who also was the comoderator of that particular group came to me and said, "I can really help you. Why don't you come and see me?" She worked for the Department of Vocational Rehabilitation; she was a caseworker for them.

I decided at that time I would like to go to school. I'd never been to college and was thirty-five years old at that point, and I thought that might help me reenter and resocialize. I didn't even know if I could be around people. It had been many years since I socialized with anybody when I was sober. There was a small college in the town that I lived in, and I thought that would be a good place to ease back in. So I did. I enrolled in that school with the help of the woman from the Department of Vocational Rehabilitation. I got on the work-study program, and between the money that brought me and the help from vocational rehab, I was able to go to school full time and pay my way and get by. And it was an incredible experience. I ended up going to school for two years, getting an associate degree, being on the dean's list, which I was really proud of because I never thought I could even learn again. I didn't really have much faith in myself that I could do anything. But still, the less I drank, the better I felt. And by no means did I stop drinking immediately and forever. It seemed like I was going to school and liking it a whole lot, but still, on the weekends, I would sneak off and get a six-pack of beer and drink it. And then, of course, that would usually end up meaning another six-pack of beer, and I'd usually end up getting drunk, although I was somehow able to handle that and stop at that point. I was making some friends at the school. It was a whole new life, like the beginning of my life, because for all the years before that it was as though I walked around numb all the time. The only feelings I really had were guilt and remorse because of the horrible person that I thought I was. I got a lot of that from my dad, especially after my pregnancy. At that time he

told me that I was a whore; you name it—he called me it. He
said I would never amount to a thing. After a while I guess I
really believed that was true, and that's the way it was for me.
During those horrible drinking years I just went around apolo-
gizing to people all the time, and I felt kind of like a puppy dog.

Anyhow, I finished school, and things got better as far as
my drinking went. I was able to go for several months without a
drink. Yet the first year was terribly hard. I went to a lot of AA
meetings out in the country, and I got really tired of hearing those
drunk stories all the time. In fact, many times when I left those
meetings, I went out and drank. It reminded me of my drinking
days, and some of it was beginning to sound like fun again,
although none of it really ever was. So I'd go out and drink. I
think living alone really had a lot to do with how hard it was for
me because there wasn't anybody around to see that I wasn't
drinking. After the first year I decided I wanted to continue college
and moved to Albuquerque. I was making new friends and slowly
easing back into some kind of a life that was structured, and it
was really good for me. I think the structure of school helped me
with my sobriety a lot. And the better I did at school, the better
I wanted to do. That made me regain a lot of self-confidence and
self-esteem because, believe me, I had none, I mean, zero, none.

In the meantime, the nurse also helped me tremendously,
financially and in a whole lot of other ways. We became lovers.
It was the first lesbian experience for her, and it was kind of hard
on me. But she was so good and supportive. I called her my angel
from heaven because, if it wasn't for her, I don't know if I would
have made it through those first couple of years. She helped me
a lot.

When I moved to Albuquerque, things started to go downhill again. I entered the University of New Mexico, and it was
really much more difficult than I thought it would be. I also started
smoking a lot of marijuana. I didn't realize how many times it
would lead me back to drinking again. It seemed like I could
make it for eight or nine months, but I couldn't make it past that.
And I sincerely believe that the marijuana smoking, being a sec-

ondary addiction, really did trigger my primary addiction, which
was alcohol, on more than one occasion. And I made it through
about five more years the same way. I smoked a ton of marijuana.
I ended up quitting school. I just couldn't deal with it anymore.
It was too much for me. I felt I wasn't doing well. I got a C, and
that was devastating. My marijuana smoking was getting in the
way of all the work I had to do for school. I still had a terrible
time with AA, although I knew I needed something. So I had
some very difficult years. Then I got a job. I was also still living
alone. I never really lived with anybody for the first five years of
my recovery, but I did begin to make friends. I got involved in
some lesbian groups. I became real involved in a peer counseling
group, which involved a lesbian and gay hot line, which I worked
on for three years and volunteered my services. And through that
group I met a counselor who was a lesbian and started going to
see her. That seemed to help me a lot. I just tried to be more
active in the things I wanted to do, which was to be involved in
the gay and lesbian community. It was also a way for me to meet
women.

I started working two jobs. I wanted to buy a new car, which
I did. I had never owned a new car in my whole life, and I was
feeling really good. I think I had it for eight months and probably
went that long without drinking—and swore I was never going
to drink when I had that new car, but I did, and I wrecked the
new car and I ended up in jail again. That seemed to be a turning
point again in my life. At that time I had no insurance, so I was
sued by a lot of people. In fact, to this day, I am still paying for
the car that I wrecked. I have lots of reminders of my past.

That year I moved into a house with a woman. I was later
to find out that she was a really sick person. I had turned forty,
and I kind of had the feeling that maybe I was never going to
find anyone else. So she came along, and I guess I fell in love
with her. I started drinking again almost every weekend, and it
was getting out of hand again, and I knew it. So we decided
together that I should go into treatment. I started to work with

an incredible therapist. I felt really spiritually awakened when I was in this treatment center, a beautiful place out in the country. I was outside by myself one day, and I was really looking around me at the mountains, the beautiful blue sky, a stream running by, things growing all around. It was incredibly beautiful, and I was silently praying to God to enlighten me. I was overwhelmed by the beauty that surrounded me and how lucky I was to be living in the midst of it. Something overcame me that I will never, ever forget. I felt my whole body start to grow. I felt the warmth of God in my soul and heart. And I've been a really different person since that time.

Other things started to happen to me in treatment. There was an incredible group of people, a real special group that I was in treatment with. Everyone was so supportive and loving of each other, and that was almost overwhelming in itself. I finally got something out of treatment, I guess, because I was really ready for it and wanted desperately to be sober.

Some of the things that started to happen to me in treatment felt like a catharsis. A lot of things came together for me. I believe for almost the whole two weeks I was there I cried hysterically almost every day for about four hours. I thought I was losing my mind, and I came very close to doing that after talking to some of the nurses and learning some of the symptoms I seemed to be having, which they attributed to the tons of marijuana smoking I'd done. This was probably the most critical time in my recovery, but I got through it with all the help of those loving, supportive people. All those people in that group knew I was gay, and it didn't seem to matter to anybody. In fact, one of the most beautiful things someone said to me several months later was that everyone fell in love with Rita. That made me feel really good. I realize now it was a unique situation in a treatment center because I know a lot of lesbian women I've talked to who were never treated that way. In fact, quite to the contrary. They were pretty much treated like castoffs, or they weren't able to be fully involved with most of the other people in treatment.

I feel like I resolved some things with my family, especially my father—going all the way back to the time I was five years old. Some of the deep hatred I seemed to have had for him seemed to dissipate through that therapy. And I guess I just grew up a lot.

After I got out of treatment, I was determined this time to be clean and sober. And I did go to AA a lot—sometimes two and three meetings a day. I was sort of lost and wasn't quite sure what to do, so I clung to AA, and at that time that's all there was. We had Gay AA, and I became quite involved in that off and on for five years. I was the secretary-treasurer of our gay and lesbian AA group for a year. And I was very involved. I also did 12-step work for probably a year and a half, and that helped me more than really AA itself did. I think AA is a good program, but I had a hard time with it because of the moral aspect that they seemed to interject after all those years. And there were a lot of things I couldn't do—like the moral inventory and character defects that I really didn't feel that I had. The reason was that I knew my alcoholism was a disease that poisoned my mind, not because I was really that kind of a person. So I did have a hard time with it. I think AA is a good program, but I think a lot of it has to do with the people. They seem to want to give you advice, and they want you to do things their way. Well, I have a hard time with that.

One night the woman I was living with beat me up terribly. It really upset me, and I knew it was definitely the end of that relationship. Not only that, I found her saying things like she was taking on my personality, and I decided that there was something quite wrong and I needed to get out. The next day I moved out. I didn't have a place to go. I went to stay with a friend. I didn't have a job at the time either. I didn't have much. I think I was getting an unemployment check, and that was about it. I moved out ten days before Christmas. It was very devastating to me. I thought I was in love with her, but I knew in my guts it was not going to be and that she was really a sick person.

I started to drink again, right around Christmastime, and I also tried to kill myself; I tried to cut my wrists one night. I got crazy again, and I went back into treatment. I was in treatment for New Year's, which was probably the best place I could have been. I went through two more weeks of treatment. This was the fourth time I'd been in treatment. I was still really serious about being sober, and I came out of treatment a little after the first of the year.

I did have lots of supportive women friends—also some men friends I had made in Gay AA. I moved in with some other friends for a while, and that seemed to work out okay. I continued to go to AA. I had a sponsor who was making me write out all the steps. I felt like a schoolchild in grade school all over again. I just felt all that was totally unnecessary. One day she called my roommate and told her to tell me that she didn't want to be my sponsor anymore. Not too long after that I went to a few more AA meetings, and I just felt like everybody was screaming their own advice and what they wanted me to do, not what I wanted to do. One day I just ran out of an AA meeting crying. That was the last time I went to AA for a very, very long time.

A couple of months later I heard about Women For Sobriety. I also met Nancy. I had known Nancy for quite a few years before then, but she was the lover of a very good friend of mine, and I would mostly see her coming and going out of that friend's house. I always liked Nancy, and thought she was really neat, and wished I could have gotten to know her better.

Well, I heard that her relationship had come to an end with this friend of mine, and so I went to visit her because I felt she needed a friend. We started to see each other as friends and later on became lovers. Nancy is the only woman, the first woman, I've ever had a total relationship with sober. I shouldn't say totally because I did get drunk one more time.

The first time I was in treatment, back in 1975, the day I got out of the hospital, I had a phone call at work, and it was from my mother. My father had died. So I went home, and that was the first time I was sober, too. I felt really good about it, but I also felt really bad that my dad had died and didn't know that I'd quit drinking. My parents had reached the point where when I called them drunk, which I did a lot when I lived in California, they didn't even talk to me on the phone anymore. In fact, my brother had his telephone number changed so I couldn't call him either. I was desperate for someone to talk to during those horrible days when I lived in California. My family was burned-out and nonbelieving and distrusting of me.

I was relieved when my father died. My brother was, too. Neither one of us had a lot of love for him, although later on I forgave him. He lied to me a lot, especially about my adoption. All my life I knew I was adopted, and they never really told us until I was thirty-two years old. But I knew it all the time. I used to hear my dad scream things through closed doors: "Those goddamn kids, I wish we could take them back to where we got them." He was a miserable man, and I'm really glad I'm not related to him.

I'd have to say that the most supportive person through my sobriety was the nurse I met in the hospital the very first time I realized I needed to do something about my drinking. She helped me incredibly. And she was so supportive. I suppose that's why I fell in love with her. We had a quite beautiful relationship for almost five years, and then she left me. I think I abused her a lot by my periodic drinking because I knew she would come and take care of me, being the nurse she was and the type of person she was. I think she was almost on the verge of a nervous breakdown, and she knew she had to end our relationship. I talked to her a few years later, but she still felt a lot of anger toward me, and I thought it best not to try and renew the relationship, even on a friendship level. I haven't talked to her since then, but I think about her a lot, and I always will.

Most of my nurturing has come from women and mostly from lesbian women. They're like my family. I consider a lot of women in our group my family, and I know a lot of them feel the same way.

I was introduced to Women For Sobriety in March of 1981. I also met Nancy then, who has been the most incredibly supportive, loving, nurturing person that I have ever known. Nancy and I don't live together. We live about a block and a half apart, but we see each other almost every day. We both lead our own lives. We're both very independent. And I guess what I decided when I met Nancy was to have no expectations of anybody anymore, and especially not of somebody I cared a lot about. I was in love with Nancy a long time before she was in love with me, but we were really good friends before we were lovers. I think that made a big difference in our relationship. We've had a few rough spots, but we've managed to work them out, talk them out, and it's been quite an incredible relationship. And also, it's been my first relationship during a lengthy period of sobriety, which next month will be three years. Hurray and hallelujah!

I immediately fell in love with the Women For Sobriety program. It just seemed to fill all my needs, and I drag Nancy along with me to meetings. At that time we were both still smoking marijuana. I stayed away from it for almost nine months, and I started smoking it again. Nancy actually gave it up before I did. About six months after I'd been in the program for Women For Sobriety, I drank one more time. And it was the most devastating drunk that I think ever happened. It didn't take me very long to get drunk. I'd downed several pints of tequila, and I was flat on my face and I threw up my guts for about three days. I really thought I was going to die that time for sure. It scared the hell out of me. I've never been so sick in my life. I had a constant problem with heartburn and indigestion. I think I'm very lucky that I didn't rupture my esophagus because that's what it felt like was happening. I also felt like I threw up my liver, which I know is impossible, but it was that bad. And that was the last time that I ever drank.

Anyhow, using the WFS program really helped change my whole way of thinking—from totally negative to a positive attitude about everything. I always think of when Nancy and I were both new in the program. On the way to work we used to ride together, and she'd look at me and say, "Remember, enthusiasm is my daily exercise!" And I'm usually a pretty grumpy person in the morning. Also, I hated the job I had. So, we used to laugh on the way to work. And I used those statements like I've never used anything all day long, and I mean all day long, to get me through that job I hated. And I realized that it worked. It was incredible to me.

Also during that time I finally decided to give up marijuana smoking. I realized how ridiculous that was. And one day I just thought, *Why am I doing this?* It was really depressing me all the time. I think about it now, and I just can't even believe that I did that. It was totally self-destructive—another self-destructive thing that I just replaced, I guess. It's taken me a long time to get rid of all those addictions—all those self-destructive addictions I had. I guess that was my whole attitude for years. I also decided I liked living. And it was as though something really snapped. I felt good about being alive. My attitude kept changing for the better. Things were definitely more positive because I made them that way. My time together with Nancy was becoming more important and really precious to me. Life was just beautiful, and I started to feel that there really wasn't anything I couldn't become if I wanted to. I also kept up with my therapy. I probably have done six or eight weekend workshops. I'm not in therapy on a regular basis anymore, but there's lots of times that I feel I still need to be doing that. And I may do it periodically.

My self-esteem—I'm trying to think back—I know it's only three years ago, but it's hard to see how all these things changed. But again, I have to say it's the WFS program. I really worked at it. It was easy to use the WFS program. In fact, sometimes it almost seems too easy. I hear other people say that to me every single week in our group now. That, hey, you know, I thought about how happiness is a habit I will develop, and happiness is created, not just to be waited for. I just worked really hard at doing all those things to change my old negative thinking. I had a hard time with my emotions, and sometimes I still do. I've always thought maybe I've been an overly emotional person, or maybe it's just because I never grew up until the last five years of my life.

I did everything I could possibly do to help myself grow and become the person I wanted to become. I always was a very insecure person—that's totally changed. About a year ago I decided that I wanted to be in business for myself. I didn't really plan it when it happened. I had some time on my hands, and I didn't have a lot of money, so I started cleaning houses for my friends for something to do and for some extra money. I realized that's something I really loved to do. I've always loved to clean. I'm a really clean person—not compulsively so; maybe I used to be, but not anymore. I realized that, in no time at all, by word of mouth through friends, I had this overwhelming number of people calling me and asking me if I wanted to clean for them. So I started doing cleaning on a full-time basis, and I realized that I could have my own business from doing what I was doing. I have really pursued that and made it a legal business, and now I'm branching out into commercial cleaning for businesses, and I'll be having employees within the next month, and things couldn't be going better.

Every time I become discouraged, I just change my thoughts around, and one of the big things that I'm aware of in my sobriety and recovery is that nothing—absolutely nothing—is a crisis anymore. Things aren't monumental problems. Nothing is to me anymore. I'm just so aware I can change that around so fast now that it's almost automatic for me to change anything negative into something positive. I don't dwell on things. I realize that's a real bad place to be. I don't like feeling negative, I don't like feeling depressed, so I've learned to turn it around. No matter what it is. Another thing I've noticed: I just don't feel that my problems are really problems compared to the way I used to think when I was drinking all the time.

One of the hardest things for me in my sobriety was dealing with my emotions. It's as though they were falling out all over the place all the time at first, and I cried an awful lot. I feel like

I cried the whole first year of my real sobriety. I've cried a lot because I've grown a lot. I think that's been really good for me. I've gotten rid of a lot of stuff that I held in for so many years, and that's the reason why I drank, so I didn't have to feel anything. I stayed numb all the time so I didn't have to deal with any of my emotions, which seemed to be just too much for me to handle.

Through the progress of my alcoholism, toward the end, where I think it was becoming terminal, I did notice the emotion that did start to come out and which got me in a whole lot of trouble. It landed me in jail many times and I lost every friend I ever had. The emotion was anger. Every time I got really drunk and lost control and was in a blackout, my anger was incredible. I was hostile and furiously angry at the whole world. There was a period of ten to fifteen years where I really never cried, and when I did cry, it was only when I was drunk, of course, and it just felt as if I was the only one in the world that had feelings like I had, and that I couldn't express them or nobody would understand me. It was just devastating to me that nobody really knew how I felt inside. My mind was really, really going.

The thing that I have the most difficulty with in my sobriety, the thing I have to work on all the time, is to remember to think, act, and feel, instead of feel, act, and think. I've a tendency to do that a lot, and I have all my life. Just the other day I had a chance to experience that when I was talking to my mother on the phone. My mother still has a tendency to talk to me like I'm a child, and so when I was talking to her the other day, she brought up something that I had said (And I just feel that she doesn't know me at all—however, she has gained a lot more trust in me over the last three years, I know that, and I do know that she loves me. And she even said that I was dependable, which was nice to hear, but it rather amused me). Anyhow, I felt myself just seething when my mother said something she probably said to me a whole lot as a kid, and then I realized that she has absolutely no idea how I have really changed emotionally and how much I have grown up. So instead of getting angry at my mother, I just kind of seethed for a minute and cooled down and said, "Yes,

Mother." It had something to do with how things take time, and if there's anything that I have learned in my sobriety, it's a whole lot of patience and tolerance. I'm not in a big hurry like I used to be all the time. I'm not in a big hurry for things to happen, and I think that also goes along with my feeling about living. It's precious to me. I love it. I love every day, I love every minute, and I don't need to be in such a big hurry anymore.

Another difficult thing for me was being responsible for myself, especially financially. I've always had a terrible time with money. I love to spend money. Now it's become important to me that I save money and I pay all my bills on time; I've worked hard at doing that over the past few years. There still are a few obstacles. I didn't want to pay some bills for some reasons that I felt were unfair, but needless to say, I ended up paying them anyhow. And I seem to have that squared away pretty well now. My bills come first, and I don't spend money like I used to. I just don't have any need to. I realize that material things really aren't that important anymore. I just hope for some comfortable years in my old age, and that's not very far away because I'm now forty-five. I feel that I'm a very independent person, but in a way I feel that I've really been independent most of my life for the reason that I've been single. Somehow I managed to survive a lot of those years, and it's really quite incredible to me now. I did manage to find women along the way who, for some reason, wanted to support me at times when I was totally incompetent and not able to work. My father also bailed me out of many situations for many years. At the drop of a hat he'd send me just about any amount of money I needed. And that didn't help. Now I can honestly say that I am a financially responsible person. I think I am an honest person, and that's important to me. I've found out that if I'm not honest, I'm just not anything. I think honesty is incredibly important.

That also goes along with liking myself now. I like myself, I like who I am, I like the way I feel, and I believe that I'm an incredibly confident woman, and there isn't anything I cannot do if I make my mind up to it. I still have a lot of love and support, mostly from Nancy. I joked the other night about finding Nancy and Women For Sobriety, and it seems those two things saved my life.

It's been a very long, long struggle but worth every single minute of it. And I'm really happy to be alive, and life is just truly great and wonderful for me now. And I have a lot of people to thank.

LOIS: THE HOUSEWIFE

My name is Lois, and I am sixty-eight years old. I was born in St. Paul, Minnesota, where I still live. I had three brothers, and no sisters. Both my parents are dead; they died when I was in my sixties.

We were a very close family, a very loving family. I don't think there was any rivalry between myself and my brothers, although I always wished I was a better tomboy so that I could beat them at sports. I got very interested in sports because my brothers were, and I was the only girl. Now, in later life, they tell me that I was spoiled. My dad thought I was pretty great, and my mother and I had a great companionship. We went shopping together. We did everything together. I now think that probably my mother was an alcoholic, but she was such a sweet little French lady—very quiet and always in the kitchen cooking— that no one realized. In later years, when I was in treatment in 1971, they asked if there were any alcoholics in the family, and I only could think of my one brother who now lives in Montana. I think my mother was a secret alcoholic. She always had a little whiskey in the kitchen, for her coughing, she said. At night, by her bed, she had a little. In her later years she was hard-of-hearing, so whenever we all gathered, she would go out in the kitchen and cook and make hors d'oeuvres. No one ever saw any behavior changes in my mother, but I think she was very dependent on alcohol in her late years. She lived to be eighty-four.

My dad lived to be eighty-seven. He went to Georgetown University and graduated president of his class. My mother did all the artwork for the Georgetown University books. She was a very creative person. I think my mother did not fulfill her own dreams because then women never had careers. So she used all her creativeness in her cooking, for which she was very well known, and in her sewing. But she could have been an artist in her own right. My father was very outgoing. Everybody loved him. He formed the Cosmopolitan International Club and also the Business and Professional Men's Club in the Minnesota area. I think I take after my dad because in high school and in later years I formed clubs, too. I formed a national sorority that is still going. I enjoy people, and I like to be in groups of people. This comes from my father's side of the family. My mother's family was very quiet but very sweet people. They never rocked the boat, never said anything to disturb anyone. I now believe that at least two of my brothers are alcoholics. One just died of diabetes, but he was very much into drinking, and the doctor never saw that. He was on a lot of medication, way too much medication, but none of the family believed that. My other brother is a very outgoing person. He was in the FBI for many years. He was head of espionage. Now he's in Montana on a ranch, but he and his wife have been heavy drinkers for years, and they always think that drinking is the only way of life and that it's too bad that I fell off the deep edge! This bothers me to some extent, being the only one who went through treatment.

I have forty-five first cousins in the Twin City area, and I'm the only one that ever went into treatment. So it's always "Poor Lois, she really hit that bottle hard. Just think, she had to go for treatment." But I have to let that go, and someday maybe they'll get the message. There's so much talk about drinking here in Minnesota.

I don't remember when I took my first drink, but I know I never drank until after I was thirty-five because I just always drank Coke. Everyone always kidded me about that. "My God, how can you have fun at a party and just be drinking Coke?" I think it came on very gradually because my relatives always had cocktails at parties, and they always had drinks before they ate.

I would say that three-fourths of my cousins are probably over the deep edge in alcohol. They're all very social people, and they all have very good jobs, so none of them turned into bums. They're protected by other family members. But I went into treatment when I was fifty-five.

I was an executive secretary at a big computer corporation, Univac. I worked part time for twenty-eight years. I never drank in the morning and never got drunk at parties. In later years, when I was drinking heavily, I'd have some drinks before we'd go to a party. My husband would always monitor. He was just a beer drinker. When he used to pick me up for dates, way back in 1940, he'd always say, "Hurry up, we have to get to the tavern so I can have a couple of beers." And my mother'd say, "You know, you better watch it, he might be an alcoholic." Well, to this day two beers is about all he drinks, and he doesn't drink during the week. Many times he never drinks at the weekend either. If we go out, he'll have a few beers. I used to envy that. I used to see him sit in a chair and he'd say, "Oh, I think I'll have a beer. . . . You want to get me a beer?" Of course, I'd go out and make myself a nice strong highball and drink it quickly and then come in with a Coke or something and sit across from him in the room. Then I would say, "Don't you want another beer?" He'd say, "No." He apparently just liked the taste of beer. And it bothered me that anybody could stop after two. That's when I really got into drinking.

I had no special fears as a child. My dad went through the depression, but he always kept the family together. He'd find something to keep us going. We lost a couple of homes during the depression; we couldn't pay the mortgages on them. But we went to private schools, and my dad sacrificed everything so we could all have good educations. My brothers all went to college. I didn't. At that time they didn't think girls needed college, and they thought I was going to get into the art field. So I went to art school after high school.

I always hated my nose—I had a big nose. My dad always said I looked like his aunt Margaret, and Aunt Margaret was the homeliest of his sisters. I don't think I had any good feelings about my looks. But I always managed to have a bunch of boys around. I'd invite a whole bowling club up to our lake home at Big Pelican Lake. My dad went there and bought the property. It was a real wilderness in 1919. I was only two years old, and we'd spend every summer up there. Later, when I got married, I went up there and spent all my summers with my two daughters, and my mother was there, and her other grandchildren. One of my sisters-in-law worked, so I took care of her three children all summer. I never felt any great fear. The jealousies I think I had arose when I married my husband. He was a graduate of St. Thomas College and was supposed to be a teacher. His dad had a home electric wiring company, and he decided he could make more money working in an electrical field, so he went to a vocational school and learned to be an electrician and worked with his father for a while until he dissolved the company. Then he went to work for a big contractor and then he taught night school. So he didn't use his teaching degree. But it seems like my brothers always had such glamorous jobs. One brother was head of the FBI and was a law graduate and lived in Washington, D.C.; another brother was a certified public accountant and was regional director of Internal Revenue. He was on the news all the time, always on TV. For forty years he made the headlines in the paper. My third brother was an accountant for Northwest Airlines, and he traveled all over for the company. And I kind of always felt jealous that they made all these trips—they could see everything. There was a jealousy there that we would never do it. My husband always had a straight salary and worked on the union wages, and our biggest thing was to go to the lake every summer. So I guess the fear was that I wasn't going to have any money to retire on. We still have that fear. We just about ate up our salary all the time as we were living. His folks left us money, but then my mother-in-law went into a nursing home, and that used up every cent we ever had.

A fear I had was that I might not get married. I really wanted to get married and have children. And I remember when I picked my husband he was the best-looking of the boyfriends I had. Later, when I was drinking and having a lot of trouble with my husband, my mother (who almost never commented adversely and always made us feel good about ourselves) said, "Maybe you shouldn't have married the good-looking one." And that was the only comment she ever made. I never even knew that she felt that way about my husband because she always told me to be patient, put up with him, and remember he was an only child. His mother had adopted him. Her sister had died and left this baby. She adopted him because she had no children. So he was quite spoiled and a very hyper person with a lot of anger if he didn't get his way. That was the hardest thing to accept in my marriage because I was a people-pleaser. He'd go to a party, and if he didn't like something, he'd tell somebody off. He was always putting people down, and I couldn't stand this. I was always trying to change him. I wanted him to be affectionate toward my mother. My mother was French. She loved to kiss and hug everybody. He isn't an affectionate person at all. He hardly ever kisses. He would never say, "I love you." That bothered me in later years. Why doesn't he say that? He said it when we were going together, and now he never says it. He can't seem to say it. When I went through treatment, I finally found how much he cared for me. He went to everything they told him to go to. He's been going for fourteen years. He went to Al-Anon a whole year before I went into treatment. He never misses. He has sacrificed. He doesn't like to get all dressed up and go to these meetings. He came to hear all the speeches I wanted to hear. And in these later years I am beginning to see, through his actions, that he really cares about me. I never thought he did. I just thought he was always disappointed in me. I was disappointed in him. We argued terribly. We argued about money. He never let me touch the money, but he handled it very poorly. His mother always handled the money. This, I think, was at the root of my anger, some of my fears.

I was very proud of my children. One graduated with a four-point average at the university. The other was in everything: head of all the societies at the university, she was a model, she was up for Miss Teenage America, and she was making the newspapers all the time. Now I see a lot of rivalry between my two daughters. They're three years apart and the youngest one had to wear braces and glasses, and the elder one was a beauty. The elder one got very jealous when the baby came along, and I think she has alcoholic tendencies; someday she's going to have to face it. She is also going to have to face the jealousy she feels for her younger sister. And her sister feels she never got the breaks that her older sister got. I can see it with them, but I don't really see that I had it in my family. I was real proud of my brothers, and the only jealousy was that I thought they had [a] lot easier and more glamorous lives than I had. I suppose I always was jealous of every trip they made and all the beautiful big Christmas presents they could afford to buy.

I had a beautiful relationship with my parents. They were always kind. When I look back, I wonder why my poor mother didn't ever tell me how she felt. She had to live this public life with my dad. He was chairman of the Democratic National Committee when Roosevelt ran and had tons of people at the lake— political people she'd never see again. She was constantly cooking and baking. Everybody I ever met said my mother was an angel. She just never complained; everybody loved her. She was a very pretty woman, always kept herself looking very nice. I was always proud of her, always wanted to show her off to everybody. I wish we had had a more open relationship where she could have said to me, "I don't feel like cooking today, I wish Dad wouldn't invite all these people. I'm so tired I can't stand it." But she never did. She kept it all inside. This might have been why she got into drinking—because she never expressed her feelings. She always came on as if everything was great, everything was fine. Now that I know a little bit, that problems shared become half problems, I wish she had shared them. She kept it all inside and probably took her little drink till she went to sleep at night. No one ever noticed that she drank except my younger brother, who lived at home and began to notice all the whiskey bottles that were going through the place.

My dad drank a lot socially. He was an attorney and in later years was the oldest practicing lawyer in the state. We were always proud of him. He was always written up as being one of the greatest orators the state had ever had. I don't think they would have ever accepted my alcoholism; they both died just before I went into treatment. They would have never forgiven my husband and my daughters for putting me in treatment. My brothers didn't for a long time; they thought it was bringing disgrace to the family name.

My family was very supportive. My one daughter studied to become a counselor when I got out of treatment so she'd understand alcoholism. Unfortunately she married an alcoholic. She left him after four months. She didn't know he was alcoholic, and the anger that she has toward him I see as old anger she still has toward me. I don't think she really understands. She often says, "It can't be an illness that makes people act that terribly." When she tells me this, she's talking about her husband, but I can interpret that it's the way she still feels about me. My daughters send me congratulation cards to tell me how much they like me sober.

I became very active in AA. For nine years I orientated new patients, telling them about their illness, and then for another five years I did the same thing at St. John's treatment center. I was the main speaker. More and more I saw that women were saying, "I went to AA, and it didn't seem to do anything for me." (I myself was in an AA group with fifteen men. I was the only woman for about seven years.) Finally some of those women said, "Why don't we make our own group?," so we became a women's AA group. Then they said, "We need to get our self-images back." We started reading all these books—*I'm Okay, How to Get Rid of Anxiety, How to Be Assertive*—and finally we almost became a book club until, in 1978, I discovered the national Women For Sobriety program. Many of the women said, "Oh, we have to stick to AA." Finally, however, they decided to accept the WFS program, and then we had a problem because the AA group wouldn't let us meet at their premises anymore because we weren't using their program. They threw us out, and we had a very hard time finding a meeting room at no charge. But we eventually did, and the women that came (many of them had been in treatment as often as ten times) finally achieved sobriety because they can now share with a group that really cares.

To most of the women their relationships with men are a big deal: with their husbands, with men at work, and so forth. They can't discuss it at an AA meeting, so they cannot share this major part of their lives, which sends a lot of them back to drinking. Most of them carry terrible guilt because they have so little support. I am so lucky; my husband is one of the few men that keeps going to Al-Anon. All the other women, whose husbands I get into Al-Anon, come for three or four meetings and never come back. I feel that I'm very lucky.

My other daughter married an alcoholic, too, and I think she drinks with him. They're very social; they're up with the big society crowd and go to all the cocktail parties. And they think that they're managing, that they're okay because they're just drinking wine. She never talks to me about it. I don't know if it's because she's afraid that she might have a tendency that way, but she's real proud. I told her a couple of times that her sister once in a while brings up the past, and she said, "Well, Mother, I forgot the past. I never think of it anymore." But I really wonder. I don't think she knows how to share her feelings. Sometimes I think she takes after my husband, although now I read that a lot of adult children of alcoholics don't know how to share their feelings and don't have a lot of trust.

I see what has happened to both my daughters. The younger one became a "laugh clown laugh." She was always making jokes about everything to make the family laugh and be happy. But she often remembers the terrible fights and tells me she couldn't bring boyfriends home. We fought a lot about money. My husband thought he was managing it; he never let me know what he earned. When I went into treatment, I didn't know what his salary was, what his paychecks were. And then he never paid anything. He was so used to his mother's taking care of that side of things. Now, since treatment, the counselors made him come and they said, "Together you're going to work out this checkbook." I manage all the checks now; I pay the bills; he gives me a portion of all of his paychecks. It's wonderful. We never have an argument. I don't know why I lived twenty-five years like that. Just figuring, I guess, *Well, it's his money, and I can't do anything with it.* I had to beg for anything I wanted. I was always running to my dad for extra money to buy something for myself and the kids. This made me feel very sad. I seemed so out of it. I felt like I wasn't a responsible person, that he wouldn't trust me.

I suppose I still have guilt feelings, although I try to get rid of them. I really drank the heaviest when the girls were dating and they were in high school and college. They forced me into treatment. They finally didn't know what to do with me because I was drinking up north at the lake, and one day I had jumped in the lake and told them I was going to kill myself because they were all hollering at me. I swam straight out, and of course, they did what I wanted. They all came running down the beach, screaming, "Mother, Mother, come back, we love you, we love you." And I just kept swimming. I had all my clothes on, and that was in the fall, and that lake almost had ice on it. It's a miracle I didn't drown. Finally they said the magic words, "Mother come back, you can drink all you want." And I swam back just like Esther Williams in a movie. And then I drank another whole year after that. But I was getting very scared. I thought, *What is this, that I do these crazy things when I drink?*

The next summer, when I went to the lake, they knew I was drinking a lot more up there than I do at home because I wasn't working. So they called a treatment center and said, "Whatever you do, get her in there some way." So they told me my husband had had a terrible accident and was in the hospital at St. Mary's and I was wanted immediately. So I drove sober 150 miles and ran into the hospital to see my sick husband. They said he was in room 323. I ran in, and the girls were bawling, and I thought sure he died, that I didn't get there in time. Finally the nurse said, "You know, I want to tell you something. Your husband's all right, but you're very sick."

And I screamed, "What do you mean, I'm sick?"

And they said, "This is the AA part of the hospital, the treatment center."

And I said, "No one is going to keep me here." I ran to the window and said I was going to jump out. I looked down. We were on the third floor, and I was afraid I was going to get hurt, so I didn't jump. I stayed in the hospital, and it took me only about two days to realize that I should be there. The doctors thought I was going to carry guilt forever because my daughters tricked me into treatment, and so they worked all the time, always telling me what terrible daughters I had, that they had betrayed me and so on to get all the guilt and resentment out of my system. They couldn't believe that I really didn't feel resentment. I was so grateful. I guess I worried a lot more than I thought I did. I was using a lot of defenses. I was going through menopause, the girls didn't know what that was like, and I was always saying that I had the flu, that something was wrong with me. To this day I'm so grateful because it really saved my life.

My husband is very proud of me. He comes to every speech I make. He's always bragging. I hear him talking to other people about my sobriety date, and I think how fortunate I am because I really do have a lot going for me. I have a very supportive family. I don't think my other relatives, my old aunts and uncles and cousins, accept it at all. I always come right out and tell them that I'm an alcoholic. I laugh when they're all drinking. They'll say, "What will you have?" And I'll say, "Oh, I'd like a straight bourbon, but I'm going to have a Coke." I'm trying to educate them not to show any shame.

I'm very happy to have this program to live by. I would have given anything to have a program like this when my girls were little, to have guidelines on how to get rid of negative feelings, how to get happiness in your life, how to keep enthusiasm in your life, how to make the past gone forever. But the best guideline of all is "I am what I think." I have to work on this. I work all the time with women who are in their fifties who have a terrible time getting their self-images together. I think that the Women For Sobriety program is just tops. I can't believe that people can keep going with the old humility statements in the AA program. I never knocked AA. I still go to my old AA meetings because I know some of the fellows there so well, and I get a big kick out of them. They're always ridiculing me because I ask any woman that comes if she wants to go to Women For Sobriety, and they say all I come there for is to solicit for Women For Sobriety. But then they often ask me to be their speaker at meetings—I always put a lot of humor into any criticism I have. I kind of turn it around and laugh at it. I don't know, but to me that works pretty well, if they have some laughter going. If you're all right with yourself, I always feel you can take criticism.

This summer my daughter was going to drive from Montana to see us with a tiny, colicky baby, a dog, and a brand-new car pulling a great big boat. She was going to drive 1,000 miles, and she was going to drive all night long. I worried. I told our group how worried I was about her. I said, "Driving at night in those circumstances." I talked about it, and finally, one day a woman in the group said, "Lois, don't worry about it. She's your daughter, she'll make it." And you know, that was the best thing somebody could say. It gave me back my self-confidence and my good image. Maybe I *had* done something right for my daughters. The older one never talks about her feelings, she never tells me anything, she just pretends that everything is happy, but I know, with a drinking husband who's got diabetes, there's got to be worries. But she won't talk to me about it, and that's a real hurt to me. I can't seem to break her down, but I don't think she knows how to deal with her feelings.

My other daughter tells me everything. She's now going to Al-Anon; she's trying to get her husband into AA. She's trying to do something out in Montana. She is very open, too, to tell me about her worries and how she didn't like the years I drank and all the fighting we did, and I think she's begun to see that our marriage is like a lot of marriages, maybe even hers because she is having arguments now, too. I guess she thought that we were the only family that ever fought.

I really feel good about myself. I don't think I'm homely anymore. I always used to have a feeling that everybody in the room was prettier than I was. I look at photographs, and I think *Gee, I'm not bad-looking even if I have got a big hooked nose.* I tell you, I don't know what the program has done for me. I feel like I'm still forty years old. I have all the zip and pep of forty. My husband and I don't fight anymore. We joke; we kid. He still is a very short-tempered person, but I know how to handle that. I just don't get involved with it. I just walk away. I used to try to calm him down and change him. Now I have learned to accept him. I've lived with him for forty years, and I'm not going to change him now. I think we're both getting pretty mellow and figure it's better to make life worthwhile these last few years and not spend them fighting.

A major part of my recovery, I think, is my involvement. I don't know if everybody could get as involved as I am, but I'm on a hot line for Women For Sobriety. Almost every day people call. I really get out of myself by helping others. There's something about helping people. I still have a ninety-year-old aunt and uncle left of the older generation. Every day I go over and bring them their meal. They both drink, too, very heavily. And all the relatives want to put them in treatment—at ninety years old! I'm trying to help them not to be so lonely. I'm trying to stop them being hungry. They never cook unless I bring something, and now they're really getting better because of it. Sure it takes two hours out of my day to cook and take a meal over, but I'm so busy thinking about them I'm not thinking about my own problems.

I've got arthritis now, and a few other things are showing up. They told me that I had such a lack of vitamin C after I got out of treatment that I could hardly walk. They put me on vitamin C, and I think this is so important. Alcoholism is absolutely a physical illness, and I talk about it. At AA they don't like it when I go to the meetings and I say something about the physical illness.

It's all got to be spiritual in their book. But it *is* a physical illness, and you have to get well from the inside out. Get on a good vitamin program; get good exercise, good nutrition. If you have a tired body, you have a tired mind, and all the old habits are there. I always explain to the women in my self-help group that getting sober is like being a right-handed person who suddenly has to learn to be a left-handed person. That means everything you do, you have to concentrate on it. Now I can't do it this way, I have to do it the new way. And sure, some people have relapses. All of a sudden they automatically grab for that drink, just like you'd automatically use your right hand if you'd been a right-handed person your whole life.

I've never had any psychiatric counseling. I think sharing with other people is the answer. I had a very caring family, a very loving emotional relationship with my mother, my father, my three brothers. We never had a fight. My dad was German; my mother was French. We really had a lot of closeness in the family.

The worst thing is what people say to me when I tell them — and I tell everybody. I met a friend that I knew from high school, and she said, "What have you been doing all these years?"

I said, "You know I was an alcoholic and I went through treatment in 1971?"

And she said, "Oh, Lois, what was your problem? I always thought you had a wonderful family."

I said, "I did have a wonderful family. My problem was that I had a defect in my metabolism. I have a physical illness." I didn't have to have a problem to drink. My problem was created when I drank. I began to hate my husband. I slowly put walls up around myself. I didn't get close to anybody anymore.

Anyway, back to—you said please discuss your marriage, when did you get married? I covered all that. "Did you have sexual problems?" No. "Financial?" Yes. "Emotional?" Probably yes. "Did your drinking affect any of these?" Well, I suppose any little money I could get I was trying to buy liquor with it. "Were you ever sexually molested?" No. "Have you ever been battered?" No. I do think when I was drinking we used to get kind of violent.

Sometimes my husband would grab me by the throat and choke me and say he was going to choke the liquor right out of me, and hit me on the arm or kick me in the leg or something, but a lot of times when that would happen, I would jump in the car and race away. We had a little sports car, and one time, when I was really feeling down (my dad and my mother had just died), I went and sat behind their apartment building and cried and cried and cried, thinking they're the only ones who ever loved me. Then on the way home I hit a parked car. There was a Volkswagen that came alongside of me with some kids, and they wanted to race me because I was in the sports car. I turned to look at them, and I hit a parked car. My husband said later, when they called the police, that the police said that it looks like this lady's been drinking. But they didn't do anything about it. Of course, at the time I told them that my eyes were so filled with tears crying over my folks that I didn't see the car. You know how alcoholics can always think of good excuses—and they work.

Emotionally I guess I still am working on self-image. I wanted to be the perfect mother and have my kids only remember the wonderful things. At times they've said how bad I was, how goofy I was, when I was drinking. And I always think, *Well, I couldn't have worked every day if I was as goofy as they make out.* They kind of make me think that all I did was lay on the davenport all day and drink. Yet I was chairman of the mothers' group at the University of Minnesota, I was president of a lot of clubs, I chaired a lot of big parties, sent out invitations, so I wasn't always just laying around like they picture it. The oldest girl never says too much about it. She became a superachiever, which the oldest often is, but I think part of it was that she felt that would bring harmony in the family if we could all get together and say how great she was. And she was. I often wish she would let me know if she feels like I hurt her in any way. She's in the drinking society, and she likes to drink, so maybe that's why she doesn't even want to bring it up.

As I've said, the support I got was very good. My daughter took the chemical dependency courses. My husband and I attended a growth group at St. Mary's that was aimed at getting the communication back in the addict's family again. We were in it for two years, and he went faithfully; even if I didn't want to go, he went. That always made me think that he really must care about me, to make such an effort, because he isn't one that likes to dress up and go out at night after he's worked hard all day. We had to go every Monday. And then every Saturday I went over and orientated the new patients who had been in less than seven days on what alcoholism was and how they had to go to AA, and my husband orientated the Al-Anon group. We were very active, and I think that's where a lot of the support came from because we were able to talk about the same people, we were able to talk about the same things. He understood. He wasn't the only husband with a drinking wife; he heard how others had reacted. These growth groups were written about—I think it was in *Reader's Digest*—as one of the best treatment methods because they were able to get communication going again in the family. We were asked to be growth group leaders after two years, and so we went for another two years. We had to take a lot of courses and seminars and workshops to do that, so there was a real togetherness. I don't think I would have lasted if I'd had to do that alone all the time—especially driving in Minnesota in the winter. I would have just given up the whole idea.

The only problem I know in growth groups is that in some cases the women are afraid to talk up because all the way home the husband will say, "Why did you say that?" and they get in a big argument. Couples have told us later they fought more than they communicated because often a wife was intimidated by her husband sitting there and was afraid to say what he was like at certain times. I think the men were more open to say what the women were like. They would sit there and really say, "Well, you know, some days she looks like she's gonna drink again, and she's still..." The husbands always thought the alcoholic wife was going to become Mrs. Perfect. The expectations were just ridiculous. What was good about the group was that they all heard other people. If a woman has certain habits, she's going to have them whether she's drunk or sober. A lot of my habits are still the same. I think I was always an organizer. I like people. I liked them when I was drunk; I like them now I'm sober.

My biggest problem in sobriety? Well, I still like to drink. I use that protein diet drink—it's got all the minerals and all the vitamins in it—and I mix it with cranberry juice. And if I drink one of those around four o'clock when I get tired and my blood sugar is down, I don't have any urge to drink alcohol. It just seems to take the urge out of me. I don't know if it's the vitamins in it. It's like a strawberry float or malt. It does stop me eating too much, but the most important thing is that the physical craving for alcohol goes when I drink it.

Like I say, I work a lot on my guilt. When I was in treatment, they said I carried so much guilt. They wouldn't even let me leave until I went and asked *everybody* how they got rid of their guilt. I think that's because I always thought my mother was loved by everyone, and I wanted to be just like her, and now I felt there were people that didn't love me.

Well, that's just about it. I love my recovery, and I think I have so much going for me that I will definitely make it—with a husband who's involved and a loving family behind me all the time.

WHERE TO GET HELP

Self-help is the most popular method of recovery.
There are two self-help programs, Women For Sobriety and Alcoholics Anonymous. The location of Women For Sobriety groups can be found by calling 215-536-8026 or writing to Box 618, Quakertown, Pennsylvania 18951. In some cities, WFS groups are listed in the Yellow Pages. Alcoholics Anonymous is listed in the Yellow Pages in every city and hamlet of this country and many others, a result of fifty years of growth.

I believe the WFS Program provides more help for women alcoholics because it was developed from a woman's experience, while the AA Program was the result of a man's experience. The WFS Program takes into account the special problems of women, which the AA program was never meant to do. In fact, women were turned away from AA in its first years.

The AA program instructs the alcoholic to:

1) turn problems over to God
2) admit moral defects
3) seek humility

Although this program works very well with men, it does not help women overcome their feelings of helplessness, guilt, humiliation, and powerlessness. The founder of AA, Bill W., believed he needed to find humility to stay sober, but I believe this concept is unworkable for women. In *Twelve and Twelve*, an AA publication, Bill W. writes, "The attainment of greater hu-

249

mility is the foundation principle of each of AA's Twelve Steps. For without some degree of humility, no alcoholic can stay sober at all."

To preserve this humility, AA believes that an alcoholic must keep his drinking experiences vivid, often reciting them at AA meetings.

As yet, Women For Sobriety groups are not as numerous as AA groups. In the early weeks of sobriety, when the alcoholic needs the most support, the availability of AA is very important. At this stage, being with other alcoholics is what makes sobriety possible, not specialized programs.

Women For Sobriety groups are very small; ideally, each is made up of fewer than ten women. They are "conversations in the round," led by a woman thoroughly versed in the WFS Program.

ALCOHOLICS ANONYMOUS*

1. Admitted we were powerless over alcohol, that our lives had become unmanageable.
2. Came to believe that a power greater than ourselves could restore us to sanity.
3. Made a decision to turn our will and our lives over to the care of God as we understood Him.
4. Made a searching and fearless moral inventory of ourselves.
5. Admitted to God, to ourselves, and to another being the exact nature of our wrongs.
6. Were entirely ready to have God remove all these defects of character.
7. Humbly asked Him to remove our shortcomings.
8. Made a list of all persons we had harmed, and became willing to make amends to them all.
9. Made direct amends to such people wherever possible, except when to do so would injure them or others.
10. Continued to take personal inventory, and when we were wrong promptly admitted it.
11. Sought through prayer and meditation to improve our conscious contact with God as we understand Him, praying only for knowledge of His will and the power to carry that out.
12. Having had a spiritual experience as the result of these steps, we tried to carry this message to alcoholics, and to practice these principles in all our affairs.

WOMEN FOR SOBRIETY

1. I have a life-threatening problem that once had me.
2. Negative thoughts destroy only myself.
3. Happiness is a habit I will develop.
4. Problems bother me only to degree I permit them to.
5. I am what I think.
6. Life can be ordinary or it can be great.
7. Love can change the course of my world.
8. The fundamental object of life is emotional and spiritual growth.
9. The past is gone forever.
10. All love given returns.
11. Enthusiasm is my daily exercise.
12. I am a competent woman and have much to give life.
13. I am responsible for myself and for my actions.

© 1976, 1988, 1993

(A modification of the WFS Program is also now available to men.)